History of Crime and Criminal Justice Series

Written in Blood
Fatal Attraction in Enlightenment Amsterdam

Pieter Spierenburg

The Ohio State University Press
Columbus

Copyright © 2004 by The Ohio State University
All rights reserved.

Library of Congress Cataloging-in-Publication Data

Spierenburg, Petrus Cornelis.
  Written in blood : fatal attraction in enlightenment Amsterdam /
Pieter Spierenburg.— 1st ed.
    p. cm. — (History of crime and criminal justice series)
Includes bibliographical references and index.
  ISBN 0-8142-0955-6 (hardcover : alk. paper) — ISBN 0-8142-9040-X
(CD-ROM)
  1. Murder—Netherlands—Amsterdam—Case studies. 2. Gogh,
Johannes Bartholomeus Ferdinandus van. I. Title. II. Series.
  HV6535.N43 A477 2004
  364.152'3'09492352—dc22
                                        2003016383

Paper (ISBN: 978-0-8142-5756-2)
Cover design by Jay Batian
Type set in Janson

Contents

Acknowledgments	vii
Prelude: First Blood	ix
Preface	xv
1. A Big City in Cultural Flux: Eighteenth-Century Amsterdam	1
2. No One Suspected He Would End As a Murderer	21
3. A New Woman	47
4. How to Dump a Body When There Are No Cars?	67
5. Nathaniel's Ascension	95
6. An Unsuccessful Career	117
7. An Infamous Infatuation	138
8. Honor, Shame, and Notoriety	169
9. Van Gogh's Last Blood	191
Notes	199
Bibliography	219
Index	229

Acknowledgments

Although the two cases dealt with here are well known among Dutch historians of crime, hardly anything had been published about them when I started the investigation. Two articles deal explicitly with Van Gogh: Zevenbergen (1985) was instrumental in directing me to the Ghent University Library, which has the only extant copies of several crucial pamphlets (which Jan Art was so kind to photocopy and send to me); and Jongenelen's contribution to De Haas 2002, which is mainly concerned with the literary production ascribed to Van Gogh, appeared while I was revising my manuscript.

In the various archives I visited, I enjoyed the friendly guidance of several persons. Let me mention Rob Huybrecht in particular, who assisted me, as often before, in the archive of the Court of Holland and without whose help it would have been hard to find the petition for the annulment of Nathaniel Donker's marriage. I am grateful to Manon van der Heijden for reading and commenting on an earlier version of the manuscript.

While I wrote the book a number of persons advised me on matters of detail: Jan Buisman (the weather), Rudolf Dekker (various), Sjoerd Faber (guardianship), Willem Frijhoff (universities), Irene Groeneweg (clothing), Frank Huisman (medical matters), Astrid Ikelaar (Donker's last boat trip), Johan Kamermans (probate inventories), Inger Leemans (novels), Corrie Ridderikhoff (Franeker students), Jan de Vries (barges), and Jan Luiten van Zanden (wages).

In completing the manuscript I owe thanks for their support and comments to the series editors, Jeff Adler and David Johnson. Especially valuable comments came from an anonymous external reviewer. Notably, this reviewer made me realize that the original manuscript contained too many distracting passages which, upon second thought, were there for no other reason than to show that I had the information. I am also grateful to the acquisitions editor at The Ohio State University Press, Heather

Lee Miller, for her support, and the copyeditor, Leslie Evans, for her careful checking of the manuscript.

My final thanks are for my friends Eric Johnson and his wife, Mary Orr Johnson. Eric first suggested it might be a good idea, after several works of a more analytical nature, to do a microhistory. It turned out to be great fun to perform the research and write the book. Eric has given his warmest support throughout this project, and he and Mary checked the final manuscript to smooth its style.

Prelude: First Blood

On June 28, 1775, the magistrates of Amsterdam announced they would purge the city of mad dogs. Concern about rabies had been mounting for several weeks. The infection had spread among the city's canine population from the surrounding countryside. Eight days earlier, the authorities in the village of Ouderkerk, where Van Gogh's mother lived, had issued a similar ordinance. It encouraged the inhabitants to club stray dogs to death. The Amsterdam purge was to begin the next Monday, when every owner of a faithful quadruped had better keep it in the house or else on a leash. All other dogs would become outlaws.[1]

In the evening Van Gogh sat alone in his home: a simple room in the house of a craftsman who made felt slippers. Van Gogh probably did not worry about mad dogs. Since January his obsessive mind had focused on only one person: Annie. For him it had been love at first sight. He had paid her debts so that she could leave the brothel where she lived and she had promised to stop seeing her former favorite. But had she? Van Gogh reviewed the events of the past six months: her compliance and pleasing behavior, which soon turned into hesitation about the engagement; the frequent occasions when he had caught this other man in her room; his well-founded suspicion that she continued in her horizontal profession; the published mockeries, which had made her realize that her fiancé was a notorious citizen; their reconciliation for a brief spell, followed by renewed doubts on her part; the stubborn efforts of her neighbors over the last few days to prevent him from seeing her. It was now clear. He had to take a drastic step.

Van Gogh had made up his mind, which gave him tranquility. He sat down and rolled up his left sleeve. He knew what to do. Although he lacked an official surgeon's license, he had mastered the art of bloodletting. His patients had been sailors and ordinary residents, but never before did he have to perform venesection in connection with lovesickness. Surely, it had never been necessary to cut his own vein. Since he was

x Prelude

Fragment of the blood letter in Van Gogh's handwriting. Photocopy in the possession of Pieter Spierenburg. The original is lost (see the conclusion of chapter 9).

right-handed, he had to take the blood from his left arm. Bandaging the arm was the hardest part of the job. The bandage had to be tied tightly enough to cause his veins to swell—that was the standard procedure. Van Gogh took his lancet and held it for a moment in the flame of the candle that lit the room. He could conveniently use the bandage to wipe away the blackened residue. A bowl stood ready on the table. With the lancet Van Gogh made one incision in his swollen vein, not too deep to avoid touching a nerve. Then he turned his arm over, to allow the blood to flow into the bowl. When he had obtained a sufficient quantity, he removed the bandage, using a clean part of it to cover the wound. According to medical custom, the patient was to take strong food and beverages to recover from this treatment. This surgeon-patient, however, had no time to eat.[2]

He had to act quickly before the human ink dried up. In his mind he had already formulated the words he was about to write. He dipped his pen into the blood and began.

In Nomen Deus, Sanctus Trinitatis
Adorable object of my purest Love
Annie Smitshuizen

Revered lady, yes adorable beauty, rightly you have made yourself the object of my reverence. This has made your worth a thousand times greater for me than it has ever been before. No tender prayers, no humble supplications, no ocean of bitter tears have been capable of reconciling your embittered heart. Well then, beautiful woman, let my own blood, which I now use for writing, accomplish it. Let my blood, shed for you and for your sake, provide you satisfaction. Grant me your tender heart again, your heart which, by senselessly acting upon an evil hatred, I have lost, alas lost. No, beautiful lover, I hope and pray to God that he will make you choose me for a husband again. I will atone for my crime through a thousand good deeds; with thousands of friendly actions I will wash away my guilt. Realize that my heart is honest and pure and that I have a holy intention to comply with that pure heart, because I swear to you and the whole world that it is impossible for me not to love you. My love is rooted so much in your virtue that death itself will be incapable of extinguishing the love I feel for you. My property and my blood, my body and my life, my soul and salvation, they all lie in your hands. Save me, I pray to you in the name of the Holy Trinity for the sake of Jesus Christ. God will cherish your soul forever, if you save my poor soul now, you, the only medium in God's hands to make me happy. I swear to you with the most precious oaths that I love you purely and sincerely, without any ulterior motive.

Take it, therefore, that everything I say and write today is sincere and pure: if I would lie just a tiny bit or withhold anything, or if there were the slightest dishonesty or ambiguity in my heart, or if I intended to draw any wrong conclusion from what has happened and it were not my holy intention to make decent use of your favor, mercy, and love, then I dare challenge the Judge of all crimes to punish me in the most severe manner. Yes, in that case I wish—and I hereby confirm this wish with my blood—that God chastise my soul and body, in this world and eternally, with all penalties that can befall upon all mortals simultaneously: may he let me live in a state of constant dying and let me die alive; may the worm of remorse continuously shake my conscience; may he cast all his thunders upon me and crush me, yet without making me experience death, by which my wretched soul would leave this miserable body; may this soul then plunge into the most horrible abyss, to be tormented eternally with all pains suffered by all the damned together. I am not afraid of these oaths, my beautiful sun, because they spring from a sincere heart; don't think that my conscience has been dulled so much that I would venture to provoke the Deity outright.

What I have presented you with words, I also present with my blood; that is, I will tolerate everything and sign for everything you desire, if only I can become your husband. Draw up a marriage settlement as detailed as you want; estimate goods worth a guilder at a ducat and so on at the same rate. Put me in wardship; nothing can be too heavy, no price too high, if only I can be married to you. Make me incapable of ever hurting or injuring you and keep all authority in your hands. On this condition, give me back your heart and love. Don't cast me away from you. Don't separate me from my blood that I believe you are carrying in your womb. No, beauty, let it be and always remain a token of our love; I have no doubts that I am its true father. Therefore, let me also be your true husband.

Leave this dismal and disastrous place with me, this place that is deadly to both of us; then we can be the happiest and most perfect spouses in the world. I am not only fully prepared to let you have your way in this, I even request it from you. Have no fear that during our marriage I will think about the things that have happened, whatever they were, but I swear with the same oaths as mentioned above that everything will be immersed in eternal oblivion. There is no suffering, no sorrow, no soul-grieving treatment, which cannot be sweetened by having your beloved person near me. Take a firm decision now in the name and the fear of God, as I have done in this matter. Pronounce now, unabashedly and without dissimulation, the final sentence, the sentence of my life or death. If it is, as I hope and expect from divine grace, that you should pronounce the sentence to spare my life, then I will consider myself the happiest of all mortals and I assure you and swear as done above that you won't regret it. In that case, keep this letter, so that you can confront me with it time and again. Yes, let this letter serve as an eternal whip for me. But if I am—and I dare say if you are—so unfortunate that you should pronounce my death sentence, then I request and demand this letter back. You can keep all others, as I will keep yours.

That's it, Beautiful Annie, the last letter that I think you will ever get from me, with the ultimate and most heartfelt determination.

Accept that this is the real and veritable truth; and, to attest this, I refer to the above-mentioned Oaths, with which I proclaim once more that I am, and hope to remain by your doing with God's grace,

    Beloved Soul-Guardian,
    Your tender loving lover

    Johannes Bartholomeus Ferdinandus van Gogh

Van Gogh dated the letter for the following day, June 29, and lay down his pen.[3] It was in blood that he had been writing and "blood" was the noun that he had used most often. With hindsight, almost every word appears ominous. Did Van Gogh have the slightest suspicion that this blood-red letter anticipated events soon to come? The phrase that the place in which he and Annie had lived was deadly to both of them would literally come true. That night, however, Van Gogh merely hoped that his words would move his loved one to tears, that she would take him in her arms again and promise to become his wife. He laid the letter in a drawer, intending to take it to Annie's home the next morning. Then he blew out the candle and went to bed.

Preface

As the prelude suggests, this book is about love and violent death. The man who wrote that letter of hope and fear would spill his blood in vain. Eventually, his name would become known throughout the entire city of Amsterdam and far beyond. It had been eight and a half years since the previous murder that every Amsterdamer had talked about. Twice, within a decade, Amsterdam had been a witness to killing for love: two cases of lethal passion in an age of Enlightenment. These murders are the subject of this book.

The dossiers of these crimes, first assembled by the city court and now enlarged upon by historical research, are voluminous. They form the basis for the two tales presented here. Obviously, a nonfictional murder story cannot be told as a "whodunit." Instead, this book's narrative elaborates on the personality of the protagonists, the events of their lives, and why they became killers; all against the background of an age of reason and sentimentality. A brief overview of the two cases follows.

The narrative beginning in chapter 2 revolves around Nathaniel Donker, born in Indonesia and sent to the Netherlands in his youth. A rich orphan at twenty, he meets Cecilia, a working-class widow, and they join in an illegal marriage contested by his older brother. They roam around and live for several years as fugitives just across the border, but finally they settle down with their two children on a country estate. Then, Dora enters the picture, a younger woman of German descent who completely enchants Nathaniel. He runs away with her to Amsterdam and, as Cecilia pursues them, they make plans to murder her. In December 1766 they lure her into their "house at the water" and strangle her. Despite some difficulties, they manage to dump the victim's corpse in the moat outside the city wall and think they are safe. A week later, however, the discovery of a truncated female body is the talk of the town. The court arrests Nathaniel, while Dora remains in hiding. But, after a month, someone betrays her. In a long trial, Nathaniel finally confesses, which leads to his execution. Dora, however, withstands the third degree of torture and survives in Amsterdam's prison for women.

The main protagonist in the tale beginning in chapter 6, J. B. F. Van Gogh, is approaching forty at the time of the crime. He has unsuccessfully pursued the careers of actor, surgeon, and hack writer. In January 1775, while visiting a brothel, he meets Annie, twenty-four, and falls in love with her at first sight. She agrees to marry him but secretly continues to work as a prostitute and to see her former lover and pimp. For six months, the engagement is on and off, with many quarrels, tears, and reconciliations. The tension escalates when a hostile hack writer publishes two pamphlets mocking the affair. At the end of June, Van Gogh writes a letter with his own blood, hoping to persuade his beloved to marry him after all. He recites it to her in the presence of the neighbors, but to no avail. Her rejection induces him to commit suicide, but at the last moment he turns his knife and stabs her in the heart. His trial, with successive appeals, goes on for years, while several writers publish accounts about him and his deeds. Some consider him a freethinker, including the prosecutor, who despises sentimentalism and depicts the defendant's deed as an ordinary crime of revenge. In the end, the public executioner decapitates Van Gogh on Amsterdam's main square in April 1778.

Microhistories often deal with only one case, but there are good reasons why this book focuses on two. In many ways, they complement each other. First, they represent the two prototypes of killing for love: eliminating a rival and turning against a lover who ends the affair. They also differ with respect to the social milieu, the character of the main actors, and the strategy used to get them convicted. Finally, the public impact of these two cases was different: a collective shuddering over an atrocious crime and great astonishment about the murderer's high standing in the first case and a lively interest in the persons of the killer and the victim in the second. But why should history writing be concerned with sensational crimes at all?

Emerging as a separate field in the 1970s, the history of crime had an ambitious program. Crime was a window to social relations. Court records revealed hidden secrets about common people's existence, the antagonism between the rich and the poor, and the position of various minorities—in short, the whole web of social relationships. Moreover, crime reflected economic conditions. Did the number of thefts and robberies rise in years of dearth or recession? Did the pattern of crime change with industrialization? Solid statistical work formed the basis for answering such questions. A key word was "serial research," a term indicating that the properties of the series itself constituted the object of investigation: annual fluctuations in the number of offenses, the ratio of theft to violence, the average age of offenders, the percentage of women prosecuted, sentencing patterns. The scholars who devised this program frowned upon the study of separate, exemplary cases. To focus on one sensational crime surely was anathema.

The serial program no longer holds sway. Although much work in the history of crime and criminal justice continues to be based on extensive data sets, few scholars belittle the study of exemplary cases. In part, this change of orientation is due to a decline of confidence in quantification. It also owes a great deal to the modern interest in questions of representation. For example, if a historian's subject is crime literature, the notorious cases obviously predominate.[1] A third important factor in the change of orientation, next to lesser confidence in quantification and interest in representation, is the increasing interest in cultural themes, such as the concept of honor. Historians now recognize that the in-depth study of one or a few trial or police dossiers can deepen our insight into the culture and social relations of the society in which they were compiled. Examples are the small dramas investigated by the papal court in sixteenth-century Rome or the much-publicized but unsolved murder of Mary Rogers in nineteenth-century New York.[2] And yet, as serious historians, we may feel uncomfortable when confronted with severed body parts found in a canal or letters written with blood. Is there a justification for focusing on these two sensational cases? Can we analyze them, look beyond their mere sensation, and use them as a source of information about the world that witnessed them?

The justification is based on a simple argument: the brutal or unexpected murders of the past are not only sensational to today's consumers of popular historiography, they equally fascinated the contemporaries who heard or read about them first-hand. That fact makes these crimes legitimate objects of scholarly research. Contemporaries were eager to learn everything about the offenders, the victims, and any relevant circumstances, so their interest mirrors their perceptions of the world. Apparently, the fascinated public recognized a familiar element in the life stories of notorious murderers. They morally condemned the crime, no doubt, but somehow they could imagine themselves in the killer's shoes. However twisted, they showed a degree of empathy. If fatal attraction fascinated Amsterdamers in the 1760s and 1770s, this was because many could imagine what it felt like. A revolution in love, discussed in the opening chapter, was taking place at this time. As extraordinary as they were, the two cases dealt with here reflected the cultural mood of the age.

But this book goes beyond the analysis of mere sensation. It also takes up the program of microhistory, first laid out by authors such as Carlo Ginzburg and Natalie Davis.[3] These historians have shown that a detailed study of an individual case can reveal hidden secrets about the larger society. What do abstract notions like gender roles or popular versus elite culture come down to when applied to real people who lived in the past? In *The Return of Martin Guerre*, for example, Davis carefully assesses the room for maneuvering available to Bertrande, the female protagonist, within the cultural and social constraints she encountered. She lived with a man who was not her husband, but she had to maintain that she had never known that he was an impostor. Otherwise, she would have lost her chaste reputation and become an outcast.

The concept of "room for maneuvering" forms a bridge, moreover, between microhistory and the epistemological work of the famous German sociologist Norbert Elias. One of Elias's main goals was to do away with discussing the behavior of historical actors in terms of dichotomies such as structure versus agency or voluntarism versus determinism. As he put it, society is just the name we give to the network of individuals who constitute it. Social processes, and specific social situations within them, result from the interactions of millions of men and women, but simultaneously these processes and situations become relatively autonomous from the wishes and efforts of individual men and women. The network, which we all form together, in its turn constrains us and limits our options. People can make choices, but at a certain risk. A French aristocrat at Louis XIV's court, for example, might choose to retire and forget about the rules of etiquette. However, if he did so, he put his social existence at stake, risking the loss of everything that gave life meaning according to his world view. It is understandable, therefore, that only a few nobles chose to avoid the court.[4]

Similarly, a jack-of-all-trades in eighteenth-century Amsterdam, fancying a prostitute, might choose to marry her, but with serious consequences for his honor in the eyes of others, who would treat him accordingly. And a married man in love with another woman might prefer her permanent company over keeping her as a courtesan, but at the cost of becoming a fugitive libertine, condemned and shunned by respectable people. Thus, the exceptional choices made by a few individuals make it understandable why the majority opted for more predictable life courses.

In sum, social circumstances leave individual persons with a limited set of options. Many people, in the past as well as today, act simply as we expect them to act in their situation. The protagonists of our story sometimes acted differently. The voluminous dossiers about these murder cases allow us to ascertain the options open to a few men and women who lived some 250 years ago and to understand what the consequences were of taking the one road or the other. The method is a dual one: we must carefully assess the motives and thoughts of the principal actors during the main phases of their lives, and we have to perfect this assessment by confronting it with the best knowledge we have of Dutch society and its culture in the eighteenth century.

1
A Big City in Cultural Flux: Eighteenth-Century Amsterdam

In the years between the two dreadful murders that are the subject of this book, if any event made an equally profound impression on Amsterdam's inhabitants, it was the great fire of 1772, which destroyed the city's theater. That disaster serves as a focal point to introduce the cultural setting in which the tragedies narrated here unfolded. Unlike the microhistories presented by other scholars, whose scene is usually a village or a small town, the two narratives treated in this book are situated in Europe's third largest city of the time. With a population of well over two hundred thousand inhabitants, Amsterdam was a place of learned as well as popular culture. Even national developments involving the Dutch Republic as a whole always had a bearing on Amsterdam, and they were widely discussed in coffeehouses and private dwellings along its many canals. We need to be concerned especially with the period from about 1750 to about 1780, coinciding with the mature years of the principal actors (and, in one case, her entire life).

On Monday, May 11, 1772, some five hundred opera lovers flocked to the theater in Amsterdam to watch and listen to two performances. The regular season, during which the city's own troupe of actors performed comic, tragic, and allegorical plays, had just finished. During the summer season the stage customarily was the domain of foreigners, often opera singers.

That night a Flemish company put on two French operas, the second of which was *Le Déserteur* by P. A. de Monsigny. It was an immensely popular piece, first performed with great success in Paris in 1769. The Flemish company was famous for its refined technique of illumination. This time they hung a huge tray containing twenty pots of wax, with two wicks burning in each, in front of the stage. During a scene situated in a prison, however, they dimmed the lights by lowering the tray down in front of the stage and partly covering it. When it somehow became overheated, a stage hand, realizing that the awful smell meant danger, ran for a bucket of water. But, when he removed the tray's cover, a shooting flame rose from it right up to the ceiling—it was already too late. The stage consisted mostly of wood and linen, and the scenery pieces were equally flammable. In less than half an hour, the entire theater was ablaze. Understandably, the audience panicked, the more so since one of the exit doors turned out to be locked. The first group that reached that door tried to ram it, but they failed because of the crowd pressing against them. Many spectators were trampled. The fire brigade could do no more than try to stop the flames from spreading to neighboring houses, with only partial success. When they had mastered the situation at three A.M., the theater and five houses lay in ashes, and thirty more buildings had severe or light damage. The death count amounted to eighteen persons who had died from suffocation, trampling, or in one case jumping down eight meters from a box.[1]

Unsurprisingly, the fire became *the* subject of conversation in Amsterdam for weeks to come, with much exaggeration and myth making. Rumors about the number of people killed, for example, ranged from one hundred to over two hundred. A periodical recording the conversations of a "nameless society" had several of its members debating the fire at their meeting the next day. Member A arrived first. He had been home the previous evening, unaware that the fuss around his house concerned the theater. Member B had stayed overnight across the harbor north of the city, where he saw the flames brightly lighting the sky. In several villages, he said, the inhabitants had rolled out the hoses, thinking the fire was nearby. Member C, joining the company a little later, had watched everything from close by. Then member D came in. He had actually visited the theater and managed to escape with torn clothes and a shoe missing. He had observed pickpockets and thieves taking advantage of the panic. In particular, they had robbed the ladies of their precious watches and earrings. Two of them had their ear lobes torn, and one robber had even threatened to cut off the ears of a Jewish lady if she refused to hand over her jewels. That night, the whole city was so bright that one could read the time from every tower clock with ease, and even in faraway places a shimmering light appeared on the horizon.[2]

The rumors, the exaggerations, and the sensationalism underline the impression this immense fire made on Amsterdam's inhabitants. Many compared the event to earlier disasters, in particular the Lisbon earthquake of 1755. Traditionally, such calamities were considered a sign of God's wrath. In the second half of the eighteenth century, however, a lot of people rejected the notion of a punishing God. Thus, one member of the "nameless society" emphasized that most accidents stem from recklessness.[3] The Amsterdam fire of 1772, then, forms a test case for the spread of rationalist or enlightened ideas. The subject of the Enlightenment is important because Van Gogh, the protagonist of our second story, consorted with hack writers (persons who made a living by producing a vast amount of writings) and, while he was jailed, people speculated that he was a freethinker.

Religiously oriented people, the Calvinists of the leading Reformed Church in particular, had always disliked the theater. In Calvinist theory, acting was pretending to be another person, an infamous habit of the devil. Moreover, plays were often frivolous, both the dialogue and the singing and dancing. Even the more permissive Remonstrants barred actors from Communion, based on the unlikelihood that any of them acted only in decent plays.[4] In 1638 the Reformed leaders had acquiesced in the debut of this temple of sin, because the profits it generated went to charity. The beneficiaries were the orphanage and the old men's home, whose regents were also regents of the theater. During the French invasions of 1672 and 1747, the magistrates temporarily closed the theater to appease God. They did so also in 1732, when they believed that God, as a punishment for the prevalence of sodomy in the Netherlands, had sent a host of worms to the country, which had eaten away the foundations of the dikes.[5]

No wonder the ruling gentlemen sensed trouble in 1772. On May 14, with the ashes still smoldering, the presiding burgomaster invited a representative of the Reformed ministers to his home. Perhaps, he suggested, his guest might be so kind as to inform his colleagues of the burgomasters' desire that no one should discuss the fire from the pulpit on Sunday the seventeenth, or let them at least preach in a restrained manner. He did communicate the request to his colleagues, but to no avail. Although relations between magistrates and ministers were harmonious in this period, such an exceptional occasion precluded ecclesiastical compliance. On Sunday, most ministers chose to comment on passages from the Old Testament, which left no doubt about their intentions: "I shall send fire to his cities"; "light the fire . . . to make his impurity melt with him"; "all their idols will be destroyed and all their whores' rewards consumed by fire."[6]

That the Reformed ministers considered the theater's destruction by fire as God's punishment for the citizens' indulgence in sinful amusement comes as no surprise. Not every contemporary commentator shared this view. Some, although religiously oriented, refused to believe it was God's habit to intervene directly in earthly affairs. Others tolerated the theater or even had sympathy for it. The views of those who denied God's punishing hand and loved the theater can be considered the most enlightened. The historian Buisman analyzed some two hundred pamphlets and poems published in reaction to the fire. Forty-one authors made a personal statement about whether or not the calamity was God's punishment. Buisman identified twenty-eight reactions as enlightened, ten as unenlightened, and three as ambiguous. Among the first group, several authors charged their opponents, who had seen God's punishing hand, with delighting in the death of innocent people. This was an arrogant and inhumane idea, they argued, in fact an offense to the deity. The views of these commentators conformed to the mild image of God that characterized the Christian Enlightenment in the Netherlands. Among the reactions to disasters that had struck the country a few decades earlier, such as a severe cattle plague, the unenlightened views still had predominated slightly.[7]

The increasing currency of enlightened ideas ranks high among the cultural changes during the years we are concerned with. In fact, all major changes of this period were cultural, pertaining either to the realm of learning or that of habits and emotions. The three decades from 1750 to 1780 witnessed few changes in the economy or demography, or in relations between social classes and the political and religious situation. Amsterdam's economy, expanding since the middle of the sixteenth century, had ceased to grow, but real decline set in just a little later. The population explosion that had made Amsterdam the third-largest city of Europe was generations ago, and the number of inhabitants was more or less stable. Despite the disagreement over preaching about the fire, church–state relations were much less conflict ridden than they had been in the previous century. There were no political upheavals between a series of disturbances and riots in 1747–1748 and the Patriot movement, which challenged the prominent position of the Prince of Orange in the country in the 1780s. Nationwide, this was also a time of quiet labor relations; a long tradition of labor unrest came to a halt by the middle of the eighteenth century.[8]

The breakthrough of the Enlightenment in the Netherlands has been documented also in a more conventional way, in studies of writing, phi-

A Big City in Cultural Flux: Eighteenth-Century Amsterdam

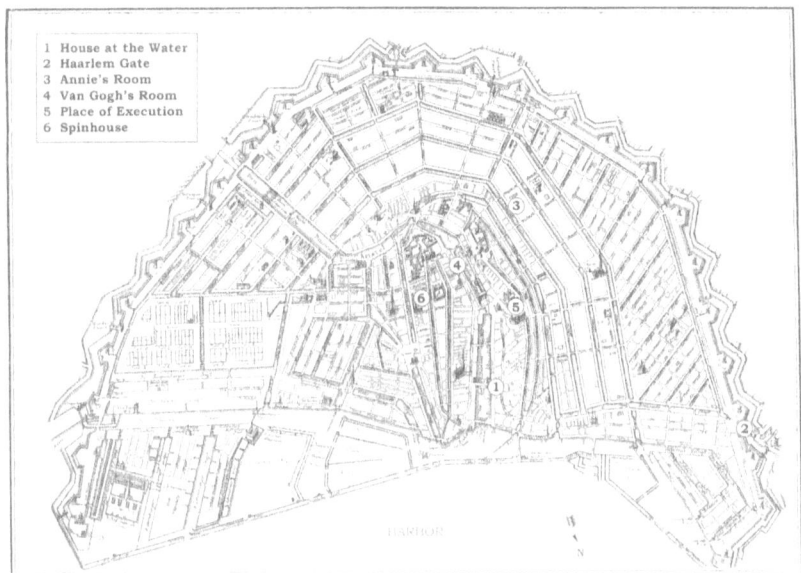

Map of eighteenth-century Amsterdam, with the principal sites of the two tales. Map compiled by Paula van Alphen, Erasmus University.

losophy, and publishing. The country's infrastructure certainly was favorable to the spread of culture: due to the high degree of literacy, the Dutch book market was of considerable size. The province of Holland—the most important of the seven that made up the Dutch Republic—had the highest density of bookstores of all European regions. Amsterdam alone boasted 121 bookstores in 1778, whereas Paris, with over twice the number of inhabitants, had a mere 129.[9] No precise figures are available for earlier in the century, but we know reading was already widespread in the Netherlands by then.

Historians usually identify the first half of the eighteenth century as the period of the early Enlightenment, and in the Netherlands Justus van Effen counts as its principal representative. This very popular writer, who believed in the perfectability of mankind, valued both reason and religion. Whereas reason was the principal guide on the road to virtue, religion served as the basis of all human morality—an ambivalence that illustrates the moderate Christian tenor of the Dutch Enlightenment. Van Effen expounded his views in a periodical entitled the *Holland Spectator*. His epigones after midcentury published periodicals of their own—a genre that Dutch historians call *spectatoriale bladen*, which might be translated as *observing magazines*. Thirteen of these magazines appeared in the 1750s and 1760s and no fewer than twenty-six in the 1770s. The authors were mostly middle class, criticizing the patrician elite for its lifestyle but never challenging its ruling monopoly. This was equally true for the learned or philosophical societies, first founded in the 1750s and 1760s and emerging in greater numbers in the 1770s. Like the "observing" writers, most members of these learned companies were solidly middle class and philosophers in their spare time.[10] Real revolutionaries and freethinkers were few in number; before 1750 they were mostly foreigners, while a few radical societies, whose members discussed the ideas of Rousseau, Diderot, and D'Alembert, emerged after midcentury. Even these societies consisted of socially respectable people.[11]

In prerevolutionary France, a less respectable figure, that of the hack writer, was closely associated with radicalism. We are well acquainted with this figure through the work of Robert Darnton, who describes hacks as poor writers leading a precarious existence, many of whom became radicals out of sheer hatred for the system. The police of Paris, however, were occasionally able to recruit one of the hacks as a spy.[12] Around 1700, London had been the first city in Europe to house a group of hack writers. They lived on or near Grub Street, which became a synonym for the milieu of hack writers everywhere.[13] After London, Paris took the lead. What about Amsterdam or, possibly, other cities in the Dutch Republic? The equivalent of a Grub Street in the Netherlands of the eighteenth century is an underresearched subject. In a volume on the Dutch Enlightenment published a decade ago, two American historians even pronounced it undiscoverable. Whereas Jeremy Popkin simply stated that the Netherlands lacked hack writers, Margaret Jacob supposed that Amsterdam had a literary underground but that it remains elusive for modern investigators because the police showed no interest in it.[14] Students of Dutch eighteenth-century literature, however, are familiar with several hacks.

The hacks' godfather was Jacob Campo Weyerman, a prolific writer who produced not only a series of books and pamphlets but also several periodicals, one of them entitled *Echo of the World*. The private lives of his contemporaries formed his favorite subject. At first, Weyerman only made a living by publishing scandals, but in the 1730s he began to extort money from public figures by announcing he was writing a book about them and promising to keep the manuscript private if they paid off. The Court of Holland had him arrested in 1738 and imposed a life sentence for his extortions the next year.[15] Weyerman, who died in prison in 1747, inspired several hack writers who were active after midcentury. The most notorious of them, Franciscus Lievens Kersteman, was rather critical of his predecessor. Kersteman specialized in semifictional biographies, beginning with Weyerman in 1756. He called his colleague a freethinker, libertine, swindler, and false player, ending however with his positive side, in particular his habit of mediating for friends in love.[16] The first edition of this book appeared while its author was staying in a private prison in Rotterdam at the request of his uncle.[17] In 1757 Kersteman published a biography of the healer-astrologer J. C. Ludeman, revealing himself as his follower and even claiming, quite improbably, to have been his student. In 1773 the Rotterdam court arrested and tried Kersteman for falsifying exchange bills, and he was imprisoned in that town for another thirteen years.[18]

The fact that both Weyerman and Kersteman were imprisoned suggests that Dutch hack writers, too, belonged to a less respectable segment of society.[19] Whereas political motives may have played a role in the former's trial, the latter served his two prison terms for nonpolitical reasons. Kersteman never attacked the social hierarchy outright. Yet he counts as a representative of the Enlightenment because his work is completely secular in tone. Even though he denounced his predecessor as a freethinker, he wrote about his own and others' adventures without moralism. This absence of moralism also characterized another hack writer of the time, Nicolaas Hoefnagel. He explicitly acknowledged Weyerman as his spiritual mentor, by publishing a periodical also named *Echo*. During most of his career Hoefnagel was equally a nonpolitical writer, but in the early 1780s, shortly before his death, he enjoyed fame as a supporter of the Patriot cause. Unlike his two colleagues, he never went to prison, save for one night in jail after a tavern brawl. Another hack writer of this period, Willem Ockers, was a radical from the beginning, fiercely attacking established religion. Since Van Gogh was acquainted with Hoefnagel and Ockers, we will get to know them better in chapter 6.

These writers operated in an increasingly hostile political climate. The relative freedom of expression that had characterized the Republic for a long time came under strain after midcentury. Faced with the radicalization of the Enlightenment into deism and criticism of the social hierarchy, Dutch authorities grew weary of dissenting voices and resented it when ordinary citizens meddled in affairs of state. Moreover, the authorities yielded more easily to diplomatic pressure concerning works displeasing to a foreign power. The prohibition of La Mettrie's *L'Homme-Machine*, by a committee of the Estates of Holland (the supreme governing body of the province), inaugurated this shift to intolerance in 1748. In 1762 the Amsterdam magistrates prohibited Rousseau's *Du Contrat Social*. No wonder that Swiss publishers became serious competitors on the market for printing illegal French books. The Dutch-language market increasingly split into two sectors. The established bookseller-publishers preferred to print works with an official approval, often ordered by church or state agencies. This provided assured sales and no troubles. Less established booksellers printed the more risky works. The movement toward intolerance affected hacks as well as mainstream writers, but the hacks' vulnerability was greater. Whether or not they were radicals, the established booksellers usually refused their manuscripts.[20]

Although the Enlightenment was above all an ideological movement, it also brought a change in the field of sensibilities and emotions. Opposition to judicial torture, for example, owed as much to a rationalist critique as to a heightened sensitivity that decried every human suffering. In a recent study of eighteenth-century emotional culture, Dorothée Sturkenboom makes use of the same observing magazines that were such a conspicuous feature of the Dutch Enlightenment. According to her, the crucial shift took place around 1760. Before that date, the authors of periodicals judged their fellow citizens primarily in terms of a moralistic typology; thereafter, the quality of one's inner feelings was an equally important criterion. This shift in emotional culture has a direct bearing on our two murder tales.

In essence, the prevailing view of human passions turned from outright negative to mildly positive. Writers of the first half of the eighteenth century had unequivocally condemned men and women whose passions controlled them. In the parade of "intemperate persons," the coquette occupied first place. She always wanted to please, was conscious of her beauty, and made a habit of flirting, but could never be had. She did not act from lust; if she gave in to a man, it was because of his seductive cunning and her naïveté. In the end, the coquette remained a decent bourgeois woman. Her male counterpart was the *petit-maître* who, even though he liked to please women, was somewhat effeminate and had no sexual desire for either women or men. He was often of patrician status. A second male type, the *lichtmis* or libertine, was noble or patrician as well, but he threatened to infect the bourgeoisie. He was the typical womanizer, potent and virile, who easily turned his attention to a prostitute if a respectable woman proved too difficult to seduce. Nathaniel Donker, of upper-middle-class descent and under the spell of a former prostitute, matched the description of the observing writers. These writers completed their catalogue of intemperate types with the masturbating youth, the miser, and the religious enthusiast.[21]

When a new emphasis on the expression of emotions broke through in the 1760s, these types continued to receive bad press. Asked to characterize

J. B. F. van Gogh, who did everything to please the woman he loved without explicitly voicing a sexual desire, an observing writer would probably have called him a petit-maître. The writers' recognition of the positive power of emotions was reserved in particular for pity and love. When referring to an "emotional person," they thought of a sensitive mind with an open eye for the world's problems. By contrast, their predecessors before 1760 had defined the "emotional person" primarily in terms of an unstable, egocentric character, dominated by his passions. The new view was compatible with the Christian tenor of the Dutch Enlightenment. God had planted pity, friendship, and altruistic love in human nature, the writers argued, in order to strengthen the bonds between all people. These feelings, therefore, benefited society as a whole. The writers even allowed men to cry, as long as they shed their tears out of compassion for the miserable. Sensitive men cried, but never out of self-pity and preferably in the company of others to make them share the compassionate mood. In this way, a man could be sensitive and remain honorable. Women, on the other hand, were expected to display their sensitivity at home, as mothers and wives. For both men and women, excessive feelings of romantic love were anathema. The observing writers partook of the European-wide new sensibility, but they distrusted the type of infatuation that was the stuff of sentimental novels. Passionate physical love was dangerous; they unequivocally ranked it with the darker side of the new sensibility.[22]

As we will see, the main protagonist of the second tale behaved much like a character in a sentimental novel. He shared the writers' positive view of emotions, but he expressed this in ways completely unacceptable to them. It makes us aware that real life might be different from the lofty ideals voiced in respectable magazines. Indeed, next to the breakthrough of the Enlightenment and a shift in emotional standards, the period 1750–1780 witnessed cultural changes of a more mundane nature. These included a transformation in the character of interpersonal violence, from a prevalence of knife fighting to a greater share of violence against intimates. The timing of this transformation was probably peculiar to Amsterdam, so an incident that took place in that city serves to introduce it.

Jan Amsins and Margaretha van Heems lived on the "French Path," an ill-reputed back street in the Jordaan quarter. He was a fifty-four-year-old porter, a resident of Amsterdam from birth. The neighbors called her Rotterdam Griet, which betrayed her place of birth. Her age remained unrecorded. Although Jan was a married man and his legal wife had borne him four children, he had been with Griet for more than ten years. During that period she had given birth to two children, whom everyone had always considered to be Jan's. After his arrest he told the court he was not sure that he was their father, possibly as a conscious tactic to cast doubt on his concubine's character. The couple did have a tumultuous relationship. When they were drunk, which was often the case, they quarreled constantly. Jan claimed that Griet once punched him so hard that he almost lost some of his teeth. All the neighbors confirmed their drunken brawls. They declared that, although both of them drank, she was intoxicated more frequently, which made her very obnoxious. In a sober state, the couple was quiet.

On a Monday night in February 1771, Jan was out drinking wine with the wife of a friend and another woman. When he came home, Griet heavily reproached him for drinking in the company of married women. She quarreled and fought with him all night, pinching his privates several times. The next morning Jan left the house, maybe for his porter's station, but he came home again in the afternoon with a lot of brandy in his stomach. When he demanded food from Griet, she started scolding him anew, calling him a sodomite and a thief. When she pinched his privates again, he became so furious that he grabbed a kitchen knife and stabbed her in the back. Seeing her bleeding heavily, he laid his hand on the wound and cried out, "my lord Jesus, what have I done?" The fuss alerted two neighboring women, who rushed in but could not prevent Griet from bleeding to death. Meanwhile, Jan had left the house. Later that night he visited a nearby tavern. Word went around that a woman had been murdered in the French Path and some customers knew that Jan had a relationship with her. Indignantly he retorted, "she is not my wife; she has been a whore of mine and all such women deserve to be killed." Those were his last words before they came to arrest him. Jan was tried and decapitated the next month.[23]

Viewed from one angle, this homicide case is modern in nature, since modern partner killings often are sudden eruptions of long, pent-up tensions. Because of the neighbors' testimonies, we know that the couple had a history of mutual conflict. The case is traditional to the extent that gendered honor played a key role. First, with the neighbors hearing a drunken Griet scolding Jan, his reputation in the eyes of the community was at stake. Second, he was keenly aware that by respectable standards his partner for ten years was a "whore." Although the inhabitants of the French Path had less concern for these standards, they surfaced in Jan's mind at the moment of crisis. More concretely, Griet had aroused his anger by pinching his privates and calling him a sodomite. These words and deeds amounted to questioning his manhood. She had probably done so earlier, and for him to go out drinking with other women served to underline his virility and independence. Traditional or modern, the case is typical of homicide in Amsterdam in the second half of the eighteenth century, a period in which many killers were intimately related to their victims. The story of Jan and Griet, then, is about gender, honor, and violence. These three themes were closely related, but we may conveniently continue with the first.

Gender relations were changing in most of Europe in the eighteenth century. For the Netherlands, this can be illustrated by a detour, that of homosexuality. During several waves of sodomy trials, conducted in Amsterdam and other towns beginning in 1730, a new conception of the homosexual gradually surfaced. According to the traditional view, prevalent until then, sodomy was just one of the perversities in the repertoire of a dissolute man. Moralists thought it unlikely that such perverts restricted themselves to sex with other men: they were considered equally eager to commit adultery or incest, and they might even be womanizers as well. From the middle of the eighteenth century onward, however, the notion of a gay identity gradually emerged. Dutch people began to speak of a person who is a sodomite instead of someone who merely practices sodomy.[24] Consequently, *sodomite* became a word of abuse regardless of a man's real sexual orientation, as in Griet's words to Jan.

The emergence of a gay identity formed part of a more encompassing transformation involving a redefinition of sex and gender. That transformation was a European-wide phenomenon, affecting the Netherlands no less than England, France, and Germany. For centuries, anatomists had viewed the difference between the female and the male body as a matter of external design. According to the prevalent image, behavior and personality shaped a person's sex, leaving room for intermediate human specimens such as hermaphrodites and viragos. The idea that intercourse between a Jew and a Christian was unnatural, for example, implied that religious differences formed the basis of biological differences. In the course of the eighteenth century, base and superstructure underwent a complete reversal. A new view of the body emerged, and according to this view sex differences were rooted in nature itself. Now it was biological sex that shaped gender. Just the male and the female body existed, and only intercourse between these bodies was natural. Heterosexuality still was a Christian prescript, but it also was now a biological norm.[25] Consequently, deviations from this norm were defined more precisely and demarcated more strictly. That is how the rise of a gay identity fits into the transformation, but more was at stake. The redefinition of sex and gender and the new biological basis for heterosexuality undoubtedly affected the character of marriage and the family. Exactly how is harder to ascertain.

Up to now, historians have vehemently disagreed about the character of marriage and the family in preindustrial Europe and the extent to which relations among spouses were subject to change. Did spouses treat each other in a distanced manner and were parents largely indifferent to small children? Did "modern," affective bonds between family members take the place of this indifference from the late seventeenth century onward? That is one extreme view. According to the opposite view, spousal and parent-child relations always were warm and caring. Only the fashion of expressing them changed. The parties concerned posited these extremes largely without a mutual debate. Even though several historians have tried to bridge the gap, the great question concerning marital affection essentially remains unresolved. Fortunately, there is no urgent need to resolve it here. Whatever the "real," innermost feelings of spouses and parents, the cultural significance of marriage and the family unmistakably changed in the course of the eighteenth century. Again, this development was visible in the Netherlands as well as in most other European countries. Especially among the upper and middle classes, family life became a fundamental part of a person's identity. It moved from a semiperipheral to a central stage of culture. This change owed something to the new biological base for heterosexuality, but it had wider ramifications. It owed at least as much to the increasing emphasis on sentimentality and romance.

In the Dutch case, a few clearly identifiable trends support the idea of cultural change concerning marriage. For the children of the elite, free choice of partners was the rule in the eighteenth century, whereas among the upper classes in the sixteenth and early seventeenth centuries, parents had played the key role in bringing a couple together. Similarly, in the eighteenth century, husbands wrote intimate letters to their wives and vice versa. Women and men addressed their spouses informally, calling each other by their first names or by private sweet epithets. There is little information, however, on the modes of address prevalent before 1700. The third trend was the decline of litigation over marriage vows. It had been a venerable custom to sue another party for breaking a promise of marriage that he or she had once given. Mostly women did this, but men did as well, and often the vow had been made years earlier. Courts and consistories frequently handled such cases until the middle of the seventeenth century. Women and men who wanted to embark upon a union against the desire of the other party obviously could not claim mutual affection. In Amsterdam two judges held a session each week as the committee for marital affairs. In the first half of the seventeenth century, the majority of plaintiffs demanded the implementation of a marriage promise. In the first half of the eighteenth century, mostly couples in love called upon the commissioners, in order to overrule parents or guardians unwilling to give their consent.[26] The observing writers of the second half of the eighteenth century tuned in to this development. They propagated the ideal of marital bliss, enjoyed preferably in the safe haven of one's home.[27] Although this ideal had been around for a long time, it received a much greater emphasis and was expressed in a purely secular context now.

Seen in a broader perspective, the above trends represented an acceleration in a long-term process covering the sixteenth to twentieth centuries. The character of love itself changed. Once, to love somebody primarily meant performing your duties toward your partner, according to a set of cultural expectations. Nowadays, the psychological dimension of love is paramount, couples mutually exploring their innermost feelings. As a major step on the long road from then to now, the eighteenth-century revolution in love primarily concerned the affection expressed in marriage or courtship. This revolution encroached upon a pattern of behavior that historians call *homosocial*, a somewhat awkward term. They mean that, outside the marital bed, men were mostly in the company of men and women of women. During the eighteenth century, on the other hand, it became common for husbands and wives to spend more time with each other. This new custom first arose among the middle and upper classes. Note that husbands and wives, or engaged couples, were expected to stay in each other's company. When this revolutionized love befell a man and a woman who, for whatever reason, were unable to marry each other, that couple was bound to get into trouble. The new sensibility demanded that they stay together anyway, but social customs still were a formidable barrier to that. The ensuing predicament was the stuff of the sentimental novels of the period. In these novels, the solution sometimes consisted of suicide. About actual suicide in the Netherlands, we have little information, but we do know that in a few cases the predicament of impossible love led to murderous conflict; this may be called the darker side of the new sensibility.

The phrase "revolution in love" serves as shorthand for the interrelated changes regarding marriage, gender concepts, and emotional standards that were going on as the affairs dealt with here unfolded. This narrative examines the revolution in love from the angle of love gone wrong. Of course, the two murder cases cannot "prove" that a revolution in love took place in the eighteenth century. The evidence for that is contained in the works of the scholars referred to here, directly or indirectly. The murder stories shed new light on the character of the revolution in love by exploring its darker side. More important perhaps, they reveal how, in individual lives, modern sentiments remained inextricably intertwined with traditional views. Historical change never means a total reversal in the behavior and attitudes of all women and men making up a society.

About extramarital love, for example, conventional views persisted throughout the eighteenth century and beyond. Not surprisingly, preachers and religious moralists continued to condemn adultery and premarital intercourse. The active moral discipline at consistory meetings, however, was on the wane by this period.[28] The secular courts occasionally tried women and men for such offenses. Equally conventional, but in a different sense, was the double standard, which allowed men an unofficial freedom denied to women. A large part of the population still endorsed it. As a rule, the more religiously inclined a person, the less likely he was to condone the double standard. Among "respectable" workers and shopkeepers, it was also a matter of honor to be a faithful husband. The observing writers accused the French-influenced elite of thinking lightly about adultery, but even in the beau monde, discretion was everything in extramarital affairs. Had Nathaniel Donker just kept a mistress whom he cautiously visited at times, few people would have bothered about it. For all appearances, he had been an honorable husband and father.

Conventional views certainly remained prevalent concerning sex for sale. Honor played a key role here at several levels. The world of venal sex forms an integral part of our story because a prostitute or former prostitute was involved in both murder cases, in the first as a co-killer, in the second as the victim; this fact, in particular, led to the intertwining of modern sentiments and ancient attitudes.

For today's visitors, Amsterdam's number-one attraction is its red-light district. Try to pass through the crowd there on a Saturday night! Eighteenth-century Amsterdam was equally famous for its brothels, although their physical presence was more concealed. We are well informed about prostitution in early modern Amsterdam through the work of Lotte van de Pol.[29] Since 1578, when the city embraced the Reformation, prostitution was an underground business. The degree to which it was nevertheless visible varied over time. The period 1670–1720 was the "golden age" of night life in Amsterdam, exemplified by the music hall. Music halls were no straightforward brothels. They were taverns where men and women drank and danced and some men sought a sexual rendezvous. Popular books spread the fame of the music halls (and the prostitutes who lived there), which attracted an increasing number of foreign tourists. Yet, disembarked sailors formed the most conspicuous set of clients in this period. Whether or not because music halls attracted tourists, the authorities left them practically undisturbed. But around 1710, a concern over Amsterdam's reputation for vice prompted the city fathers toward rigorous action. The court's attention shifted from novice prostitutes to recidivists and the organizers of the trade. Many proprietors of music halls went bankrupt through the confiscation of musical instruments and whores' clothes. By 1720 most music halls had disappeared.

Demand on the amusement market remained high, however, and the factors pushing women to offer their services on this market, if anything, only grew stronger. Until about 1700, Amsterdam was a center of the textile industry, in which many women found employment. Most arrested prostitutes had been working in that industry earlier or had looked for a job in it. When the textile industry moved to the countryside, domestic service remained as the only major respectable employment for women. Historians estimate the number of domestic servants in eighteenth-century Amsterdam at twenty thousand, but the demand in that sector did not increase after 1700.[30] Moreover, the city constantly witnessed a surplus of women. Many women migrated to Amsterdam independently and stayed there, while many men went to sea. Within the adult Christian population, the sex ratio was probably as high as four women to three men; among the lower classes possibly even three women to two men. The Jewish community had a more equal sex ratio, because Jews prevented their women from migrating alone and the men did not enlist as sailors. After 1700 the combined factors of an unequal sex ratio and the disappearance of the textile industry caused unemployment and poverty to strike many women. This induced a number of them to try their luck in the illegal sex trade. The tighter control of Jewish men over their women meant that few Jewish women became prostitutes, while Jewish men did contribute to the demand. Consequently, some Christian women accepted Jews as clients, even though sex between Jews and Christians constituted an offense in its own right. The total number of professional prostitutes active in the city lay between eight hundred and one thousand.

After the waning of the music hall's golden era, then, prostitution remained a flourishing sector of the urban economy. The second and third quarters of the eighteenth century were the period of the secret brothel. Brothels always had existed in sorts, some more covert than others. In the decades after 1720, the covert establishment became the rule. Many brothels looked like ordinary taverns, but the door leading to the back room was open for steady or trustworthy clients, whose wishes went beyond wine and beer. Some procurers exploited their business under the guise of a store or even an ordinary dwelling. In *The Amsterdam Libertine*, written around 1730, an Amsterdamer leads a stranger to a place that in no way looks like a whorehouse. No women are living there, but the hostess asks a man who occasionally helps her to call a prostitute.

After midcentury, however, music halls reappeared, but in a more modest format than their predecessors. Women came in at night and danced, but if a client wanted sex, the woman took him out to some shabby room nearby. These establishments had a lower-class imprint, while secret brothels continued to cater to the wishes of a wealthier clientele. The nameless society, which we met in connection with the theater fire, once discussed the pleasures of different classes of people. The rich gentleman, one member said, liked to go out at midnight. He knew where to find such a house that, from the street, looked like a decent clothing or jewelry shop, but it stayed open at least until four A.M. and it lodged "beauties with very low heels, who tumble backwards more easily than a stone statue."[31]

Throughout the early modern period, the management of brothels in Amsterdam was largely a female affair, although several male procurers figure in our first tale. Even when married, women usually managed brothels alone. The husbands of arrested madams routinely claimed they had nothing to do with their wives' affairs. Although this sounds like a convenient excuse, it appears to have been true in most cases. Madams with thriving businesses hired the services of strong fellows with a reputation for violence, to protect the whores against clients who made trouble. Streetwalking women enjoyed no such protection. They were the most vulnerable group, because the judiciary pursued them relentlessly and they earned a meager income. Their standard fee was a *sesthalf* (five and one-half stivers). In a brothel, the client easily paid six to twelve times that amount, not to mention what he owed the madam for drinks, room rent, bed clothes, and the tip. The net income received by the prostitute herself was often zero. As a rule, she was heavily indebted to the madam, who provided her with "whores' clothes" and sometimes jewelry, too. Pregnancies, of streetwalkers as well as women who worked in brothels, were infrequent, due to bad health, venereal disease in particular, more than to contraception. According to a contemporary saying, grass seldom grows on heavily trodden paths.

As everywhere in Europe, contemporaries used the word *whore* in a broad sense. Any woman considered dishonorable might be called a whore.

Professional prostitutes counted as infamous without exception. The stigma of dishonor even extended to women who worked as seamstresses, charwomen, or domestic servants in a brothel. There were considerable numbers of them, according to the judicial records, but again the claim was a convenient excuse in at least some cases. Whereas outsiders considered all whores as infamous, within the world of prostitution subtle degrees of dishonor existed. These had to do with the type of sex and the status of clients. Most women only offered the standard service of simple coitus in the missionary position, with half their clothes on. They found it perverse when a client proposed to do it entirely in the nude. If a prostitute agreed to special variants, her colleagues certainly looked down on her. Women who insisted that their clients should be single men or widowers equally looked down on less discriminate colleagues. "Married men's whore" was a formidable insult.

It is hardly surprising to hear about these degrees of disreputability. Their existence followed from the undemocratic character of honor as a cultural commodity. Honor presupposes infamy or, at least, lesser honor. Ultimately, from an individual perspective, personal honor can be ascertained only in terms of other people who lack it or possess less of it. This characteristic formed the basis of a mechanism by which honor determined the lives of ever lower groups. If you have doubts about your reputation, look for others with an obviously baser character: others who are even more infamous than you fear you yourself are. For an ordinary Amsterdam prostitute of the eighteenth century, the infamous other was the married men's whore.

Up to now, we have discussed female honor, as ever centering on the woman's sexuality. In the world of prostitution, male honor was at stake, too. Most married men who visited a brothel did so as secretly as possible. If it became public knowledge, this was highly embarrassing, especially if they were active church members. This applied to almost every married brothel visitor, since men who could only afford the services of a streetwalker came from a milieu in which the neighbors (if not their wives) did not frown on this behavior. If a respectable housefather had anything to do with a prostitute, it was a severe stain upon his honor in the eyes of his peers. Even if his servant got pregnant, the only way to avoid suspicion was to dismiss her immediately. This code resulted from a gradual broadening of the base for male honor during the early modern period. Likewise, economic solidity had become an important source of honor for men. Once, this had been different. Male honor originally depended on a reputation for violence, bravery, and a patron's capacity to protect the women and men dependent on him. An echo of this older conception of male honor resounded in Amsterdam at the beginning of the eighteenth century in the milieu of knife fighters.[32]

The typical knife fighter always carried a stabbing weapon in his pocket, and he was prepared to use it whenever someone challenged him. Ordinarily, the challenge was a phase in a conflict that arose among a company of men in a tavern or in the street. Insults often were the immediate cause. This made knife fights akin to the official duel, fought with sword or pistol, even though that was uncommon in the Netherlands. Far from issuing written challenges, however, popular duelists settled the matter on the spot. In a tavern, the words "follow me outside" constituted an unmistakable signal. The yell *sta vast* (stand your man) was the sign to start fighting.

Popular duels were ritualized and bound to a code of honor. First and foremost, it was anathema for any third person, friend or foe, to intervene, except for the purpose of separating the combatants and convincing them to stop. Only a one-on-one combat was a fair fight. If one of the men intending to start a duel was in the company of a friend and the latter stated his intention to refrain from interfering, it usually earned him the compliment of being an honorable man. The fight as such was a test of skill, in which the combatants proved their manhood. It was over when one man had cut the other or obtained a clear advantage, but sometimes it went wrong with a lethal result. When a popular duel ended in the death of a combatant, this counted as a pardonable accident in the milieu of knife fighters. The court, however, took it as seriously as any other homicide. Once, a considerable part of Amsterdam's population had been involved in knife fighting, but around 1700 its practitioners occupied a social position along the border of the "respectable" and the "disreputable" segment of the city's lower classes. About half of the protagonists in popular duels also were petty thieves or they committed property crimes on an occasional basis.

Honorific knife fights, hardly visible since the 1720s, play no direct role in our murder stories. Their demise, however, was another feature of the cultural changes that affected Amsterdam in the eighteenth century. For one thing, the popular duel was the last major manifestation of an honor code that obliged a man to be brave and violent. Its disappearance shifted the balance of views of honor definitively toward a more bourgeois conception of respectability, which predominated in the years 1750–1780. The disappearance of the popular duel also meant that the character of violence in the city changed. This coincided with a considerable drop in Amsterdam's homicide rates, from about nine per one hundred thousand in the first quarter of the eighteenth century to about three in the third quarter. Thus, the change was most pronounced with respect to homicidal violence: from knife fights gone wrong to killings in the domestic sphere or property crime. A simple count of killer-victim relationships illustrates this shift. In the first half of the eighteenth century, 44 percent of homicide victims were strangers and 15 percent intimates. In the period 1751–1810 this ratio had reversed: 18 percent strangers and 43 percent intimates.[33] These figures, obtained from trial records, are probably a little biased, but the trend is unmistakable. The typical homicide in Amsterdam after 1750 was the killing of an intimate person, usually in a domestic setting. Our two murders were characteristic of their time.

To be more precise, these two crimes represented a distinct subcategory of violence against intimates. They were not just the culmination of domestic quarrels; they resulted from vehement desire and subsequent frustration. This takes us back to the darker side of the revolution in love.

Of course, the desire of a man for a woman, and vice versa, has been around for a long time, and this desire has sometimes led to the spilling of blood. In the Old Testament, King David wants the beautiful Bathsheba, so he arranges for her husband to be killed in battle. The knights of courtly romance put their lives into the service of their favorite ladies, but they seldom met these ladies, constantly roaming around to perform heroic deeds for them. Elizabethan courtiers praised their peers who had committed suicide because of a lost love. To take matters into your own hands and eliminate a rival or kill the one you cannot get implies an entirely different attitude. It combines the romantic desire to be with one loved person all the time with a firm resolution and conscious planning to reach that goal. It also requires an overwhelming feeling that the deed, however abject, is inevitable.

Such feelings, that is the contention here, were new in the eighteenth century. Earlier periods—possibly with the exception of the Italian Renaissance[34]—hardly witnessed such expressions of an intense longing and desire for another person, coupled with the compulsive idea that you have to be and remain with this person all the time and no matter what. Such an attitude presupposes a touch of romanticism, which many historians consider a relatively modern state of mind. Literary evidence supports the idea that something new was around in the eighteenth century. In most of Europe, before circa 1700, popular literature as well as published speeches and sermons routinely described wife or husband killers as drunken men and wanton women. Their inspiration, if any, came from the devil rather than some romantic compulsion. It is only after that date, also in the

Netherlands, that the latter motif gained prominence. The revolution in love affected a large part of Europe's middle and upper classes. Needless to say, for the majority of men and women the consequences were less drastic. The average tragic lover might shed a million tears or confide his or her feelings to a diary. Couples with a third person standing in their way could ignore or run from that person. Even though murder was unrepresentative in quantitative terms, as a corollary of the revolution in love, it nevertheless reflected this cultural transformation.

2

No One Suspected He Would End As a Murderer

Palm trees waved gently in the tropical breeze. Anyone who ventured to the shore would have had a broad view on either side. To the north lay a large bay, part of the Java Sea. On the inland side, a plain, overgrown with thicket that hid its muddy soil, stretched about a kilometer to the fort. Solid sandy beaches lay further along the coast, and on the horizon one could see wet rice fields and mangrove forests. The fort, erected by the first group of European adventurers led by Jan Pietersz Coen, dominated the skyline with its huge, square-shaped structure, a bastion at each corner. South of the fort, the second generation of colonists, mostly merchants, had built the city and surrounded it with walls. It had a rectangular shape, nine hundred meters wide from west to east and thirteen hundred meters deep into the inland. Its streets formed a simple grid, as in modern Manhattan, but they alternated with canals. Names like Church Street and Amsterdam Canal reminded one of the mother country, but there was also a Malay Canal and the stateliest was called the Tiger Canal. Everything was a mixture of Dutch and Asian. Houses with gables and stone stairs up to the front door alternated with dwellings in Chinese style with their graceful roofs. The town hall looked traditionally Dutch, as did the mills, the wharf, the quays and drawbridges, the taverns, and the boardinghouses hosting sailors. But coral sand and gravel covered the streets, and the trees along the canals were tamarinds. Native oarsmen crossed the waters in their praus, and Chinese *wayang* players performed at the corner of the market square.

Chapter 2

It was 1730, the last year before the great silting up set in, which eventually filled the air with stench and germs. On their way down from the mountains through the forests, the rivers had always dragged loads of mud to the coast. For ages, they had dumped it straight into the sea, but the intervention of the Europeans had put up a barrier. At the time they built the fort, it bordered on the beach; the muddy plain had silted up behind a pier. Worse, the silt continually filled the town's canals, fed by several rivers. Throughout the eighteenth century, the city employed Javanese dredgers, delivered by the island's princes, to deepen the canals. From the 1730s onward, the struggle against the mud and the stench seemed lost. Moreover, the sugar mills outside had started to pollute the fresh water flowing into town. The combined effects of pollution and silting up made the climate ever more unhealthful. After 1730 the mortality of Europeans sharply increased. More frequently than before, they succumbed to tropical diseases, called by names such as rotting fever or red diarrhea.

But in 1730 the mood was still optimistic. Trade prospered. Twice a year, big ships sailed off to the homeland, loaded with spices, sugar, and other Indonesian products. Most Europeans freely admitted they had ventured to the tropics for one reason only—to make a fortune—and many, though not all, succeeded. No less than twenty thousand people crowded into the urban rectangle of barely over one square kilometer, and another one hundred thousand lived outside the walls. About a quarter of this population consisted of slaves, mostly Indonesian; the rest were mostly mestizos and free Chinese, wearing the characteristic long queue at the back of the head. The Chinese also owned slaves. The Europeans constituted a minority, but they ruled the town. The rich and respectable among them rode in stately coaches drawn by a pair of horses. They dressed in black and wore wigs, that is, when they walked the streets or paraded to the Reformed church in the company of slave women.[1]

This was Batavia, the place where Nathaniel Donker was born and spent his childhood years.

"Donker" means dark, and darkness descended upon the family in the end. Our first protagonist had one thing in common with the defendant in the second part: at his arrest for a capital offense, he was ignorant, or pretended to be ignorant, of his exact age. In December 1766 he declared he was between thirty-three and thirty-seven years old. Batavia's baptismal registers, of which the Dutch national archive has copies, cannot help.

No One Expected He Would End As a Murderer 23

The records of the 1720s and 1730s are in such a bad state that most entries are illegible. By sheer luck, one of the few legible fragments concerns Pieter Gerbrand, Nathaniel's older brother. The parents, Pieter Donker and Petronella Jeronima van der Laan, had him baptized on February 10, 1729.[2] Two later documents allow us to establish Nathaniel's date of birth by approximation (or Nathanael's; the two spellings were equally common). His father's testament of May 1745 said he was fourteen years old. In July 1755 Pieter Gerbrand stated that his brother was to reach majority (i.e., become twenty-five) later that year.[3] So, Nathaniel was born toward the end of 1730, the last year before the great silting up set in. Although not even a full two years older, his brother was destined to take a father's role. But that is a later part of the story.

The earliest document revealing the status and wealth of the Donker family is the father's testament. In 1745 he was captain of the western division of Batavia's civil militia and vice president of the college supervising estates. His body was weak and sick, notary Petrus Dobbelaar recorded, but his mind and memory were strong. Possibly, Pieter Donker suffered from either the notorious rotting fever or the red diarrhea. On May 6, at five P.M., Dobbelaar took his pen to write the words directly from his client's mouth in the latter's home on the Rhinoceros Canal. He opened with the standard phrase that the testator revoked all previous testaments—not surprising—but the document continued: "in particular the one drawn up yesterday in the presence of the same notary." Within twenty-four hours, Pieter Donker had changed his mind. The document itself hints at the reason why.

Before mentioning the principal heirs, the testator reserved considerable portions for several others. Foremost among them were his three "natural" daughters, Anna, Petronella, and Catharina, all born in Batavia. Anna, her age unrecorded, was obviously the oldest, being married to "the citizen Gerrit van Reene." Petronella was eight and Catharina three. The little girls' mothers were the former slave Dina from Batavia and the testator's slave Bunga from Macassar. Although in terms of the total capital the three received a minor part, the amounts were generous, if we realize that a fully employed male worker in Holland earned about three hundred guilders a year.[4] The oldest daughter received three thousand guilders and a house in Utrecht Street in Amsterdam. She and her husband probably intended to move to Holland, or perhaps they already lived in that house. The two younger daughters each inherited a sum of seven thousand guilders. The testator reserved the same amount for the child with whom Bunga was pregnant, if it turned out to be from a European man. Lesser sums went to Dina, Bunga, some other slaves and servants and their families, the testator's assistant, his godson, the father of his first wife, and the persons who were to lay out his corpse. Several slaves, among them Bunga, were to receive the necessary sum to buy emancipation. Finally, Pieter Donker remitted a number of debts. The remainder of the inheritance went to his three legitimate sons, the oldest of whom was twenty-four-year-old Gerrit. The younger two, the notary added, presently were staying *in patria*. The sons also received their father's clothes, and when they married their wives obtained the clothes of the testator's wife.[5]

So there had been a number of women in Pieter Donker's life, not least Indonesian women. A few simple calculations and deductions put the relationships in place. His second wife bore all three legitimate sons; otherwise, it made no sense to promise her clothes to their future spouses. Since the oldest daughter had a husband, she was probably about the same age as the oldest son. Unless she was the fruit of a brief liaison between Pieter's first and second marriage, at least once he had had a mistress while married. Possibly, his relationship with the slave Dina, too, dated from before the death of his second wife. Moreover, given the rate of infant mortality, his spouses and mistresses probably had borne him more children who did not survive.

In the mother country, such a sexual appetite would meet with disapproval from his peers, save for a few libertines. The mores of colonial society were different. Partly this had to do with the highly unequal sex ratio among the European population. In Batavia, only a few European and mestizo women were available as suitable marriage candidates. Incidentally, ambitious young Dutchmen often preferred an older woman—a rich widow—over a younger bride. Perhaps Pieter Donker's first wife had been such a widow, European or mestizo, but with her father still alive in 1745, she cannot have been very old. Less lucky or less wealthy European men lived with native female "housekeepers." Poor males had to be content with the cheap whores from the isle of Bali who plied their trade in town. All this contributed to a certain lightness about sexual liaisons. The rich among the European married men also had native concubines or favorite slave women. This was a common practice in many colonial societies. In Batavia the ministers and elders of the Reformed Church were forced to acquiesce in these social customs.

Understandably, only the final testament Pieter Donker authorized was included among a pack of documents to be shipped to the mother country. We can only speculate about the contents of the revoked testament of the previous day. Perhaps the reason for his change of mind was trivial, only having to do with his last lover, Bunga, whom he apparently suspected of unfaithfulness. For Bunga's unborn child, he reserved the same amount that the two little daughters received, so the phrase "from a European" really meant from the testator himself. This suggests that she still was his lover but that he had competition, or feared it, from one or more native men. Possibly he had first intended to disinherit her. Alternatively, the testament of the previous day ignored his native lovers and illegitimate offspring altogether. Maybe someone had tried to dissuade him from spending large sums on them, someone who first succeeded but whom he overruled a day later. It is unlikely that this person was a representative of the Reformed Church: although the Church condemned extramarital sex, they did encourage Christians to accept their financial responsibilities. Perhaps the testator's oldest son, in the interest of himself and his brothers, had tried to persuade his father to keep the entire estate within the legitimate family. In the absence of other documents, we can only guess.

Despite his weak health, Pieter Donker lived for another two years without changing his testament again. He died in Batavia on June 18, 1747.[6] In November 1748 Batavia's orphan masters, whom the testament had designated as executors and guardians over the two young daughters, made a probate inventory, possibly assisted by Gerrit, who had reached majority in the meantime.[7] The inventory, totaling 131 pages, consists of three sections. The first sixty-nine pages concern the goods auctioned in Batavia after the testator's death, with the buyers' names. The proceeds amount to ƒ36,305. A description of some fifty houses and premises Donker owned in Indonesia follows, and the third section mentions the proceeds of still other goods. The grand total amounted to ƒ122,385, the annual wages of 408 workers.[8]

When their father died, Pieter Gerbrand and Nathaniel had long left Indonesia. As vague as Nathaniel was about his age at his arrest, he was sure he had come to Holland late in 1739. If he was right, he had spent his first nine years in Batavia, enough to have a recollection of the town in later life. Perhaps it was the death of their mother that prompted the father to send his two youngest sons to the homeland; in any case, he had sent them separately. Nathaniel had sailed to Holland on a Company ship under Captain Pieter Swaandregt, to whose care father Donker had entrusted his youngest son.[9] Swaandregt lived in Delft, where Nathaniel spent the next ten years of his life as Swaandregt's ward. After the father's death, the Amsterdam Orphan Chamber (the institution deciding in matters related to orphans), representing the Batavia chamber in the homeland, administered the brothers' goods.

This institution confirmed the brothers' respective supervisors, officially becoming parental guardians now. For a long time, the Orphan Chamber was to be Nathaniel's only link with Amsterdam.

In the homeland, the family story was to revolve around two persons. Gerrit stayed in Indonesia and died there between 1755 and 1761. He had probably married, since his brothers did not inherit from him.[10] Later records remain silent about their half sisters, save for one brief mention by Nathaniel of a brother-in-law married to a natural daughter of his father and living in Amsterdam in 1766.[11] This brother-in-law's name was not Van Reene, so he either was the second husband of the oldest half sister or married to one of the other two. Just Pieter Gerbrand and Nathaniel were to set the stage, in conflict and cooperation.

The older brother's conduct was exemplary from his youth onward. After Latin school he went to the small Frisian town of Franeker to study law at the university there. Pieter Gerbrand registered as a student on January 3, 1747, shortly before his eighteenth birthday and five months before his father's death. In 1750 he passed his candidate's examination.[12]

Information is lacking about Nathaniel's adolescent years. Delft, halfway between The Hague and Rotterdam, counted about twenty thousand inhabitants at the time, a marked contrast with the bustling life of Batavia. Did Nathaniel get bored? It is always hazardous to juxtapose the impression the environment makes on a five-year-old and a fifteen-year-old. In the tropics he had been a child, playing most of the time, attended by a host of servants and slaves. Maybe his education in Batavia was restricted to learning to read and write. In Delft, no doubt, he had to go to school. Although he lacked the intellectual capabilities or motivation, or both, of his brother, he surely received the education appropriate to the son of a wealthy entrepreneur. Then, around his eighteenth birthday, he realized he was a rich heir. It probably undermined whatever authority his foster family had over him. Yet until 1750 he met their expectations by working in a merchant's office.[13] Either this office was in The Hague, or Nathaniel visited that town. At any rate, he met Cecilia there.

For all we know, Cecilia Klos had humble origins. Her parents, Jacob Klos and Maria van der Linden, came from the south of Holland and published the banns in Rotterdam on February 4, 1725, each listing the same address in that town.[14] They married in the Reformed church seventeen days later. Cecilia was baptized in the same church on September 13,

1725, less than seven months after her parents' wedding. Three witnesses were present, among whom was another Jacob Klos, probably the father's uncle, and his wife Anna Cecilia. The latter gave her name to the child, who was baptized Anna Cecilia as well. However, in every document between 1747 and 1759, she appeared as just Cecilia. Then it suddenly became Johanna Cecilia Klos. Did she recall her full baptismal name, but incorrectly? In any case, Cecilia was the constant element, and everyone she knew, including Donker, called her by that name.

When Cecilia's parents had a son baptized in July 1727, they lived at a new address in Rotterdam. Again the witnesses numbered three, with the same uncle and aunt among them, who were probably godparents to both children. Cecilia lost her father three months later, shortly after her second birthday. Her brother died in February 1728. At the time of the father's death, the family had returned to the address where Cecilia was born, and they still lived there when her mother remarried. Now she became the wife of a Rhinelander, Jan Hendrik Steffens, a bachelor from Solingen. They published the banns on February 24, 1732, married on March 11, and had a son baptized on March 30, truly a last-minute wedding. Nevertheless, all these ceremonies took place in Rotterdam's Reformed Church. At the time of the baptism, the Steffenses had moved to a new address again. They had two more children baptized, in 1737 and 1740, each time at still another address. Cecilia was now fifteen. During the 1740s she moved to The Hague, possibly to work as a domestic servant. Her last Rotterdam address once more was a new one.[15]

The mother's two premarital pregnancies and her frequent changes of address, with both husbands, definitely suggest a lower-class milieu. To the extent that honor mattered for these people, it did not demand that engaged couples abstain from sex. Cecilia grew up as a poor girl, but her beauty was her asset. She had the unusual combination of black hair and blue eyes.[16] In The Hague her looks drew the attention of a London-born immigrant, James Woodrouffe. Cecilia and James published the banns in The Hague on March 12, 1747, and in Rotterdam a week later.[17] They married in The Hague on April 2. The couple only spent a brief time together, since James died shortly afterward.[18] How did Cecilia make a living upon becoming a widow at such a young age? Some years later, Nathaniel Donker's brother claimed she had been a prostitute, but no independent source supports this allegation. The records do not disclose under what circumstances Nathaniel and Cecilia met, just that it happened in 1750.[19]

Nathaniel was barely twenty, his future wife five years older than he. An adventurous young man, about to break loose from the bonds of his foster family and as yet sexually inexperienced, he found himself in love for the first time. He fell for the pretty widow with long, raven hair, who reminded him of the Indonesian women he had seen in his youth. At this stage, we may assume, Nathaniel Donker was not acting under the influence of the new romanticism; in any case, few sentimental novels had been published yet. As a background to this youthful infatuation, a sense of adventure and, possibly, rebellion against his foster parents are more likely factors. Whereas he was far superior to her in social status, she surpassed him in practical knowledge of the world. Cecilia probably took the lead in their common activities, albeit with his approval. Nathaniel's supervisors painted a negative picture of a sly woman, ruthlessly taking advantage of a gullible youth. Whatever her original state of mind, the later record shows she always remained true to him. Supposedly his status and money played a part when she took him as her lover. Without a description of Nathaniel's looks, there is no point in speculating whether Cecilia was also physically attracted to him.

Although decried by his supervisors, Nathaniel's first step under Cecilia's guidance was by all means patriotic. In late 1750 or early 1751 he left his merchant's office to enlist in the Dutch army. Lieutenant General Hoeuft van Ojen accepted him as a cadet in his regiment of mounted guards, stationed in The Hague. The recruiting agents, it appears, refrained from asking questions about his family background. After a few days Nathaniel showed up at his guardian's home as a soldier. Swaandregt was furious. His ward tried to calm him down, insisting that a military career was his best chance to make a fortune. He promised to act according to his "quality," his social status. Swaandregt acquiesced, provided the money for his ward's equipment, and found him a convenient lodging house in The Hague.[20] Making a fortune, however, was not his primary reason for becoming a cadet. Nathaniel and Cecilia believed his enlistment in the cavalry cleared the way toward marriage. It made the lieutenant general his surrogate parent, and they hoped to persuade him to give his permission for the wedding. They soon found out they were wrong. With their original marriage plans thwarted, Nathaniel and Cecilia started scheming to obtain their goal fraudulently. Leiden, they thought, was the right place to mislead the civil service.

On February 12, 1751, the couple had the banns published in Leiden. To assume a completely false identity would make their marriage certificate worthless, so he said he was Nathaniel Donker, bachelor from Batavia, she Cecilia Klos, widow of James Woodrouffe. The rest was fictional. He pretended to be a journeyman glazier, living at Leiden's Long Bridge, and the witness accompanying him, supposedly, was his cousin, Nicolaas Mol. She said she lived at the Rapenburg and introduced the two female witnesses as her aunt and an acquaintance. The minister of Leiden's church joined the would-be glazier and the widow in matrimony on February 28, 1751.[21] They were a legal couple now, at least for the moment.

When news of the wedding reached Pieter Swaandregt in Delft, he took immediate action. In vain, he had tried to dissuade his ward from joining the cavalry, but he used the military authorities now to reassert his control. He petitioned the High Court-Martial to have Nathaniel Donker imprisoned. In May 1751 that court provided Swaandregt with an "act of confinement."[22] This document authorized the guardian to incarcerate his ward in a private prison of his choosing in Holland. To do this, Swaandregt had to lay hands on him and that, precisely, was the problem. Nathaniel was gone. It is unclear whether the army discharged him or he deserted his regiment; the Dutch authorities never called him a deserter and no court ever tried him for desertion. Whatever happened, the act of confinement, issued by the High Court-Martial, ensured that he remained under the court's authority. To bolster his case, Swaandregt took action against Cecilia as well. On May 18, 1751, the court of The Hague authorized its bailiff to apprehend her for fraudulently having the banns published in order to marry a minor under tutelage. This is the only criminal charge ever issued against her. Since the authorities also didn't manage to capture Cecilia, she escaped trial. On May 30 the court of The Hague sent a message to the Rotterdam magistrates, but three days later the magistrates replied they could not find Cecilia in her native town. The authorities in The Hague left it at that.[23]

Although searched for separately and in separate places, Nathaniel and Cecilia were happy together. Landlords and innkeepers sold their goods and services on credit to this rich heir, expecting to get their due later. So the young couple roamed around from one village to another in the southern territory of Brabant. Nathaniel later recalled several locations but exaggerated the time they spent there. At some point, they considered the Republic unsafe for them. They crossed the border, where another army recruited him.

Meanwhile, the older brother, Pieter Gerbrand, had finished his study of law, receiving a Doctor's degree in Franeker on July 22, 1752.[24] He felt that at least he had to demonstrate an ability to follow in his father's footsteps and make a career. Yet the delay of two years between his graduation as a candidate and his doctorate is puzzling, since the usual interval was a few days or two weeks at most.²⁵ Because the amount of time Pieter Gerbrand had needed to get his candidate's degree was about average, we have reason to assume he took his studies seriously. Perhaps reports about the behavior of his younger brother distracted him immediately after his graduation. Pieter Gerbrand's name is absent from the records of the university's disciplinary court.²⁶ In this period, young men from the middle and upper classes considered their student years first of all as ones of merriment. Their families often allowed them this freedom: All over Europe, the social expectation was for students to have fun. In Germany, for example, they engaged in the sport of teasing aristocratic army officers, provoking them to issue a challenge even though an officer's status was too superior to that of the average student to fight a duel with him. Dueling was less common among the Dutch, but its few practitioners often were students. For the rest, they tried to enjoy themselves, drinking, roaming the streets at night, making noise, threatening passers-by with their rapiers, and taking liberties with young women from the lower classes. In short, their role was to act irresponsibly.

Pieter Gerbrand, we may assume, despite the delay until his doctorate, acted responsibly. Soon the Court of Holland admitted him to the bar; he took the oath on February 12, 1753, two days after his twenty-fourth birthday.²⁷ Eager to protect the family honor, he then took action to replace Captain Swaandregt. The young lawyer possibly thought that Swaandregt had failed, first in keeping Nathaniel under control, then in tracing him. In any case, Pieter Gerbrand's manifest determination to act in support of the family honor enhanced his personal reputation, a necessary precondition for furthering his professional career. He had two concrete aims: official appointment as his brother's guardian and annulment of the marriage. To that end, he petitioned the Court of Holland twice, on May 24 and June 4, 1753. In the first petition, he listed Leiden as his place of residence.

The older brother was worried primarily because Nathaniel had chosen a lower-class woman as his partner. He had made a misalliance, causing an ugly stain on the family's reputation. To state this all too bluntly, however, was inadvisable. Pieter Gerbrand couched his worries in a legal and moral tale, stressing one party's wicked cunning and the other's youthful delusions. Taking the two petitions together, we read a compelling narrative, one intended to impress the Court of Holland as much as possible. After a brief introduction, explaining their father's death in Indonesia while they were wards in Holland, Pieter Gerbrand came to the point. Unfortunately, Nathaniel had drifted into bad company. His would-be friends only liked him for his money, shamelessly profiting from his simple mind. The narrator took his brother's simplicity for granted: the fact that he loved to entertain these friends served to prove it. Through them, he had become acquainted with Cecilia, unnamed in the first petition but called by her name in the second. In both she had epithets like "bad," "infamous," and "corrupt," suggesting she engaged in prostitution.[28] It was the villainous friends, however, who had taken all the initiatives: inducing Nathaniel to quit his office, enlist in the cavalry, and, finally, court Cecilia. At this stage, her role acquired greater weight: she abused his "foolish love" and profited from his youthful ignorance:

> To the utmost sorrow of the petitioner, she managed to influence and mislead the said Nathaniel Donker to such an extent that he, setting aside all probity, lapsed into the vileness of not only binding himself to her with a written promise of marriage but, moreover, although they both lived in The Hague, to go to Leiden secretly. . . . There, he . . . had his marriage to the said Cecilia Klos registered.[29]

Pieter Gerbrand qualified this fraudulent marriage as illegal, clandestine, nonexistent, null and void. Both Swaandregt and Amsterdam's orphan masters, who could hardly bear the machinations Nathaniel was the victim of, wanted to save him from corruption. Their efforts were to no avail. Presently, Nathaniel and this woman roamed around outside the territory of the Republic. He refused to give her up and return to the bosom of his family. An official annulment of the marriage might help, but the gentlemen of the Amsterdam Orphan Chamber wondered whether they were legally competent to sue in this matter. So they suggested that, as the person most interested in saving Nathaniel from ruin, the older brother might become his guardian. The Court of Holland was the superior authority to decide this.

Thus far the narrative. The Court heard the petitioner in person in a session at which Swaandregt was also present. Since no record was kept, we are ignorant about the latter's words, but he probably just consented. He had taken Nathaniel into his home and raised him out of sympathy for the father. Things had gone wrong, and now he was glad to be relieved of his burden. It meant an exit for Pieter Swaandregt from Nathaniel Donker's life and exit also for Cecilia's wicked friends, whose principal role had been to play Nicolaas Mol and the other witnesses at the wedding. The verbal session enabled the justices to scrutinize the petitioner, following the brief encounter three months earlier when they had admitted him to the bar. Satisfied, they appointed Pieter Gerbrand as guardian and authorized him to take steps toward the dissolution of his brother's marriage.[30] Hence the second petition, technically a request for a *mandement*, an order to overrule a decision, in this case the decision of the Reformed Church of Leiden to join Nathaniel and Cecilia in matrimony. A mandement procedure usually was a tedious affair; this one still was undecided in July 1755. Pieter Gerbrand's appointment as the guardian of his brother, not even two years younger, was curious for one reason in particular. The guardian was twenty-four, hence a minor himself.[31] Possibly, he lied about his age to the Amsterdam Orphan Chamber and the Court of Holland, neither of whom had the registers from Batavia at hand to check.

The newly appointed guardian knew that his brother had taken refuge abroad. Since an heir on the run with a woman was expected to roam around perpetually, perhaps Pieter Gerbrand hoped Nathaniel would move back and forth over the border. Did he also know his brother had joined a foreign army? Even after he had traced him, he wrote that Nathaniel "claimed" to have served the king of Prussia. In fact, a Prussian lieutenant named Van Aken had recruited Nathaniel as an underofficer in his cavalry regiment stationed in Cleves. Maybe he needed the money, but just after enlisting he bought a silver-embroidered saddle cloth and two holsters—on credit. Whatever Nathaniel's occupation abroad, in order to lay hands on him, it was necessary to catch him in Dutch territory. With the 1751 act of confinement in his pocket, Pieter Gerbrand could request any Dutch magistrate to arrest his brother. As soon as he became guardian, he personally directed the investigation, with the help of his friend Jan Gaubert, later an Amsterdam *makelaar*, that is, an intermediary or middleman in large-scale commerce. Accompanied by Gaubert, he made two journeys, in August and October 1753, to the border area where villages belonging to the Republic, the southern Netherlands, and the Empire alternated. The second time, it seems, the two brothers met, in a village just across the border. Secretly, Pieter Gerbrand had arranged for Nathaniel's arrest, paying the local magistrate a handsome sum, but his brother got away.

Finally, in May 1754, Pieter Gerbrand succeeded. Knowing his brother was in Nijmegen—opposite Cleves at the Dutch side of the border—he warned the town's magistrates, who ordered Nathaniel's arrest. He later claimed they had lured him into Dutch territory. The claim has credibility, given the fact that, on May 18, Pieter Gerbrand, staying in Nijmegen himself, paid a gratuity of twenty ducats to a man with an Italian name "for bringing my brother here." It took some effort to keep him in the country, because the Nijmegen authorities considered the option of extraditing Nathaniel back to Prussia, which obliged Pieter Gerbrand to hire a lawyer. He had already induced the High Court-Martial in Holland to renew the act of confinement on May 8. Convening in a special session, for which they charged the beneficiary twenty-five guilders and five stivers, the Nijmegen magistrates decided to hand over Nathaniel to the Dutch military authorities.[32] On May 21, 1754, he arrived in a Delft *beterhuis* called *De Drie Taarlingen*.[33] Nathaniel was back in the first town in which he had stayed after his arrival from Indonesia, this time as a prisoner.

Beterhuis, literally "house for improvement," was a typical Dutch term, but the system of private confinement existed in other European countries as well.[34] If a person severely offended the norms of good conduct, without explicitly breaking the law, an interested party, usually a relative, could petition to have him locked away for a time. A hierarchical relationship was no necessary precondition: mothers imprisoned their sons, but also sons their fathers, sisters their brothers, and nephews their aunts. It was a private affair, but one needed the consent of the authorities, in the Netherlands always from a court.

Although separate wards of urban prisons sometimes carried that name, the typical beterhuis of the eighteenth century was a privately run institution. Only well-to-do families could afford to pay the warden's fee for keeping and feeding their black sheep. Thus, confinement in such a place was private in a double sense. The regime of the beterhuis compared mildly with that of the prison workhouse, in which criminals performed forced labor. The inmates of private prisons were allowed to read books, smoke their pipes together, and receive visits from family and friends, and they got good food. Private prisons were of modest size, housing ten to fifteen inmates at a time. They had the appearance of taverns or inns, an appearance reinforced by names like The Gilded Cable, King David, and New Rome. De Drie Taarlingen, Nathaniel Donker's prison, was named after the three original owners, but no Taarling had been warden since the first decade of the eighteenth century. For the inmates' relatives, it only mattered that the black sheep were safely locked away, no longer able to harm the family reputation. They need not suffer the physical degradation of forced labor. Indeed, had they been incarcerated along with criminals, this would also damage the entire family's honor.

Until the first quarter of the eighteenth century, it was common to keep men and women together in one prison, but later private institutions specialized in either male or female prisoners. Interestingly, two-thirds of the inmates of privately run prisons were male, whereas among the total population of persons confined by their families, including inmates of urban institutions, a 50 : 50 sex ratio was the rule. Among the patriciate and the higher bourgeoisie, women were more readily controlled preventively. Male adventurers presented the greatest threat to family reputations. They roamed around, refused to come home at night, and spent hours or days in taverns and other dubious places, drinking excessively; they had loose morals, leading a highly promiscuous life; they had bad tempers, threatening their peers or betters. Or they simply squandered their money, often inherited capital for which their forbears had worked hard.

The sort of persons who deserved imprisonment reminds us of the bad characters identified by observing writers, whose typology still held full sway in the 1750s. It seems logical to rank these black sheep with the "intemperate persons controlled by their passions." Yet the writers' bad characters and the descriptions of the behavior of black sheep by their families match one another only imperfectly. One reason for this is obvious. Whereas the writers had construed a moralistic typology, petitioners for an act of confinement focused on concrete examples of misconduct. They told a story, describing the consequences rather than the causes of moral failure. The mismatch goes deeper, however. Several of the habits denounced by the observing writers were positive traits carried to excess. Take the miser. In a less radical version, he was simply a man sensibly saving his money: the opposite of squandering, one of the major charges against Nathaniel Donker. Or consider the flirting coquette. Conscious of her beauty, she always wanted to please everyone. Understandably, a desire to please people never appeared among the reported mistakes of private prisoners. The relatives of a young woman suspected of promiscuity complained she stayed away from home at night or they decried her dubious company. Neither did petitions for confinement ever call a man effeminate, one of the characteristics of a petit-maître. The libertine, the virile womanizer, was the best match for descriptions of the misconduct of black sheep. Yet, for all we know, Nathaniel Donker stayed with one woman in the 1750s. He was to become a real libertine only later in life. Finally, petitions for confinement always showed a great concern for the family reputation, a factor that the observing authors mentioned only in passing. With their moralism, they put the emphasis on guilt, whereas the relatives of black sheep had their thoughts fixed on shame.

On the average, persons committed by their families stayed in prison between two and four years. Although it was common for the authorizing magistrates to set a term, they regularly consented to its prolongation when the family requested this. In a request to that end, the petitioners claimed there was no sign of improved behavior on the part of the inmate, nor much hope for the near future. If they stated their case convincingly, the court usually granted a prolongation. Alternatively, the relatives might ask for release or at least refrain from seeking a prolongation. In the first case, they mentioned two standard reasons, sufficiently valid for the court to consent to a release: the prisoner's repentance and improved behavior. Since the black sheep were in no position in captivity to repeat the activities that had caused their misfortune, the two reasons in practice amounted to the same. In any case, the petitioners expected their relatives to misbehave no longer after returning to the free world.

The inability to engage in undesirable activities while incarcerated had practical consequences, especially in the case of inmates committed for squandering their money. As an alternative measure, a court might place the squanderer under guardianship, as the Court of Holland first did with Nathaniel Donker. However, while a ward, he still contracted debts—and he was not alone in this. The modern observer is struck by the ease with which contemporary landlords, tavern keepers, and shop owners gave credit to people of "quality" or who simply dressed well. They left a jewelry shop with a golden ring or traveled from one inn to the next in another town, leaving only a written declaration of debt behind. The creditors, it seems, never inquired into the legal status of their clients. They might be of minor age or under official tutelage but contract debts anyway. Perhaps the shop owners and innkeepers acted wisely in selling on credit without enquiry. When they subsequently approached a debtor's trustees, they usually received their due. Such was the policy of the Amsterdam Orphan Chamber, faced with Nathaniel Donker's creditors. When the creditors showed up, this institution reimbursed the creditors from the Donker estate, which it administered. The trustees could have chosen to declare the debts, illegally contracted, null and void, but for what purpose? To keep their ward's capital intact, allowing him to waste even more money? That made little sense, so guardians in the end always paid off the debts. In practice, this meant that a ward could freely dispose of his capital after all. Only in captivity he could not.

A final function of the private prison was to prevent a person from ending up in a criminal prison, or worse, on the scaffold. Men and women petitioning for a relative's confinement often expressed the fear that, should he continue in his harmful and semilegal ways, he might fall into the hands of justice. Some black sheep had lower-class friends who the petitioners thought, correctly or not, engaged in criminal activities. Others gambled away their money, which made their relatives suspect they might try to recover it fraudulently. In such cases, imprisonment in a nonjudicial institution served as a preventive measure to save the family honor. As private prisons were nonjudicial institutions, the offenses for which the inmates had been committed, as a rule, were not punishable crimes. Alcoholism, the offense mentioned most frequently, was not illegal. Madness, another reason for confinement, differed from crime since it carried the notion of diminished responsibility. Most forms of sexual deviance, on the other hand, were liable to punishment by a court, but petitioners described their misbehaving relatives' sexuality in terms of a dubious lifestyle rather than in reference to concrete behavior. Courts always registered petitions for confinement separately from criminal trials. More important, they rarely prosecuted former private prisoners for a crime. From a Leiden sample of 310 private prisoners, only two or three were involved in a criminal procedure in the town at some other point in their lives.

Even when Nathaniel Donker was a prisoner in De Drie Taarlingen, then, contemporaries had no particular reason to think he would end up as a murderer.

A wealthy prisoner under tutelage was the financier of his own stay in prison. Another person directed his affairs, paying the warden's bills from the estate he controlled. Nathaniel financed his imprisonment, as well as the preceding effort of tracking him down. The trips his brother and Gaubert made in vain in 1753, their stay in Nijmegen in May 1754, the costs of legal counsel there and at the Court of Holland: everything was presented for reimbursement to the Amsterdam Orphan Chamber, as well as the debts contracted by Nathaniel himself. In 1755 the Orphan Chamber received new declarations for legal costs at the Court of Holland and in Delft, along with warden Jan Cordy's bills. In that year, Gaubert twice traveled back and forth between Nijmegen and The Hague. Pieter Gerbrand's total declarations in Amsterdam, from August 1753 until August 1755, amounted to over fifty-four hundred guilders.[35] Excluded from this total was another considerable sum taken from his brother's estate to buy off a Prussian claim.

If Pieter Gerbrand refused to believe his brother had taken up arms for a foreign power, in October 1754 he found out for sure. The Prussians demanded Nathaniel Donker back! It is an open question whether his regiment badly needed his services or the officers just wanted satisfaction for his abduction. Since Nathaniel Donker had enlisted in their country's army, they argued, he counted as their king's subject. Hence, he was extraditable. As expected, this argument was unacceptable to Pieter Gerbrand and the Amsterdam Orphan Chamber. The latter's clerk wrote an extensive plea to convince the Prussians that their presumed subject's interest was best served if he remained incarcerated in Delft until he showed signs of improvement.[36] This document failed to impress the Prussian authorities. Instead, they sent Lieutenant Van Aken, in whose regiment Nathaniel had served, to the Netherlands with the order to arrange his extradition. Realizing his efforts at appeasement had failed, Pieter Gerbrand consulted experts in international relations, who advised him to make a deal with the foreign officer. The latter was willing to waive his claim for no less than seven thousand guilders. Shocked by this exorbitant demand, the Orphan Chamber referred the case to the burgomasters, but they thought it wise to accept the offer. On June 10, 1755, the Chamber's secretary stored the original German document, two seals attached to it and signed by Van Aken's superior, in his drawer: Lieutenant General Heinrich von Hauteharmoy, commander of the city and fortification of Brieg, discharged Nathaniel Donker of all his obligations. The Court of Holland, not consulted in this matter, approved of the deal a month later.[37]

In its turn, the High Court-Martial was no party to the deal. On April 21 the military tribunal had prolonged Nathaniel's confinement in Delft. Nine days later, when his brother approached them about the guardianship, they told him to write to the Court of Holland instead.[38] This ended the High Court-Martial's involvement in Nathaniel's case—henceforth the justices in The Hague would deal with the problems he caused. Nathaniel's entire military career was soon over, as his formal discharge as a Prussian hussar was under negotiation. Having served two armies in a period of peace, between the War of the Austrian Succession and the Seven Years War, he had never faced an enemy in battle.

For some time Pieter Gerbrand, too, was to disappear from Nathaniel's life. His brother had two reasons to approach the Court of Holland about the guardianship. First, Nathaniel would reach majority later that year. Pieter Gerbrand's official function until then was *voogd*, or a person who replaces the parents of an orphan of minor age. A court could put a mature person under guardianship as well, if it considered that person unable to manage his own affairs, notably his financial affairs. In that case the guardian was called *curator*. Pieter Gerbrand was unable to continue his guardianship in this new capacity, which was the second reason why he approached the Court of Holland. He planned to make "a trip abroad." In other words, he was about to embark on his Grand Tour through Europe, the customary way for young men from the elite and the wealthy bourgeoisie to conclude their education. Originally an aristocratic custom, the Grand Tour had already been adopted by Dutch patrician families by the middle of the seventeenth century.[39] In the eighteenth century it was common among the higher-status groups throughout the Republic. By making this tour, with Germany and Italy as the principal destinations, Pieter Gerbrand demonstrated that the Donker family belonged to high society. And in order not to jeopardize that pretense, his brother ought to remain in prison and under guardianship. Because the Amsterdam Orphan Chamber managed Nathaniel's inheritance, it was logical to propose the Chamber's administrator, Jan Bitter, as guardian. Bitter's legal representative in The Hague was the lawyer Leonard Thomeeze, two decades later the attorney in Van Gogh's appeal trial.

Pieter Gerbrand backed up his request with the standard lamentations about his younger brother's bad conduct and his failure to improve. The petitioner had hoped that incarceration would make Nathaniel meek, but alas, he remained obstinate. Each time the elder brother visited him, Nathaniel boasted that the king of Prussia would get him out of prison. Jan Bitter, appointed as guardian on July 14, repeated the story three days later, in a request for the Court of Holland's confirmation of Nathaniel's confinement. Bitter's petition contained one new element: the prisoner had been diagnosed as suffering from a "dirty disease." Was this an unsubstantiated accusation, made in the confident expectation that the justices would never ask for a doctor's certificate? If it was true, either Cecilia had infected Nathaniel with venereal disease, or he had contracted it from intercourse with another woman. Whereas the first possibility suggests there was some truth in the allegations against her (unless she got it from her first husband, dead for a number of years), the second makes him a libertine earlier than we had assumed.

On July 17 the Court of Holland prolonged Nathaniel's confinement by a year.[40] It also annulled his marriage to Cecilia; the exact date cannot be ascertained.[41] We do know another exact date, February 27, 1756, when the Court of Holland questioned Jan Cordy, warden of De Drie Taarlingen. The previous day, the justices had angrily summoned him to appear at noon, to provide details about the news that reached them: Nathaniel Donker had escaped from prison.[42]

Without a record of the Court's conversation with Cordy, we cannot tell whether Nathaniel was just lucky to find a door negligently left open or if he had planned his escape with the assistance of others. Neither do we have any information on the whereabouts of Cecilia during the twenty-one months of his captivity. Spouses and relatives had the right to visit the inmates of a private prison, but with the marriage contested and finally annulled, it is possible that the warden refused Cecilia access as an unentitled visitor. In that case, if she helped her partner get out, she could only have done so from a distance. Whatever the circumstances of Nathaniel's escape from De Drie Taarlingen, it brought him and Cecilia together again. They went back to the town where Nathaniel's regiment had been stationed. While the great "reversal of alliances" among the European powers, which made Prussia side with England and turn against France, was taking shape, Nathaniel returned to Prussian territory, but no longer as a soldier.

Kleef in Dutch, its present German name Kleve, commonly referred to as Cleves in English: with five thousand inhabitants, it was a small town, lying half a mile west of the Rhine.[43] Since 1741, when a mineral spring had been discovered nearby, Cleves ranked among the health resorts of Europe. Yet urban life there remained sober. A contemporary author praised the town for lacking balls, concerts, operas, and plays, events that emptied a visitor's purse in the more worldly resorts. The nearby countryside, however, was said to be very pleasant and good for hunting. Although under Prussian rule since 1614, throughout the eighteenth century Cleves was predominantly a Dutch town.[44] The peaceful coexistence of several religious communities also reminded one of the Netherlands. All this was conducive to Dutch immigration. A number of rentiers from the Republic, many of them Catholics, lived in Cleves with their families. Protestants as well as Catholics welcomed the favorable interest rates and the low prices of foodstuffs. But the town's assets attracted not just rentiers. In 1741, noting that too many poor people came into town, the magistrates obliged every newcomer to appear before them and produce an attestation of good conduct. Posting a bail of one hundred or two hundred *reichsthalers*, depending on one's status, was a further precondition for residence.[45] The bail was no problem for Nathaniel Donker, but at his escape the Delft warden had failed to provide him with an attestation of good conduct. Maybe he forged one. He probably rented one or more rooms in someone's house or he stayed in an inn; his name is absent from Cleves's registers of residents, listing only a house's owner or its principal tenant. Near the mineral spring, a furnished room with one bed cost five Dutch guilders per week, with two beds six guilders and another guilder for the accommodation of a domestic servant. Such prices Donker could afford, that is, on credit.

Arriving in the spring of 1756, Nathaniel and Cecilia lived in Cleves for more than three years. Apart from financial strain, they had a happy time together. In 1757, Cecilia gave birth to a son. At his baptism in Cleves's Reformed church on February 24 of that year, the secret commissioner Strunck and a Miss Van der Heijden acted as godparents. More remarkable was the child's name: Pieter Gerbrand.[46] Nathaniel named his son after his older brother, who had chased him and had had him incarcerated! Was it a gesture, a sign that he was prepared for reconciliation? The boy's first name, of course, was also his grandfather's.

At the time of his son's birth, Nathaniel had been in touch with his guardian, Jan Bitter, who was trying to clear up his financial situation and apparently knew his address. Unlike Nathaniel's brother, the new guardian adopted a realistic approach, which is understandable because he was less directly concerned about the Donker family honor. Bitter had summoned all of his ward's creditors to inquire into their claims and passed on the resulting list. In a letter of January 12, Nathaniel had commented on this list. He considered some claims justified, leaving the remainder to the Court of Holland's arbitration. In March the justices fixed the total of recognized debts at $f21,034$, authorizing the Amsterdam Orphan Chamber to pay off the creditors. They numbered forty-nine altogether, including six lawyers, five attorneys, two coach drivers, two tailors, and of course Cordy, the warden. The latter, who possibly had suffered no sleepless nights over Nathaniel's escaping from his house, did insist on receiving his last fee.[47]

No doubt, Bitter had also informed Nathaniel and Cecilia that the Court of Holland had declared their marriage null and void. In their new hometown, this was an inconvenience they found easy to repair. On August 21, 1757, the couple renewed their marriage vows in the Reformed church of Cleves. Two ministers, one Dutch-speaking and one German-speaking, served that church, and it was the former, we may assume, who joined them in matrimony again. The register listed no witnesses, nor is there any indication that the minister knew about the first marriage and its annulment, although he had baptized the couple's son six months earlier.[48] Nathaniel and Cecilia had become husband and wife for the second time.

The documentation about the couple's vicissitudes in Cleves is scant. From other settlements of debts, we know that in 1758 Nathaniel had bread, groceries, butter, bacon, and meat delivered and clothes made on credit, while he owed rent to his landlord. He also owed money to the keeper of a boarding school in the village of Meersel, presumably because his son stayed there.[49] On the whole, it seems, the couple felt at home in Cleves. Had they remained in this small town, just across the Republic's border, their story probably would have ended quite differently.

Two reasons prompted them to move. The principal problem was the ever recurring one of a lack of cash. Realizing that creditors would always find their way to Amsterdam in the end, Jan Bitter granted his ward an allowance, but Nathaniel found it insufficient. So he contracted new debts. It was a vicious circle of buying on credit and hoping that one day his trustees paid off. Unless he could settle his affairs in Holland, this might go on forever. Second, the nice town with its beautiful surroundings, as described by enthusiastic travelers, lost some of its attraction. The Seven Years War had broken out in September 1756. Until 1760 the main battles between Prussia and its enemies took place in faraway regions such as Saxony and Silesia. The French did not send an army into the Rhineland until spring 1757 and even then their main drive was toward Georgian Hanover. There were troop movements in the countryside around Cleves, but no attack occurred on the town itself.[50] Yet the citizens felt unsafe while war conditions led to a slump. Mail coaches still took off for Nijmegen or Arnhem and from there to The Hague. Along with one of them, Nathaniel sent a letter that reached the Court of Holland on December 15, 1758.

His petition related events since 1751, as his successive guardians had done earlier, but set in a more positive light. Quickly passing over his escape from a private prison, he called himself and his wife residents of Cleves. The settlement of March 1757, he explained, had been of no avail because he had subsequently received an insufficient allowance. The total of his new debts amounted to $f11,573$. The petitioner enclosed a certificate from the burgomasters and council of Cleves, stating he "had governed himself very properly for a considerable time." Whereas Nathaniel had arrived in Cleves without a certificate of good conduct, its magistrates now granted him one for his return. The petition concluded with a request to end the guardianship, or else to allow him to settle his debts and receive another thirty-five hundred guilders to buy necessities. In a corollary, the Amsterdam Orphan Chamber stated its readiness to provide Nathaniel, semiannually, with the net revenues of his capital. The Court of Holland consented to the demands on the condition that Nathaniel Donker take up domicile under its jurisdiction.[51]

This condition made Nathaniel and Cecilia suspicious. What if the justices changed their minds and ordered him taken back to the Delft prison? First, Nathaniel arranged for an administrative bombardment on the Court of Holland. In February–April 1759 it received three official letters from the Cleves-Mark regional government urging the Dutch magistrates to allow their resident free disposal over his goods, so that he could satisfy his creditors in Cleves. Annoyed at receiving a document in German, without translation, the Court sent a negative reply and communicated this to Nathaniel's lawyers. The justices postponed a decision on the next two letters, also written in German. The death of Jan Bitter, in May, caused further delay. Another administrator of the Amsterdam Orphan Chamber, Abraham Follé, took over as guardian. Finally, on July 25, 1759, the Court of Holland took note of the fact that Nathaniel Donker now lived in The Hague. The justices decided not to bother any longer about the letters from Cleves and cleared the way for a definitive settlement of debts.[52]

Back in The Hague, Nathaniel and Cecilia lived separately. That was one more ordeal they had to pass in the process of putting their affairs in order. They had hoped the Dutch authorities would recognize the Cleves marriage, concluded by two adults according to local law, but the Court of Holland argued that someone under guardianship could never marry without its permission. The couple had no option but to request the Court to consent to their third wedding, the first in the eyes of the Dutch magistrates. Once more, Nathaniel construed a narrative, as favorable to himself as he possibly could, explaining his behavior during the past decade. This one opened with his meeting and falling in love with Cecilia in 1750. We know the story's sequel. He reminded the magistrates that a valid marriage facilitated the legitimization of his son, entitling the latter to inherit from his father. Over the past months in The Hague, the petitioner and his partner had behaved decently, as attested by witnesses. He could not live without her and the child, he said. These were prophetic words indeed, but in 1759 even Nathaniel himself was ignorant of their ultimate meaning. He ended with another moving phrase: the years he had spent with Cecilia, for better or for worse, "had only increased his love and affection for her."[53]

Although written to obtain a favorable disposition, the narrative reveals a few genuine concerns. As the magistrates in Cleves and, presumably, his neighbors had treated Nathaniel as a respectable man, a rentier, he aspired to gain respectability in his home country, too. The legitimization of his son was a major precondition for this, which additionally ensured that the boy could live comfortably in the future, also after his father's death. Obviously, he expected to have means left to pass on to his son. We can rank the allusions to love among the expressions of sentimentality about to become fashionable. Nathaniel, or his lawyer, supposed that the justices would appreciate these sentimental phrases. In this period, mutual love was accepted as a basis for marriage among the upper classes and the bourgeoisie of the Netherlands. So the appeal to it was a rational move, but Nathaniel's feelings were sincere nevertheless. Why else would he seek approval for a third wedding with Cecilia? Had he wished to part with her, he could have appealed to the earlier objections of his guardians, without jeopardizing the efforts to gain control over his estate. As only he petitioned the court, we lack Cecilia's narrative. With nothing to go on, let us assume she still loved him, too. Moreover, a fully legal marriage sealed her career of social climbing, from a poor Rotterdam girl to a lady rentier.

While negotiating consent to his marriage, Nathaniel made peace with his older brother, who had returned from his travels. By the mid-1760s Pieter Gerbrand worked as a lawyer in Amsterdam, and possibly he had already established himself in that town. The Court of Holland summoned Nathaniel, his guardian, and his brother to appear in person. Neither Follé nor Pieter Gerbrand objected to the wedding when they saw the Court's conditions: the guardianship would continue, the couple was obliged to settle within the Court of Holland's jurisdiction, and its commissioners advised in the matter of a marriage settlement. The second condition referred to the area of the Court's immediate jurisdiction, comprising just a section of The Hague. On November 15 the justices formally consented to Nathaniel and Cecilia's first valid marriage under Dutch law.[54] At the end of the month the couple drew up a marriage settlement—no copy extant—in the presence of the commissioners.

Nathaniel and Cecilia (listed as Johanna Cecilia for the first time) published the banns in The Hague on December 2, 1759. Eight days later, guardian Follé released a sum of thirty-five hundred guilders from his ward's capital to furnish a household. On December 16 the couple married in the church of Scheveningen, a seaside resort bordering on The Hague. It was almost nine years after their first, clandestine union. The church's clerk took note of the marriage settlement, adding that the bride offered a sum of two thousand guilders to her only child.[55] It is unlikely that the bride wore any clothes that had belonged to her late mother-in-law, as provided for in her late father-in-law's testament. As to the location, the couple obviously found Scheveningen a nice place for their wedding, which provided the additional satisfaction of celebrating it outside the Court of Holland's jurisdiction. For the third time, a minister had pronounced them husband and wife. He was twenty-nine now, she thirty-four. This was their last wedding.

To acquire full respectability, Nathaniel had to await the complete ordering of his finances and his release from tutelage. Already before the wedding, his guardian had started to work toward the first goal. Nathaniel's lawyers in The Hague, who had helped him obtain judicial consent to his marriage, presented a bill of one thousand guilders, and in Cleves a number of unpaid debts remained. Not every creditor was known by name. In November 1759 Follé put an advertisement in the newspapers, calling upon everyone who had a claim on Nathaniel Donker to report it within six weeks. After the expiration of this term, no claim would be recognized.[56]

With creditors from the Republic and abroad, the settlement of debts took longer than six weeks. The Court of Holland registered its approval to the final arrangement on December 15, 1760. Twenty-three creditors had shown up at the Amsterdam Orphan Chamber, among them three lawyers, a notary, and the heirs of the deceased court official Groneman. The commercial creditors included a wig maker and someone who had repaired a golden watch. Donker also owed money to a doctor and a surgeon, for forty visits and six bloodlettings, respectively. The document does not reveal who—father, mother, son, or the whole family—had needed these medical services. The gentlemen of the Orphan Chamber had done their best in the interest of their ward, managing to lower several claims. After their bargaining, the debt totaled ƒ3,328. With additional costs included, Follé sold securities from the Donker capital to the amount of five thousand guilders.[57]

The next step in the normalization process for the Donker family was to settle down according to their status as rentiers. They found a country house along the canal between The Hague and Leiden, named Visvliet. On April 21, 1761, Nathaniel reported that the owner intended to sell the house at a public auction. Instead, he wanted his guardian to buy it for him and, of course, he needed permission from the Court of Holland. The justices agreed, although the estate was outside the Court's jurisdiction. They told Follé to offer no more than about five thousand guilders. Two weeks of bargaining followed with the outcome, on May 4, that Donker could have the house plus the surrounding land for sixty-five hundred guilders. With additional costs, this meant liquidizing securities to the amount of eight thousand guilders from his capital. The Court of Holland notified the local authorities that the new resident was under its tutelage.[58]

Now that they were established on a country estate, it was time for the last step in the normalization process. This took another year. In their session of May 3, 1762, the justices of the Court of Holland ended Nathaniel Donker's guardianship. In the same session they considered the "pretensions that certain Jews had on the said Donker" and decided to hand over the documents in question to the attorney general. The request that Nathaniel had submitted concluded that the petitioner had arrived *ad seniorem mentem* (older and wiser). Three persons, one of whom was the lord of two adjacent manors, testified that Nathaniel behaved like an honorable and kind man. This was the first time that any of his peers had officially conferred honor on Nathaniel. Now he contrasted favorably with the anonymous Jews, suspected of cheating on him. The justices framed one last condition for turning him into a completely free man: a capital of ten thousand guilders, invested partly in his country house and partly in state bonds, should be reserved for his children. He was not allowed to alienate this capital without the Court of Holland's permission.[59]

Indeed, the justices spoke of children, in plural. The Donker family was enlarged to four at the end of 1761 or the beginning of 1762. The second child was baptized Nathaniel Jacob.[60] Whereas the parents had named their first son after his learned and respectable uncle, the father conferred his own name on this one. The child's second name was his maternal grandfather's. This son was legitimate from birth on. At last, Nathaniel and Cecilia had settled down as completely respectable citizens. The interval of five years between the two births could be due to Cecilia's diminished fertility. She was thirty-six when she bore her second child. Alternatively, they had used contraceptive methods during the interval. By the middle of the eighteenth century, many married couples among the upper and middle classes of Western Europe practiced *coitus interruptus* for contraception. If Nathaniel and Cecilia did so, they conformed to the trend set by their social peers.

In retrospect, the year 1763 was their finest. Without judicial interference, they lived with their two little sons on the Visvliet estate. Two official documents mentioning Nathaniel's name in that year are extant. In March he designated an Amsterdam lawyer as his plenipotentiary, to recover all cash and bonds still kept at that city's Orphan Chamber.[61] In June the Court of Holland's attorney general finally concluded his investigation into the dealings with the Jews. He reported to the justices, "although such negotiations are rarely free from cheating, there are no sufficient grounds for undertaking a criminal action against any of the Jews." Clearly, they were the suspects. Despite the lack of proof, the attorney general suggested that the Court undertake preventive action "against such covert deceptions, which often lead to the ruin of young people." Noting that the two parties had failed to reach a settlement, the justices decided to drop the case from consideration.[62]

The tone of anti-Semitic stereotyping in the attorney general's advice is subtle, but unmistakable. This was the first time that Donker had been involved in a conflict in which neither he nor his wife but others played the role of offender. The tale of Nathaniel and Cecilia might have ended here, with an "and they lived happily ever after." Something, someone intervened.

3

A New Woman

It came by surprise. In its session of January 22, 1765, as usual, the Court of Holland dealt with several petitions. One was signed by Johanna Cecilia Klos, living on the Visvliet estate, acting on behalf of herself and her minor children. Did her name ring a bell with the justices? She informed them:

> My husband, Nathaniel Donker, left for Amsterdam on January 4 of this year, pretending he had some business there. He never returned. After making inquiries, I learned he had gone on from Amsterdam to Utrecht with some woman. As you can imagine, this is all to my utmost sorrow and distress. Moreover, I fear he has diverted all his bonds. Whether or not this is the case, in the present uncertainty someone ought to provisionally represent his person during his absence. This is all the more necessary in view of the dowry agreed upon in our marriage settlement of November 30, 1759, drawn up in the presence of your Court. Lacking independent means of subsistence, I am obliged to rent the Visvliet estate. May I also remind you of the act dated May 4, 1762, which determined that a sum of ten thousand guilders, invested in Visvliet and deposited in bonds, was reserved for my children. Making this sum liquid requires your Court's consent, which I request herewith. Further, I request your permission to handle my own affairs, or else for the appointment of a trustee. In the latter case, I propose the notary Hendrik van der Ven.[1]

The phrase "I fear he has diverted all his bonds" was an understatement. When Cecilia opened Nathaniel's drawer, she found nothing but empty folders, and all his clothes were gone.² For their part, the justices remembered the runaway husband well enough. This was the first and only time his wife approached them. They agreed to the trustee she proposed.

What went wrong with so strong a love? The year 1763 had been their finest. In all probability, Nathaniel and Cecilia were a happy couple during most of 1764 as well, but toward the end of that year, at the latest, he met the woman she referred to in the petition. It was a reenactment of the events of the early 1750s, this time with Cecilia in the role of accuser, blaming an intruder for viciously casting a spell on Nathaniel.

As in the first case, we are not well informed about the circumstances under which he got to know her. He met his new lover, like his wife, in The Hague. This time, we are sure she worked as a prostitute. A woman who knew her well said she pretended to be a skirt stitcher, but it was common knowledge that she earned her income as a "girl of pleasure." A brothel keeper and a prostitute confirmed she lived in a house known to be a music hall.³ And in December 1766 Nathaniel himself admitted that she "had been a whore," with whom he "had an affair for over two years, even before he left his wife." He also claimed that Cecilia had made him do it, because she acted "dishonorably" in her turn, but this statement, made to exculpate himself, deserves little credence.⁴ In all likelihood, Nathaniel first saw his future mistress when he visited her as a client. Who was she?

All official records list her full name as Dorothea Bosselman or Borstelman. At her first interrogation, she said she was "from Hatink, a village about seven hours from Essen in Germany."⁵ Did she mean Essen in the Ruhr region? And did the seven hours refer to the distance on foot or by coach? Apparently, the Amsterdam court was satisfied with this imprecise geographic indication. If she gave her age correctly, she was born in 1741. At eighteen, she tried her luck in the Netherlands, where everyone knew her as German Doortje.⁶ She first stayed with an infantry corporal, then with a widow who had a grocery store, next in two successive homes of her own, all in The Hague. Then Nathaniel came into her life. He and his compatriots called her with the familiar Dutch form of Doortje. If we turn this into Dora, we lose the diminutive, but that is actually congruent with her character: Not only did she take the lead, she was determined and steadfast, a real iron lady. She never broke, not even on the rack.

The secret of her appeal remains elusive, too. The Amsterdam gossip chronicler Jacob Bicker Raye called her the beautiful Dora. Was it her voice, for example, or her charming gestures? Was she a coquette, as defined by the observing writers, except that she was conducive to seduction? For eighteenth-century people, the power of physical attraction lay in other features than it does for us, accustomed as we are to an erotic body culture. Yet, from the description of her looks, it is a little hard to imagine they were a source of fatal attraction. A dry Amsterdam court clerk, admittedly, drew up the description, two years after Dora met Nathaniel. But it was meant to help people recognize her; hence, it ought to be realistic. The clerk described her as of mediocre height; rather buxom; a light face; dark brown hair; no thick eyebrows; a snub nose with large nostrils, slightly curved inward at the upper end; broad jaws; the cheeks somewhat shrunken; a good mouth with teeth, not very white; chubby hands; thick and coarse legs.[7] Probably, as far as physical appearance was concerned, her mouth was her major asset. To have all your teeth intact counted as a mark of beauty. With dentistry hardly developed, this held true for the social elites as well. Her buxomness, too, may have attracted men. The actual word the clerk used, *gezet*, now means a little fat, in a slightly negative sense, but in the early modern period it rather meant well rounded: Dora resembled a female figure in a Rubens picture.

Did Nathaniel's flight on January 4 take Cecilia by surprise, or did she already harbor suspicion? In any case, she acted resolutely. Some time elapsed, obviously, between writing her request to the Court of Holland and its treatment by the justices. Meanwhile, Cecilia had traced her husband and his lover further than Utrecht. She found out they stayed in a lodging house in Nijmegen, kept by a certain Daniel Siebert. It looked as if they were on the way to Cleves. Did Nathaniel hesitate to travel there straight away, because the town reminded him too much of the wife he had just left? When he heard she was coming after him, he had to run from his lodging house in a hurry, leaving half of his luggage behind. He dropped the idea of moving to Cleves, going to Amsterdam instead, where he checked into an inn called The White Mill.[8] Meanwhile, Cecilia had an excellent opportunity to lay hands at least on his goods.

The court of Nijmegen dealt with her case on January 20, 1765. Its clerk recorded the plaintiff's name as "Cecilia N. N.," legal wife of N. Donker, with J. G. C. Stalman as her attorney. The plaintiff's demand: seizure on all goods, securities, credits and bonds that her husband had or might have within the city and its jurisdiction, in particular in the packs and suitcases in the house of Daniel Siebert. She claimed the property thereof, awaiting further disposition about which share was hers. Because Donker had maliciously deserted her and their children, he was legally unauthorized to take those goods with him. Anyone keeping any other goods of Donker's, the demand continued, had to leave these untouched. Finally, Siebert should be forbidden to break the seal of the suitcases in his house. The court agreed to these demands, renewing its arrest three times, until it was published at the front of the town hall on March 12.

A legal battle ensued, lasting until November, whose outcome, alas, is unrecorded. Nathaniel and Dora came forward with a clever countermove. Whereas he remained in hiding, on April 20 she alone appeared in the Nijmegen courtroom. Its clerk wrote her name as Dorothea van Borstelman, adding that C. Altrogge acted as her attorney. The plaintiff demanded nullification of the arrest obtained by Cecilia N. N. on January 20, published on March 12. The argument was simple: Whereas the other party claimed that the goods in the lodging house were Donker's, they really belonged to the plaintiff. Since they had stayed there together, how could the judges decide? They postponed their decision for the time being. On May 1 a third party intervened: Adriaan van Kerkhoven, trustee over the property of Nathaniel Donker and Cecilia Klos, appointed by the court of Stompwijk, under which Visvliet was administered. It is unclear whether he replaced or supplemented Van der Ven, the trustee appointed by the Court of Holland. Van Kerkhoven also demanded that the goods at Siebert's place—and others, seized by a court official—remain sealed. He laid a claim on Nathaniel's possessions, to supply any deficit at Visvliet.

On November 14, Cecilia filed another claim with the Nijmegen court, which now listed her full name. Her husband's departure, she argued, had made her the legal guardian of their two minor sons. This time, the coveted objects were two suitcases in particular, still at Siebert's lodging house. No doubt, she knew they contained securities. The court noted that the two opposing parties—Cecilia and Dora—had submitted themselves to the judgment of burgomasters, whom the judges had asked to decide about the ownership. Once more, the plaintiff demanded that the suitcases be allocated to her, or else to Donker if he showed up. Of course, the subsidiary clause did not mean she allowed Nathaniel free disposal of his capital. She emphasized he had to compensate for the deficits at home and supply the ten thousand guilders to which his children were entitled. The court registered her claim the next day, the last time the case was on record.[9]

Thus, we are ignorant about the outcome of the legal battle at Nijmegen. We do know that none of the participants profited from it. Cecilia's financial difficulties continued, while Nathaniel contracted new debts in his turn.

It was a remarkable change of roles. For years Cecilia had been Nathaniel's companion, and during much of this period they had been on the run. Now he was running from her: she had turned from his companion into his pursuer. What were Cecilia's motives in pursuing Nathaniel, and what prompted him to go away with Dora in the first place?

When Nathaniel began his affair with Dora in 1764, supposedly his love for Cecilia finally had faded. We may ascribe it to the trivial factor of age. She was approaching forty, while he was in his early thirties. Dora was twenty-three. Nathaniel conformed to a stereotypical cultural pattern of exchanging one's mature wife for a younger woman. This pattern, of course, is more common in our own time, with easy access to divorce, than it was in the eighteenth century; that is, in the European context. Had Donker been a prosperous merchant in Beirut or a wealthy farmer in sub-Saharan Africa, he could have taken Dora as his second wife, or maybe she would have already been his third. In such a situation, his first wife would have resented losing her prime, but she would have accepted the new union as inevitable. And the community as a whole would have considered it just natural. As Donker lived in Christian Europe, this option was unavailable to him, although he might have taken advantage of the practical liberties allowed elite men. If he had kept Dora as a courtesan, he could have visited her frequently, without encountering much opprobrium. Cecilia would either be ignorant about it or acquiesce.

Obviously, Nathaniel was not content with just visiting Dora frequently; he wished to stay with her all the time. This was fatal attraction. Although he no longer loved his wife, he also gave up the company of his children and the control over part of his property for this attraction. The desire for a new woman, and of this woman for the man, may be universal, but social expectations and cultural stereotypes shape its outcome in different societies. In a polygamous culture, the man, if he can afford it, adds another spouse to his harem. In our case, the outcome had Donker cast in the traditional role of the libertine, running away with a woman of dubious repute and (again) squandering the patrimonial capital. Additionally, if we venture into psychological speculation, Nathaniel indulged in being on the run with Dora. After serving in the military twice, escaping from prison, and roaming around with Cecilia, it was hard to get accustomed to a settled life. This constituted a subconscious motive to start the affair.

To a certain extent, Cecilia's motive is self-evident: she wished to hold on to her husband. Alternatively, her love was over, too, but she needed the money to live decently with her children. This is not the whole story, however. We must take into account the importance attached to honor and respectability. Cecilia had worked her way up. In the early 1750s Nathaniel's relatives had accused this working-class girl, rightly or wrongly, of prostitution. Her honor was contested. In the 1760s she had finally become a respectable woman, the lady of a stately country home. Even with control over their capital, but as an abandoned wife, she suffered a diminution of her honor and, to suppose a more altruistic motive, her children had less status and honor in the future. The only way to maintain her and her children's elevated status was to convince Nathaniel to renounce Dora and come home. Thus, she had to pursue him relentlessly—and she did.

Dora, it seems, had only something to gain. She moved up the social ladder, from an immigrant prostitute to the full-time companion of a man from a native bourgeois family, perhaps still dishonorable but at least higher up on the fine scale of degrees of honor. She certainly had more to spend now. Because she chose to be the concubine of a wealthy man, eleven years older than she, it is easy to suppose her love was insincere. This can never be ascertained, but we do know she was steadfast. She was the moving force behind Nathaniel, both in their common activities and in the final plan to eliminate her rival. She probably invented the ruse claiming the goods in the Nijmegen lodging house were hers, as she thought out other ruses at a later stage. Despite everything, she clung to her lover, even when conditions got worse.

As matters stood in 1765, the affair was bound to end, if not in murder, then with all actors simply fading into poverty. Imagine it: Cecilia and her children are obliged to leave the Visvliet estate. They are entitled to ten thousand guilders, but all the mother's efforts to obtain this sum are in vain. They live in an inconspicuous home in The Hague. The wanderlust of Nathaniel and Dora is undiminished. However, as an illegitimate couple, on the run from the legitimate wife, they have a hard time cashing bonds and securities. Sooner or later his entire capital is gone. If they have spent it soon enough for Dora to be still attractive, he induces her to take up her former trade, acting as her pimp. But one day he gets caught in a fraud. There were bleak prospects in this scenario, but murder, imprisonment, and execution were worse.

Financial trouble came anyway, now that others once more controlled a large part of the Donker capital. A trustee acting for the local magistrates administered Visvliet, now an "abandoned estate." Due to the marriage settlement, most of the estate legally belonged to Nathaniel, but even if the magistrates and trustee were willing to pay him off, they had no idea where to find him. Neither could Cecilia receive her dowry, without an official divorce or her husband declared dead. Even the ten thousand guilders for the children remained frozen; they still awaited this sum in the summer of 1767. Possibly, the absence of a record of settlement in Nijmegen meant that the suitcases with valuables were still in that town, seized by its court. In that case, Nathaniel, too, had limited means at his disposal. Soon, he had creditors troubling him again.

As Cecilia had indicated, she and the children were obliged to leave the Visvliet estate. For a time, she could afford to rent a dwelling in Voorburg, halfway between their former home and The Hague. Soon, she had to give up that house as well. They moved in with her mother, widowed again and a resident of The Hague for some time now. The mother's children with Cecilia's stepfather had either died or moved out.[10] The neighbors knew the old lady as Mrs. Steffens, the surname of her second husband. She lived in a back street near the hospital, on the edge of town, along the quay where the barges for Delft departed. This was no classy neighborhood. At age forty, in The Hague, Cecilia had returned to a milieu resembling that of her Rotterdam youth. Still, the family was not totally poor. The children, for example, wore tailor-made clothes. The tailor and his wife also dealt in secondhand goods, selling clothes and furniture to Cecilia and her mother. Since May 1766, Mrs. Steffens could afford to hire a maid. One of her duties was to comb Cecilia's hair. When she did, she noticed that Mrs. Steffens' daughter had a small bald spot, the size of a five-and-a-half-stiver coin, on top of her head. This three-generation household, then, was modest but not poor. They and their neighbors were, however, poorly educated. Mrs. Steffens, her maid, and the tailor's wife were all illiterate.[11] Of another neighboring couple, at least the woman was literate. A longtime acquaintance of Mrs. Steffens, she sometimes did her washing and occasionally wrote a letter for her.[12]

Ironically, Nathaniel and his mistress lived near his family for a while. During their wandering period, they moved back and forth between Amsterdam and The Hague several times, sleeping in inns or with people they knew. In Amsterdam, they often stayed with a man named Gerrit Deegens, whose job it was to transport rubble in a ship. His wife introduced Nathaniel and Dora to her sister, who lived in a small street in The

Hague, earning an income by making women's caps. Her husband, named Nicolaas Heemelraad, worked for a man who rented coaches. The occupations of their hosts betray that the couple stayed in modest places too, which at least had the advantage that they felt safe from discovery. In the spring of 1766, however, an acquaintance warned them that Cecilia knew their address. Quickly, they left Heemelraad's home, checking in at a Leiden inn. Cecilia tracked them down again, and this time it was a narrow escape. Lacking the cash to pay the innkeeper, Nathaniel and Dora left through the window. He helped her out holding the sheet from the bed and jumped down himself. The scene resembled a classic elopement from a boarding school, although in this case the man also left from the inside. It may have reminded Nathaniel of his escape from private prison ten years earlier. That escape had been the occasion to join the woman he now fled from.

For a while, Nathaniel and Dora went separate ways. He returned to The Hague, where Cecilia finally trapped him in another inn. She embraced him, said everything would turn out right, and took him home to her mother's place. The spouses were reconciled. Possibly, Nathaniel longed to see his little sons, whom he had missed for a year and a half. With a solemn oath, he promised never again to leave his family: if he did, let all the Biblical plagues descend upon him and vermin eat his body. However, in swearing this oath, our first protagonist was decidedly less serious than that other killer, Van Gogh, nine years later. Nathaniel stayed with his family for only a few weeks, taking the first opportunity to sneak out and go to Amsterdam. He moved in with Deegens again, where Dora soon joined him. For her part, Cecilia never tired of her efforts to win him back. She visited him at Deegens's place several times, and in between they wrote each other letters. Deegens's wife actively mediated between the spouses. In all appearance, their separation was far from definitive yet.[13]

In this triangle, Nathaniel's position was an ambiguous one. He adored his mistress, but should he have enough of her, he knew his wife would always forgive him. Each time he and Cecilia met, he made her believe she could win back his heart. But even if he really contemplated returning to her, he always had second thoughts. Nathaniel's affair with Dora also put in jeopardy his relationship with his brother, a respected lawyer established in Amsterdam. Pieter Gerbrand was extremely worried about Nathaniel's relapse into libertinage, without taking action to have him imprisoned anew. With so many odds against the affair, it is plain that Nathaniel was fatally attracted to Dora. At this stage of his life, his actions clearly reflected the darker side of the revolution in love. Even his occasional expressions of remorse toward his wife should be attributed not so much to a desire to regain respectability as to the recollection of the happy years they had spent together.

Cecilia, on the other hand, behaved according to more traditional patterns. The wife put the full blame on the concubine, not on her husband. This habit of women blaming each other was a centuries-old cultural stereotype.[14] From Dora's perspective, Cecilia was a permanent threat to her relationship with Nathaniel. "This woman will never leave us in peace," Dora hammered home to him time and again. She kept it to herself that she feared Cecilia might succeed in her efforts to win back her husband. For Dora, it was an unequivocal case of eliminating a rival. To her lover, however, she emphasized that they together suffered from persecution: "As long as she is alive, she will continue to harass us, in whatever part of the world we may be. This has to stop. The only solution is to kill her."[15]

The murder plan dated back at least to August 1766. In that month, attested to by two witnesses, the wandering couple was looking for a house in Amsterdam. This meant they had made a decision, since they needed a place of their own to commit the crime undisturbed. Dora had met a previous acquaintance, who formerly worked in a brothel in The Hague. The acquaintance told Dora she had come to Amsterdam with her boss, who now ran a music hall in the *Pijlsteeg*, close to Dam Square. Named Hendrik Hoendervoogd, but known by everyone as "The Owl," he was a big man in the prostitution business. He had named his music hall *De Pijl* (The Arrow) after the street it was on. Hoping The Owl could find them a house, Dora first approached him on a Sunday afternoon in August. She pretended she had just arrived in town on a barge and was looking for a place to sleep, whereupon he advised her to try The Black Eagle at the Tree Market. The next day, at 4:30 P.M., Dora came back with Nathaniel, finding only The Owl's concubine in, who offered the visitors a cup of tea. When The Owl returned, they asked him right away if he knew some place where they could stay. In return, Dora would procure a few girls from The Hague, to "swing" in his music hall. As The Owl had nothing for them at the moment, they continued to board with Gerrit Deegens.

On a Saturday afternoon at the beginning of October, Nathaniel and Dora knocked on The Owl's door for a second time. Excited, they told him they had found a house located "at the water," opposite the Grain Exchange. The owner planned to move out, allowing them to move in within forty days, for five hundred guilders per year. They approached The Owl hoping he would advance them the rent. The brothel keeper tried to dissuade the couple from the idea, saying that the house was too expensive and too big for them alone. They pleaded: "It is only for six months, until May, when we can rent a cheaper place, and the owner demands only three months rent now." Donker claimed he would have the money to reimburse The Owl in January. Reluctantly, the brothel keeper promised to advance them the $f125$ they needed, still under the condition that Dora get him some girls from The Hague. She had an even better idea: she would employ them as whores in the house they were to rent and allow them to dance in The Arrow once in a while. They drew up a declaration of debt, which Nathaniel signed with the name of Donk. Then the three of them went off to the house.

The Water was the name of the West side of the Damrak, one of the outlets of the Amstel River into the harbor north of town. In the middle of the sixteenth century a broad quay had been constructed there, stretching from the Old Bridge, some two hundred meters south of the harbor, to Dam Square. Later, the Grain Exchange had been built over the water near the Old Bridge. The house Nathaniel and Dora were about to rent was the fourth from the alley opposite the bridge. Everyone called it "the house at the water"; it was rather well known, since the owner, a certain Fontein, operated a toy shop in it. Fontein negotiated with Nathaniel alone. To the latter's surprise, the owner was content with $f115$, probably because the first term expired on January 1 and October had already begun. They agreed on a contract expiring on May 1, which the new tenant signed under the name of Daniel Donk. He added a miniscule abbreviation sign, allowing him to claim, if necessary, he had meant his full last name. Obviously, he had something to hide: not only his true intention in renting the house but also his whereabouts. Mr. Donk paid the $f115$ to Fontein, keeping the ten remaining guilders in his pocket. He did not try to hide the favorable deal from The Owl, triumphantly greeting him and Dora as he came out of the door. The three of them drank a cup of tea, whereupon they parted.[16]

Dora never intended to become a madam. A few weeks later, she told The Owl she was unable to procure girls. To keep her part of the deal, she herself danced in The Arrow one night in late October. At about the same time, before November in any case, she and Nathaniel moved into the house at the water. A notary from The Hague, Pieter Verhoef, involved in some dubious dealings with Donker, soon joined them. For four guilders per week, the notary rented a room in the house. It allowed the main occupants to employ a twelve-year-old girl, Kaatje, to do shopping and cleaning. The girl lived with her mother in a nearby alley.[17] For a month, this quartet stayed in the house at the water, Kaatje only for the day, without any noteworthy event happening.

On Saturday, November 29, 1766, shortly before ten in the morning, Cecilia Klos left her mother's home in The Hague, taking a barge to Amsterdam. She was in a cheerful mood. Her husband, Nathaniel Donker, had invited her to come over and discuss their reconciliation. He also intended to visit his brother-in-law with her, in an effort to obtain financial assistance from him. Cecilia and her husband were to stay in an Amsterdam inn over the weekend and possibly longer. Her rival was out of sight.

The skipper saw two women standing on the quay. The elder of the two handed over a basket to the younger one and kissed her goodbye. How could the skipper, or anyone present, know that the old widow embraced her daughter for the last time? The woman who entered his barge, aged forty-one, was dressed in a youthful and colorful manner, impressing him as a lady of quality. Her outer garment was a white coat of Haarlem cloth, with red ornaments and decorated with red and green flowers. According to the fashion of the day, she wore several garments underneath, mostly covered by the coat: a scarlet skirt with checks stitched onto it, a cotton one embroidered with bouquets, and a simple skirt with a big flower. On top of her head she wore a double calotte cap with a blue ribbon. The small bald spot underneath this cap was invisible to the skipper. Her shoes, with silver clasps and almond-colored cords, were white, as were her stockings. On the second finger of her right hand, she wore a plain golden ring without a stone.[18]

A servant spurred the horses on the towpath, and the barge took off. Cecilia inspected the contents of the basket, which her mother had packed for her the previous day. She had packed it lavishly, perhaps intending to show that the household was free from poverty. Although Cecilia lacked money, she still had the pretty clothes and jewelry from the happy days at the Visvliet estate. She probably had instructed her mother which things to include, expecting to stay in Amsterdam for a week of conspicuous extravagance. Most of her belongings consisted of clothing. On top lay a dress she particularly liked, a white chintz one with red flowers, in the English style. Chintz was a strong cotton fabric, especially popular at the time. The other clothes and textiles equally reflected the fashion of the age: two embroidered skirts, one of Indian cotton, the other English; two ordinary white skirts; three new shirts with cambric bands at the collar; white striped drawers; two camisoles, one red with a flannel lining, the other white with stripes; five muslin scarves; two white-striped jackets with buttons on the front side and ruffled sleeves; a white twilled skirt with a broad edge, embroidered with colored English worsted; a bodice with silver laces; a few pairs of cotton stockings; a cap with a red-and-white-striped ribbon; a black gauze hat, with a white silk lining; an Indian nightgown with a big flower and laces in front; two white night caps; a black calash; two linen aprons; two damask napkins; and a set of handkerchiefs.

The rest of her belongings consisted of jewelry and other luxury items: a little gold ring with a red stone and two small diamonds; a pair of silver clasps; three pairs of eardrops made of jet, one brown, one with white stones, and one with a little pearl crown; a pair of golden bracelets; a needle case, a thimble, and tweezers, all of silver; two snuffboxes, one a big square box of Saxon porcelain with a gilded edge, the other oval shaped with an ornament made of East Indian porcelain and a small mirror inside. Finally, Cecilia carried her favorite handbag, with a silver handle. In it, she had some cash: one golden coin and a few silver ones.[19]

While inspecting all of these items, Cecilia noted that one of the handkerchiefs, a red one with the image of a rider, actually was not hers. It reminded her of the occasion on which she had obtained it, when she had been embarrassed at first because of her forgetfulness. Unlike today, in the early modern period handkerchiefs were a luxury item. They signified that the owner was not one of those rude persons who blew her nose with two fingers and threw the results on the floor. Thus, they were a visible mark of politeness. In early September, Cecilia had dined in The Court of Rome in The Hague, where she suddenly noticed she had no handkerchief with her. The landlord's wife had been so kind as to lend Cecilia one of hers. Later, her mother had washed the handkerchief, and the neighbor who always wrote her letters had ironed it. Cecilia had planned to return it to the landlady of The Court of Rome many times, but she had always forgotten. Now Cecilia looked at the handkerchief anew, noticing it was marked in one corner with the letters C. W., the landlady's initials, in blue yarn.[20]

Two specimens of Cecilia's belongings can still be inspected today. The Amsterdam court had them fastened to an annex of the interrogation record. One is a colorful band, which belonged to the coat of Haarlem cloth she wore when she left The Hague. It is light blue with green yarn woven into it and red borders; the cloth looks a bit ragged and old. The other specimen is a piece torn from the English chintz dress, which she carried in her luggage, destined to play a role later in our story. It feels solid and looks rather new: a white background with a red flower motif, a fine example of calico printing. Both specimens are bright and clean; presumably the court had them washed.[21]

The journey from The Hague to Amsterdam took almost eleven hours, including the time needed to change barges. Halfway between The Hague and Leiden, Cecilia encountered the first obstacle, the Leiden Dam, not far from Visvliet where she had lived with Nathaniel and their children. The passengers had to leave the boat and cross the dam to board another, which took them to the south edge of Leiden. They arrived there at one in the afternoon. Those traveling farther had thirty minutes to walk to the north side of this town, where the Haarlem barge departed at 1:30 P.M.. This boat took them straight to Haarlem in exactly four hours. Cecilia and the other passengers bound for Amsterdam made a second crosstown walk to the Amsterdam Gate, at Haarlem's eastern edge, where they boarded a barge leaving at 6:30 P.M. and arriving at the Haarlem Gate in Amsterdam at 8:45 at night.[22]

Understandably, Cecilia did not pass these eleven hours by pondering over skirts and snuffboxes. It is likely, although we do not know for sure, that she contemplated the behavior of her runaway husband. Earlier that year, he had stayed with his family for a few weeks, only to return again to his mistress. This time, how sincere was his intention to make peace with his wife and start anew? Did this woman still have a spell on him? Her hopes were stronger than her fears when the barge arrived in Amsterdam in the evening. Even before she disembarked, she saw her husband waving at her from the quay.

Shortly after eight, Nathaniel Donker had said goodbye to his mistress for the weekend and left the house at the water. To keep her company, Kaatje, the servant girl, would sleep in the house for the next two nights.[23] Nathaniel walked to the Haarlem Gate, arriving in time to pick up his wife at the barge station. He smiled at her. They went to an inn named The Castle of Antwerp. The landlord immediately recognized them because they had stayed there together during the Amsterdam fair, on the occasion of another attempt to talk it over. Of course, he avoided the places in which he had stayed with Dora under pretense of being husband and wife. This Saturday night, in this inn, Nathaniel and Cecilia legitimately presented themselves as husband and wife. Arriving directly from the barge station, they checked in between 9:00 and 9:30 P.M.[24] Since it was late and Cecilia had made a long, fatiguing journey, they probably went to bed without taking a walk. We do not know what the couple did on Sunday, except that he took care the inn staff often saw them together. When Cecilia reminded her husband they had planned to visit his brother-in-law to ask for financial help, he protested that he lacked the proper clothes to wear on such an important mission.[25] To add a positive note, he told her he had rented a nice house, which he intended to show her on Monday.

Did Donker ever consider the alternative of shooting his wife? He was in the possession of two pistols. Already during his last stay in The Hague, he had loaded them with small lead bullets. According to his own statement, he had been afraid to cross the park outside The Hague unarmed at night. Killing his wife with one of the pistols would have meant doing it at greater physical distance from her and, hence, greater emotional distance from the act. And he could have asked Dora to fire the other, thus implicating her more fully. Whatever his true intention with these weapons, he never used them.[26]

Monday, December 1, was the fateful day, scheduled for the murder. At breakfast, Nathaniel trembled a little. Unnoticed by Cecilia, he drank a few glasses of liquor. At 10:00 A.M. he told her he had to go out alone for a short while. Of course he went straight to the house at the water; he must ascertain that everything was under control there. Dora had assured him she would take care that Verhoef was out and that Kaatje stayed away as well. He indeed found Dora at home alone. When was he going to bring Cecilia to the house, was all she wanted to know, but once more Nathaniel hesitated. Dora inveighed against him, calling him a coward and telling him he just had to do it: "Otherwise I will enter another road with you."[27] The phrase sounds a little ambiguous, but no doubt she meant to threaten him with leaving. This is the most explicit statement of "it is her or me" on record. Dora reminded her lover that they had planned the deed for months; that they had rented the house with the intention to lure the prospective victim into it; that Dora had urged Nathaniel many times to invent some pretext with which he could make Cecilia come to Amsterdam. Now he had told her he would show her the house. When they came, Dora said, she would hide in the toilet and assist him as soon as he had grabbed his wife by the neck. Nathaniel's confusion only increased. He needed another alcoholic encouragement, so he swallowed a large quantity of bitter gin. Finally, he consented. He told Dora he would arrive with his wife between 1:00 and 1:30 P.M.

Nathaniel returned to The Castle of Antwerp before noon. Instead of proposing to his wife to show her the house at the water, he suggested they visit his brother-in-law after all. This time, Cecilia refused, claiming he was incapable of finding the right words to ask for assistance. Did she notice he was a little drunk? It was a better idea, she continued, to ask the lawyer De Waal from The Hague to approach his relative on their behalf. Nathaniel rose up, as if he suddenly thought of a solution: She knew the notary Verhoef, he was sure, who could speak for them. Since Verhoef was presently staying in his home, they could go and ask him. Cecilia agreed.

If Cecilia believed they were going to see the notary, it ought to have made her frown when her husband told the landlord they intended to take a pleasure tour. Alternatively, if the couple had changed their plan in the meantime, she had no reason for suspicion. We know for sure that they left the inn before one o'clock and that Nathaniel returned there alone around six. What really happened between their departure from The Castle of Antwerp and the murder in the house at the water? To get it right, we have to listen to the contradicting stories later told in court, by the suspect on one side and four witnesses on the other. They offer us a choice between two scenarios.

The statements by the innkeeper, two male servants, and a carter were all congruent. The innkeeper said: "They told me they wanted to take a sightseeing tour across the harbor; they would skip supper, intending to be out for the whole afternoon. I did not mind, since they had already paid the bill. Moreover, they left their luggage behind, saying they would pick it up in the evening. I remember they left on a *toeslede*." A toeslede, an Amsterdam peculiarity of the time, was a closed sledge, meant for personal transport; horse drawn, it resembled a coach, except that it had no wheels. A seventeen-year-old servant of the inn had ordered the sledge: "Shortly after twelve I knocked on the door of the nearest carter; he was out on another job, but his wife told me he was about to return and would soon report at The Castle of Antwerp." Another servant of the inn said: "The carter arrived at about 12:30; I escorted the couple through the door and told my boss they had left on a sledge." The landlord confirmed that his servant had told him so, adding that no other couples had stayed in his inn that day and, certainly, no one else had left on a sledge. Finally, the carter testified: "I took them to the embarkment point for the boat to Buiksloot, which took off at one o'clock." Note that he left it open whether he actually saw the couple go on board. When confronted with these witnesses, Donker admitted he had told the landlord they planned to make a trip across the harbor, but he claimed he had added they might change their plan. He denied having ordered a sledge: he and his wife had left the inn on foot, and they had been walking all afternoon. The reason for the claim of taking a long walk is plain. Months later, however, when Donker confessed to the murder, he still insisted that they had left the inn on foot, claiming they had arrived in the house at the water at the prearranged time, between one and one-thirty.[28]

According to the first scenario, Nathaniel persuaded Cecilia that the landlord must remain ignorant of their real destination. They should order a sledge, pretending to go on a boat trip. For the later observer his purpose shines through: He was collecting witnesses whose statements were to divert judicial attention away from the scene of the crime. Why did Cecilia go along with this? Possibly, she acted as one of the "shame-faced" poor, wishing to hide at all costs that her material circumstances had sunk below her acquired social status. Afraid that their true aim, begging for money, could reveal itself somehow, she overreacted, consenting to a show of mystification. In that case, we must interpret the carter's statement to mean that he knew the boat was scheduled to depart at one o'clock. In fact, the carter left the couple at the departure point, where Nathaniel told him he could go. From the harbor's quay it was about three minutes walking to the house at the water, allowing them to arrive there at the time prearranged with Dora. This is all possible. However, if we opt for this scenario, Nathaniel's consecutive replies during his interrogations remain puzzling. To convince the judges he was innocent of the murder, it hardly mattered whether they believed he had made a long walk with his wife or a boat trip. Why did he insist on the former option, when he had taken so much trouble to make it look like the latter? And, when he finally confessed, what use was it to him to insist on this point of detail? He said they had left the inn on foot, going directly to the house at the water.

The alternative scenario, although speculative, puts all contradictory statements in place. It has Nathaniel lying to the magistrates who interrogated him afterward about the means of transport and the time of the murder. He lied until the end, sensing that the court would never have him tortured just to set straight a minor point of detail. Nathaniel and Cecilia had *not* left the inn on foot and they had *not* gone directly to the house at the water. The carter had actually seen them boarding the boat to Buiksloot. We know he returned to the Castle of Antwerp at six o'clock. In between there was plenty of time to take a boat trip, to return to carry out his plan, and to hide the body in the house. Since Dora always proclaimed her complete innocence of the crime, we lack her statement about the exact moment. Why did Nathaniel lie in court? He simply could not bear to tell the truth! Perhaps he had even repressed the memory of the events between leaving the Castle of Antwerp and killing his wife.

It probably went like this: Forever undecided, Nathaniel told Cecilia that the solution of their financial difficulties could wait. The solution of their marital problems came first. They must talk it over once more, on a romantic trip. Cecilia was eager to comply. As in their happiest days, they turned it into a festive journey, riding out on a sledge. They boarded the boat to Buiksloot, on the other side of the harbor, enjoyed a drink in a tavern there, and took the return boat. Holland has a marine climate. It was the first day of December, but the weather was mild yet. They could easily sit on the open deck and talk. Everything would turn out right between them, they assured each other. Nathaniel no longer knew whether he meant it or allowed himself this last moment before their separation. He caressed her and kissed her. Back in town, Nathaniel assured Cecilia there was time enough to visit the house at the water. They arrived there around three-thirty. Just an hour before he killed his wife, he had declared his renewed love for her! He must have repressed this unbearable reminiscence. If events really happened this way, Nathaniel and Cecilia both took the secret with them to the grave.

Cecilia entered the house at the water that Monday afternoon, never to leave it alive. Nathaniel first offered her a cup of coffee, which she declined. Then he showed her the house. He took his time, even though he realized that his mistress waited in the bathroom according to plan. When he had left Cecilia alone in another room, Dora immediately showed up and demanded to know why he had not struck her yet. He confessed his reluctance, explaining he just could not do it. Dora scolded him again, threatening him that Verhoef and Kaatje would soon be in and then their chance would be gone. When she heard Cecilia approach, Dora quickly returned to her hiding place, admonishing her lover to drop his cowardice.

This was the man who, a decade earlier, had voluntarily enlisted as an officer in the armies of two different countries. Nathaniel Donker was appalled at the thought of having to kill somebody. Was it the purely physical aversion of a man unacquainted with violence, unable to kill anyone? He had never been in a military campaign; an enemy soldier had never confronted him. Neither did he belong to those social groups who were accustomed to fighting in the streets. Quite likely, however, his reluctance lay deeper. The intended victim, after all, was his wife, the woman who had been his companion for better or worse throughout the 1750s and early 1760s; the woman he had loved so much that he had not hesitated to marry her three times.

Continuing their tour through the house, they arrived in the room adjacent to the bathroom. It was now or never. Nathaniel seized Cecilia by the neck, exclaiming, "You have pursued us long enough." Next, he squeezed her throat with both hands, whereupon she fell to the floor. It looked as if Dora remained in hiding until she was completely sure, intending to deny her presence if things went wrong. Now that she finally observed action, she rushed from the bathroom, jumped on Cecilia's stomach and grabbed her hands. While Dora held the victim in check, Nathaniel continued to strangle her. They sat in this position for no less than a quarter of an hour. Cecilia was long dead when Dora noticed the foam coming from her mouth. She dropped the victim's hands and stood up. An iron bar lay on the windowsill, for use as a support when the window was open. She took the bar and dealt several hard blows to the dead body's chest. The iron lady wanted absolute certainty! Her active participation made her a killer, not just an accomplice. Dora alone undressed the corpse. Together they moved it away, laying it in a bed, bed curtains closed, in a back room upstairs.[29]

The crime had been committed. Nathaniel's fatal attraction to Dora, bringing with it a sense that the deed was inevitable, had taken the upper hand. Note that this is his story of how the murder took place, since Dora never told hers. In order to appear less cynical and atrocious, he probably exaggerated his reluctance and Dora's constant exhortations to continue. But on the whole his confession, made in the awareness that it earned him the death penalty, seems trustworthy. While he constantly hesitated, all the evidence points at Dora being the active force, acting with complete determination. Possibly, she also invented the next trick.

The last activity of the day literally meant acting. Nathaniel's mistress was to impersonate his wife, in the clothes just stripped from the victim's body. Dora put on the English chintz dress, the skirt, and the coat of Haarlem cloth that Cecilia had worn that afternoon. Unlike Van Gogh, their successor in killing for love, Dora and Nathaniel were no professional actors. But as long as she avoided coming too close to people who remembered Cecilia's looks, they should manage to play the game.

Shortly after 6:00 P.M. the landlord of The Castle of Antwerp saw the man who had left with his wife on a sledge return alone. His spouse waited in a nearby wine bar, Donker told the innkeeper. She was ready to leave town, intending to take the barge to Haarlem that night. Donker had brought a carter to carry her luggage, which the landlord ordered his servant to get. When Donker had entrusted it to the carter, they first went to the wine shop where he had left Dora. She had been chatting with the waitress, telling her that the man with whom she had arrived was her husband. That man indeed returned to pick her up, assuring his wife that everything was ready for her departure. The waitress admired the beautiful clothes of this woman, dressed like a fine lady. She paid less attention to her customer's looks, but noted she had a slight accent, probably German.[30]

Timing was a key here. A rather precise sense of time was common in the Dutch Republic, probably earlier than in the surrounding countries. The Amsterdam court routinely asked witnesses exactly when an event had happened and most of them managed to date it within a margin of half an hour. All the city's towers had clocks. Barges, too, operated according to a tight schedule, a fact with which residents of Amsterdam were familiar. Precisely this adherence to schedule had been the innovative aspect of the system of passenger transport over water upon its introduction in the early seventeenth century. Elements of the system already existed in Europe by then; in the previous century, horse-drawn boats connected the Italian towns of Venice and Padua. To rely on a dense, dependable network was something different. Dutch barges always departed exactly on schedule, an achievement about which foreign observers expressed their astonishment.[31] In 1766 Nathaniel and Dora hoped to profit from this punctuality: To appear in places at the right time would lend credibility to the claim that Cecilia had boarded a barge.

The boat to Haarlem was due to depart at 7:00 P.M.. At 6:30, Nathaniel left the wine bar with Dora, telling the waitress he would accompany his wife to the departure point. The sledge took both of them with the luggage to the Haarlem Gate, where Nathaniel told the carter to wait until he came back. This raised no suspicion, since it was uncommon for sledges to pass through the gate. At the other side, out of sight from the carter, Nathaniel left Dora with the luggage. Returning alone, he asked the man to take him to the first sluice at the Haarlem dike. There he paid the carter's bill and said goodbye to him. A little later, Dora joined Nathaniel at the sluice. They asked a boy who passed by to carry their luggage for a few pennies. No one would ever find and question this boy, they assumed, and they were right.[32]

The landlord of The Castle of Antwerp and his servant who brought the luggage, the waitress in the wine bar, and the carter who took Nathaniel and his presumed wife to the Haarlem Gate and saw him return alone: they counted as witnesses that Cecilia had left with the seven o'clock barge for Haarlem. When this boat arrived at its destination, there were no further connections on the same day. Transit passengers had to spend the night in Haarlem. Perhaps something had happened to Cecilia there, Nathaniel might have suggested. Sooner or later, Mrs. Steffens would consider her daughter missing, and eventually a court official was to question him about it. He could reply with confidence that he had accompanied her to the barge station, invoking the testimony of several people. Whatever had happened to Cecilia, surely it had taken place somewhere between Amsterdam and The Hague. The real-life farce, Dora impersonating Cecilia, had worked perfectly, it seemed. Burning the clothes she had worn, along with the other goods and the basket in which Cecilia had kept them, was the logical next step. The only problem left was the corpse in their home.

It is a fair guess that Nathaniel Donker and his iron lady had difficulty getting to sleep that night. If either of the two slept, Dora did. She was content with the final elimination of her rival. She convinced herself she had only offered a little help, while her partner had strangled the victim. And, as revealed by her later lightheartedness, she thought they could get away with it. Nathaniel was less sure, and he had much to ponder. He had murdered the woman he had promised to be true to three times, the mother of his children, the one with whom he had never dared to part absolutely. Now he was alone with his lover, and at her mercy.

4

How to Dump a Body When There Are No Cars?

Imagine a house with a garden in a city at night. Cautiously, a man opens the back door. Is it a body that he drags out of the dining room, through the garden, into the garage? He looks to the right and left with suspicious eyes, but no one watches him. Safely in the garage, he closes the door and pauses to wipe the sweat from his brow. Then he lifts the corpse into the trunk of his car. He closes the trunk, reopens the garage door, and gets into the driver's seat. Steering his way carefully through the streets, he arrives at the edge of town, where he takes a small road into the woods. This road leads to a little stream, spanned with a bridge just strong enough to allow a car to pass over it. The man halts on the bridge. He looks around again, opens the trunk, and lifts his criminal load. Then he throws the body into the stream. After a final look, to reassure himself he is alone, he steps into his car and drives back home.

The scene is familiar. It recurs in countless crime movies and detective stories as the standard way of concealing one's implication when the murder has taken place in one's home. In 1766, Nathaniel and Dora had a problem similar to that of a protagonist in a modern crime movie who has shot a rival in the living room. Since the afternoon of Monday, December 1, the corpse of a strangled woman lay in a bed in the house at the water. The option of removing the body in a car was unavailable to them. What could eighteenth-century killers do to cover up their crime and minimize the chance of getting caught? Moreover, what could they do in a busy metropolis like Amsterdam? Dead babies, dumped by unmarried mothers, were fished from canals on a routine basis, but they had no recognizable identity that betrayed who had taken their life. To drop the body of Nathaniel's wife in the water opposite their house, near the Grain Exchange, practically amounted to turning themselves in. Donker and his lover spent most of the next day contemplating the right method. Tuesday also was the day they made their first mistake, albeit one without immediate consequences.

The mistake was to refrain from destroying all of Cecilia's belongings. Was the temptation to hold on to some of the items, the luxury ones in particular, too great? From Cecilia's possessions, Dora kept the two nice snuffboxes and two of the handkerchiefs, among them the one that the wife of a restaurant keeper in The Hague had offered as a replacement. She also took the skirt with the big flower and the new white shoes, the only pair Cecilia had with her when she departed for Amsterdam. Dora even kept the clothes she had worn when she impersonated her victim the previous day.[1] We could simply ascribe these appropriations to greed, but probably there was more at stake. Cecilia had been a rival, Donker's legitimate wife, whose place Dora had taken now. Not content with impersonating her, she wanted literally to be Cecilia. So she dressed like her former rival and used her snuffboxes and handkerchiefs, unaware that one of them actually belonged to another woman.

They pawned the rest of the victim's belongings, being at least smart enough to offer it at two different places. Together, it earned them twenty-nine guilders. In both pawn shops Dora registered under the name of Cecilia. Again, we may ascribe this to stupidity or naïveté, or alternatively Dora obsessively imagined she was Cecilia. Did she realize the inherent risk? The suggestion that Cecilia had pawned her clothes in Amsterdam on December 2 was inconsistent with the claim that she had left town in the evening of December 1. At the end of the day, Dora sold the bracelets, the clasps, and the handbag to a silversmith.[2]

A psychological explanation, that is Dora imagining herself to be a new Cecilia, should not obscure the fact that the decision to keep some of the victim's belongings and pawn or sell the rest was a matter of necessity as well. Quite likely they had considered the option of destroying everything, but they simply needed the money. From this perspective the mistake was the ultimate consequence of their role in the society in which they lived. In this society Nathaniel lacked the option of taking Dora as a supplementary wife. He had declined just to maintain her as a courtesan, because he wanted to be in her company all the time. This wish had obliged the couple to go on the run, playing the roles of a libertine and his "whore." In turn, this had caused the seizure of part of his capital, leading to renewed financial strain and debts. It was an unaffordable luxury to burn or bury Cecilia's belongings. In no way had robbery been the motive for murder, but when their crime left the killers with clothes and valuables, these were a welcome asset. To be sure, even if they remained at large with the money, a carefree life lay far in the future. Should they manage to hide the corpse for good, at least until it had become unidentifiable, the magistrates would consider Cecilia missing until they could declare her dead after some ten years had passed. Only then could Nathaniel marry Dora and try to recover what was left of his capital. The question is whether the murderous couple themselves realized this on the day after the killing.

They were safe for the moment. Pawning Cecilia's possessions was no factor in casting suspicion on Dora and Nathaniel or directly leading to their arrest. In fact, it went largely unnoticed. Both pawnbrokers entrusted Cecilia's goods to the municipal pawn shop, one on December 4 and one on December 5. They lay there stored, without the city court knowing it, until July of the next year.[3] More significant was the order that Dora gave to Kaatje in the early morning of Wednesday, December 3. The girl had to purchase a big basket with a lid that could be locked. She chose a brown and white one, which cost about two and a half guilders. It was so heavy that Kaatje had to carry it to the house at the water with the help of her little sister.[4]

After delivering the basket, Kaatje left again. It was about nine in the morning, too early to expect that the notary Verhoef, who still boarded in the house, would disturb Dora and Nathaniel in the ghastly job they had to do. With a sharp knife and a bucket of water they went upstairs to the room where they had concealed Cecilia's body. She had been dead for almost two days: The corpse was as cold as the December morning but definitely in human shape still. Robbed of all her belongings, she lay there, naked and motionless. The record does not disclose whether Dora wore the victim's clothes while she did her job. Her tool was a big kitchen knife, which she normally used for chopping parsley and vegetables. Without hesitation Dora cut off Cecilia's head. A small quantity of blood dripped from the corpse's neck onto the bed. What bothered them more were the eyes in the severed head, which were still half open. This was too much, even for the iron lady. She took one of her own handkerchiefs, a big blue one, imprinted with the image of a rider on horseback. Carefully, Dora wrapped Cecilia's head with the cotton cloth. Then, with the same kitchen knife, she cut off the victim's arms. She asked Nathaniel to help her, but he felt sick and refused. Wanting him to cooperate in some way, she forced him to provide light with a lamp. Together, they packed the body parts into the basket Kaatje had bought.[5]

With two people frequenting their home, they had to take special precautions. It was highly probable that one of them would see Nathaniel and Dora carrying the basket into the hall and through the front door. Kaatje had bought it, but the young girl harbored no suspicion. They were less sure about Verhoef, so they decided to stage another act. About ten o'clock, when they had finished their job, they hid the basket under the chimney in a back room. Then Donker knocked on Verhoef's door and asked the notary to accompany him on some business. While they were out Dora cleaned the bed and the floor of the room where she had mutilated the victim's corpse. Then she moved the basket to the hallway. Returning with Verhoef at twelve-thirty, Nathaniel expressed his surprise, emphatically asking Dora what that thing next to the front door was. "You mean this basket," she replied. "It belongs to Madam Sjoenis, whom I know from The Hague. Two women have brought it on her behalf while you were out. They requested me to give the basket back to Madam Sjoenis outside the Haarlem Gate tonight, where she will pass by in a coach. She wants to talk to me." Nathaniel pretended to be angry at her and said, "Why did you agree to this? Do you have any idea what is in this basket? Perhaps stolen goods!" Dora assured him they would get into no trouble, because she knew Madam Sjoenis well. All the while, Verhoef was present and listening.[6]

Of course Dora said "tonight," because they must wait until dark. Meanwhile, they deliberated on how to proceed. Nathaniel remembered passing a porter's station upon returning from his visits to an acquaintance. The address was in an alley just five minutes' walk from their home. That this porter's name was Michiel Stalli was unknown to Donker, and he surely would have preferred never to know it. Around five o'clock, just after sunset at that time of year, Stalli saw a gentleman entering the alley.[7] The stranger wore a white woolen cloak, a tailwig with a hair net at the end, and a brimmed hat with ribbons. Donker asked him the somewhat superfluous question, "Are you a porter?" to which Stalli replied affirmatively. Donker continued, "Can you come with a wheelbarrow to the house at the water, where Mr. Fontein used to live, pick up a big basket, and take it to the Haarlem Gate? If you accept the job, I will be back in half an hour to give you further instructions." Stalli knew where Fontein's toy shop had been, and he was happy to oblige.[8]

With no car parked in front of his house, to hire a porter was Donker's solution. The alternatives were few, practically nonexistent. In that city of canals, one might think immediately of transport over water. Today, many residents of Amsterdam own small boats, which they navigate through the canals for pleasure in the summer. Even in the eighteenth century there were pleasure boats, but neither Donker nor anyone he knew owned one and buying one was too expensive. In all other cases, at least one person would be able to link Donker to the basket. The skipper of a commercial boat might consent to transport it, but to request him to put this load ashore somewhere outside the city gate surely would raise suspicion. Transporting it in a carriage meant that the driver knew about it. To entrust the basket to a carter with a sledge, instead of a porter with a wheelbarrow, made little difference. With a load consisting of one piece, it was more logical to hire a porter. Unlike a carter, moreover, a porter was a member of a free trade, so there were no guild formalities that might complicate the matter.[9] If it looked like an ordinary job, the man was bound to forget about it soon.

In modern crime movies, the person transporting a corpse in the trunk of his car often faces unexpected frustration. A policeman stops him because of a burned-out headlight and discovers the body by chance. Or two secret lovers have picked that night for a rendezvous near a moonlit pond, unnoticed by the driver who opens his trunk and drops his load. Something similar almost happened to Nathaniel and Dora. They were not caught with the corpse, but the interruption seriously complicated the dumping process. This element in our plot looks like the invention of a contemporary playwright or, for that matter, a later historical novelist. But it did indeed happen, in Amsterdam in 1766.

After the porter accepted the job, Donker immediately went home. He conferred briefly with his lover, who had her plan ready: Nathaniel was to return to the porter's station and instruct the man where to pick up his load. She would direct the porter to the Haarlem Gate. Nathaniel was to walk directly to the gate (a shorter distance than from their home) and hide outside, until Dora had arrived with the porter and the basket and told the man he could go. Together, they would be strong enough to carry the basket to a quiet spot along the moat outside the wall and dump Cecilia's body.

At five-thirty Stalli saw Donker entering his alley again. Donker specified the address, adding that a little girl would be leaning over the lower door. Donker was unable to accompany him, he said, having some urgent business in town. Stalli did not mind, took his wheelbarrow and went off. The girl, who indeed stood there, fetched a lady, finely dressed with a silk cloak draped around her. She paid him in advance, adding a handsome tip. Stalli noticed the basket was brand new; with its contents, he estimated the weight at 150 pounds. The lady assisted him in lifting this heavy load onto his wheelbarrow.

Meanwhile, two women and a man approached the Old Bridge from the other side of the Damrak. The man was no less than The Owl, owner of The Arrow, who had advanced the rent for the house at the water. He was accompanied by his mistress and another woman, who lived on her own but who, no doubt, was one of the girls who danced in his music hall. As they crossed the bridge, they heard a door slam. Looking in the direction of the sound, The Owl realized it was the front door of Dora and Nathaniel's home. From the bridge, they saw Dora leaving with a porter carrying a huge basket. Suspicion overtook The Owl. Surely this was a dirty trick: She was leaving with her things in a hurry, and he could say goodbye to his money. Thinking how lucky he was to pass by accidentally, he told the women to be as quiet as possible, while they followed Dora and the porter from a distance.

The porter took his load around the corner through the Old Bridge Alley, continuing his way in the direction of Haarlem Street. Dora acted nervous. Sometimes she walked behind him, sometimes beside him, her eyes constantly fixed on the basket. Time and again she begged the porter to push his wheelbarrow carefully, warning him that the basket contained fragile goods. He reassured her, "Don't worry; it is well packed. I will go over the paved parts as much as I can." It took about seventeen minutes from the Damrak to the square in front of the Haarlem Gate.[10] Dora's nervousness explains why she never noticed the company following them. When they arrived at Haarlem Square, The Owl thought his suspicion was confirmed. He quickened his steps, caught up with the porter, and exclaimed, "Hold it!" Surprised, the porter stopped. The Owl immediately lifted the basket from the wheelbarrow and put it on the pavement. To Dora he snarled: "So Lady, are you leaving town just like that; you won't, Goddamn, fuck me like this."[11]

Dora was less shocked by The Owl's coarse words than by the fact that he had seized the basket, let alone the prospect that he would try to force its lock. "What nonsense are you talking?" she said. The brothel keeper retorted it was plain enough that she wanted to cheat on him. She tried to appease him: "If you go into that wine bar over there, I will join you in a minute and explain everything." But The Owl refused to be put off so eas-

How to Dump a Body When There Are No Cars? 73

Haarlem Square with Haarlem Gate (background, right) in the eighteenth century. Here The Owl stopped Dora and the porter with the basket. Behind the gate the barges for Haarlem disembarked. Photo: University Library Amsterdam.

ily. In dismay Dora requested the porter to go quickly to the gate and call the gentleman who had ordered his services, whom she expected to be waiting outside. When the porter found him and told him that someone had seized the basket, Donker expressed his astonishment. "Does this person have court officials with him?" he asked. "No, they are a fellow with two women," the porter replied. Donker followed him back to the square and recognized The Owl. Donker told him that the basket belonged to someone else and Dora specified they had to deliver it to two women in a coach, but the brothel keeper wanted immediate certainty. Finally, Dora suggested that she take The Owl and the two women back to the house at the water and show them the interior. They would see that the lamp was lit and that there was furniture in the house, even a few items she had taken back from the pawnshop that very day. It meant she had to leave Nathaniel alone with the basket, but she had no other choice.

The porter put the basket back on his wheelbarrow, ready to proceed. At Nathaniel's request, Dora opened her purse and gave him six shillings.

Then she turned around, but after a few steps she realized she still had the basket's key with her. Angrily, she ran back to Nathaniel, catching up with him just before the gatekeeper's post. From a short distance, the porter saw them in heated debate, but he was unable to hear their exact words. Perhaps Nathaniel pointed out how difficult it was to dump the body alone, urging her to come and assist him as soon as possible. He walked to the porter again, and they passed through the Haarlem Gate with their load. The others went in the opposite direction. Upon entering the house at the water, The Owl and the two women observed that its interior matched Dora's description. Satisfied, they stayed for a friendly chat.[12]

While Dora led The Owl and the two women to her home, Nathaniel was looking where exactly to place the basket. Accompanied by the porter, he crossed the wooden bridge spanning the moat that surrounded the city walls. He planned to dump the body somewhere in that moat. Without Dora's help it was impossible to drag the basket over a long distance, so the porter had to unload his wheelbarrow as near to the right spot as possible. But Nathaniel was unsure which spot was the right one. First, he ordered the porter to place the basket at the foot of a tree. Then, realizing that even in the dark too many people were passing there, he requested him to reload the wheelbarrow and move the basket to another spot, offering him a few extra coins for it. They started on this course, and then Nathaniel ordered another detour when he heard a passerby loudly wondering "where this fellow was going with that basket." When the stranger was out of sight, Nathaniel told the porter to halt once more. Finally he ordered him to take the basket to the stone dam, lying at the right side of the bridge as seen from the gate.

By now, Michiel Stalli had long realized this was no routine transport. It was one of the oddest jobs in his career as a porter. His client looked hesitant and nervous, unable to decide where to go. Fortunately, for Nathaniel, the porter had no idea he provided assistance in covering up a serious crime. Stalli thought that this gentleman was "playing bankrupt," furtively leaving town with the property he still owned. That was the only interpretation that made sense to the porter. Of course, he was loyal to every client. Dora had prepaid him and given him a tip, and he had received extra money for moving around the basket. With Stalli's help, this gentleman was safe from his creditors!

The location Nathaniel eventually preferred was commonly known as the *Steenenbeer. Beer* is an ancient word for a piece of masonry damming the water in a moat surrounding a rampart. This dam was two meters thick at the point where it connected with the Spaarndam dike. The whole construction was demolished in 1842, in order to build a station at the railroad that replaced the barge route to Haarlem. This fact, as well as the dismantling of the city walls, makes it hard for today's investigator to reconstruct the map of the terrain as it was in 1766. To arrive at the Stone Dam, Donker and the porter had to cross back over the wooden bridge. To the north of the bridge, a small strip of land lay between the moat and the city wall. A hunters' stable stood on this strip, behind which was the Stone Dam.

Upon arriving there, Donker ordered the porter to halt for the last time and take the basket from his wheelbarrow. He placed it on the dike next to the dam. From this spot a path of a few meters led to the water beneath. To Stalli's even greater surprise, Donker asked for help to carry the basket to the edge of the moat. It was dark and the path was slippery. Donker went ahead, walking down backwards and holding one side of the basket. Stalli followed, holding the other side and grabbing the Stone Dam for support. "Be careful, sir," he said to Donker, "you may easily fall into the water." Then he felt that the earth under his feet was soft and dropped the basket. Donker also dropped it. He climbed up again, saying to Stalli, "I do not think that any more people will come this way." Donker accompanied Stalli back to the city gate, where he said goodbye with the words "if you happen to see the woman who was with me, tell her I am here." Donker still hoped that Dora would quickly return from showing the furnished house and help him with the actual dumping. Although she could no longer avert the porter's suspicion, Nathaniel wished her to be an accomplice in throwing the body parts into the water. But Stalli did not see her again that day.[13]

Donker returned to the Stone Dam to finish the dreadful job alone. It was long past sundown, but the sky seemed to grow ever darker. When he took the basket's key from his pocket, he could barely see the lock, but he managed to open it. He took a deep breath and looked inside, finding everything there. He toppled the basket, which caused the torso with the legs to slip into the water. Donker quickly pushed it away from the shore. Next, he took the severed arms from the basket. He swung each one above his head and threw them as far into the moat as he could. Now he was left with his wife's head, wrapped with the blue cotton cloth with the image of a rider. Did he unwrap the packet to take a last look? If he did, he carefully packed the head into the cotton cloth anew. Like a big ball, he threw it into the water, again as far as he could. The job was done; he expected never again to look into his wife's dead eyes.[14]

As he climbed onto the dike once more, he took the empty basket with him. It felt much lighter now, in a literal and a symbolic sense. He followed the moat south, re-entering the city through the next gate. From there he had to cross the Jordaan quarter, a part of town relatively unfamiliar to him. He had no idea that the canal along which he walked, still carrying the empty basket, was the Lindengracht. He passed a narrow alley, which he thought a convenient place to drop the basket. Donker realized someone was bound to find it sooner or later, but he expected the finder to keep it as a welcome present. His expectation came true to some extent only. A grain carrier, who lived in the alley, returned from a service in the Northern Church shortly after seven-thirty. He noticed the basket and, seeing it was a new one, he supposed someone had left it by accident. He stored it in his attic, to be handed over in case the owner would show up.[15]

Donker came home shortly before eight o'clock. Everything looked normal. Dora was in with Kaatje and Verhoef, who had just returned from some business. They also had visitors, a dealer in secondhand clothes with her little daughter, to whom Dora perhaps had offered still other goods of Cecilia's for sale. The Owl and the women who accompanied him had just left. They had kept Dora from going back to the Haarlem Gate to assist Nathaniel, if she had ever contemplated this. Later that night, when the other visitors had left and Verhoef retired to his room, Nathaniel had the opportunity to inform Dora how he had fared. Understandably, he was worried about the suspicious impression he had made on the porter. For a moment he became desperate, saying, "What have I gotten myself into?" He insisted they should flee, but Dora convinced him it was perfectly safe to stay in town.[16]

In fact, it was not. The assistance provided by the porter formed the Achilles' heel in the murderers' scheme to get away with their crime. If Cecilia's corpse was discovered soon enough, Stalli would certainly hear about it and link the discovery to his job of December 3. Even if The Owl's intervention had not obliged Dora to return home and, consequently, the porter had merely delivered a 150-pound load to be picked up by someone in a coach, he might report this to the magistrates. Actually, the job had been unnecessary. Nathaniel and Dora had already been capable of inventing an ingenious plan—her impersonation of Cecilia—and with hindsight it is easy to see what they should have done this time: not hire a porter at all. Donker himself might have transported the basket out of town. To avoid suspicion, he just had to look like a porter; so many of them were active in the busy metropolis that no one knew all of them individually. His task was simply to dress in a lower-class outfit and get a wheelbarrow. To come upon this idea, evidently, required too much thinking across the boundaries of social class. It was completely outside

How to Dump a Body When There Are No Cars?

Donker's cultural frame of reference. This rich heir, who had always been used to hiring others to do jobs for him, never got the idea to play a porter. It is fair to conclude that this taken-for-granted, upper-middle-class attitude in the end contributed to his arrest and execution.

Despite this, on the night of December 3, Nathaniel could be hopeful. Admittedly, he had been obliged to dump the body alone. Four witnesses had seen him with the basket, one of whom at the very spot where he had sunk his dead wife into the water a little later. But none of them knew about the basket's awful contents. These rested at the bottom of the moat outside the city wall, and they only had to remain undetected until the head had decomposed sufficiently to be unidentifiable. Although living in the eighteenth century meant he had lacked a car, it also meant no worries that the corpse would be identified by its teeth or DNA. Despite the difficulties, Nathaniel thought he was safe: No one would ever know about his and Dora's atrocious crime. With a little luck, eastern winds might soon bring the winter frost, to cover the head, the torso, and the arms with ice. In the unsteady Dutch climate, however, one could never be sure.

It is unlikely that Donker ever read the newspaper of December 16, 1766, thirteen days after he dumped the corpse. The *Amsterdamse Courant* of that day reported: Throughout Europe, people will remember the year 1766 as one of exceptional drought. In Germany, the water level in the Rhine, the Neckar, and other tributaries is very low. In the Netherlands, the Rhine and Lek rivers can be forded in many places.[17] This was an exceptional situation indeed. Once, Amsterdam's canals were fed, indirectly, by the sea, but this was no longer the case in the eighteenth century. Hence, the water level in the canals, including the moat surrounding the city walls, was extremely shallow. In previous centuries, when the moat had a military function, this fact would be a source of concern and much talked about. There was less public discussion on the issue in 1766. Donker probably failed to notice the shallowness of the water when he threw the body parts away from him on that dark December night.

On Tuesday, December 9, 1766, Gerrit van Deventer left his home at the Brouwersgracht shortly after supper. Whatever this resident's occupation, he had time to take a stroll and see if he could spot a layer of ice somewhere. It had been freezing lightly during the previous night. No ice was visible on the Brouwersgracht or the adjacent canals, but chances were better outside the walls. His home was close to the Haarlem Gate. At one-thirty in the

A new ornamental gate was built on Haarlem Square in the nineteenth century. In the foreground is the water into which Nathaniel dumped Cecilia's body. Photo: Pieter Spierenburg.

afternoon Van Deventer passed through the gate and continued his way to the Stone Dam. He saw no ice there either, but he did notice that the water in the moat was extremely shallow. Over a distance of about ten feet from the shore, the moat lay dry. Then he saw something lying there, half in the water, half on the dry part. It was a dead animal, he thought. Van Deventer threw a few stones at the object, whereupon a passerby joined him. The two men discussed the nature of their discovery, the second concluding it was a human, rather than an animal body. At the nearby mill, they asked for a curved stick. With this instrument, they lifted the object a little, just enough to recognize it as a human body indeed. When they dragged it closer to the shore, they saw it was a woman without arms or head. Immediately, they notified the judicial authorities.

Two employees of the city hospital, assisted by two court officials, arrived at the scene with a wagon. They lifted the torso from the moat, placed it on the wagon, and drove it to the hospital.[18] Meanwhile, the gossip circuit had been activated. Within a few hours every Amsterdamer knew about the discovery of the torso of a woman outside the Haarlem Gate. Hospitals were open institutions. For the staff, it was self-evident to display the corpse they had obtained to the curious public. Many came to see it, and even with the head missing, they speculated about the woman's identity. The chronicler Jacob Bicker Raye, who recorded almost every noteworthy or sensational event in his diary, provides a glimpse of the people's interest. However, this source has to be handled with care. Bicker Raye usually dated an event on the day he knew it had happened, but often he wrote about it a few days afterwards or he later added a passage to an existing item. So we cannot take his notes to indicate the precise day on which a particular detail was known and discussed in town. Under December 9 he wrote that a female body had been found near the Stone Dam and that it was totally nude. She had been murdered in a gruesome manner, Bicker Raye added a little superfluously.[19]

The next day, the official committee of physicians and surgeons who performed autopsies on suspected crime victims examined the discovery. Their report noted that the object under examination was a "dead adult female person" without head or arms. The right side was severely bruised. After the surgeons had cut the body open, they saw that the interior cavity was full of blood and that the liver had been smashed and four ribs were broken.[20] With only a torso on the autopsy table, they refrained from speculating about the cause of death. They could not possibly know that the cause of death was strangulation and that someone had damaged the liver and ribs with an iron bar afterwards and severed the head two days later.

Supposedly, the magistrates realized right away the likelihood that the missing parts lay hidden under water near that very spot. It is a riddle why the court waited two days before ordering a search. The city had qualified personnel for it, men normally employed at dredging in sluices and along quays. It was a low-esteemed job even under normal circumstances, which may explain why they seemed not very diligent. The first pair of dredgers started working at nine in the morning, and it took them two and a half hours to find the head. Still wrapped with the blue cloth, it lay stuck in the mud. A little later, they found the right arm. Both parts lay twelve to fourteen feet from the shore. For whatever reason, they stopped searching, whereupon a deputy sent out the other team. These two probably operated from a boat, since they were said to be fishing. They found the left arm at two in the afternoon. Again an employee of the hospital arrived to pick up the parts.

The committee of physicians and surgeons examined them on the twelfth. They observed some bruises on the right side of the head and two scars, one on the left cheek, the other at the left side of the chin. They also noted the long black hair, the blue eyes, and a complete set of sound teeth, in a perfectly even row. The head and the arms, they concluded, fitted very well to the cadaver they had examined two days earlier.[21]

The hospital's staff displayed the head and the arms along with the torso, which produced an even more sensational spectacle. They even kept the blue cloth, until a court official picked it up a few days later.[22] Thousands of curious visitors streamed into the hospital. Insiders even knew the details of the first autopsy report: Jacob Bicker Raye wrote that the corpse had three or four broken ribs. They played a role in the public's speculations about the nature of the murder. Many people thought that the victim had been trampled to death, and the body was dismembered afterwards to make it unidentifiable. Despite this, the rumor went that she was a well-known woman who traveled around to sing songs, recite poems, and tell the latest news.[23] A resemblance to an existing street singer possibly was the origin of this rumor. In any case, the public's attention was drawn primarily by the atrocity of the murder, and this remained so after Cecilia's identity became known. It caused widespread astonishment about the unusual fact of an upper-middle-class killer, but it hardly raised interest in the person of the victim. That would be different in 1775.

The talk of the town can hardly have escaped Nathaniel and Dora, but they showed no signs of fear yet. While the various parts of Cecilia's corpse were discovered and displayed, the killers had footwear on their mind. On Monday evening Dora, accompanied by Kaatje, visited a shoemaker's shop and bought a pair of Spanish leather shoes for herself. Upon her request, a journeyman came to their home the next morning to measure Nathaniel's feet. It was a few hours before the discovery of Cecilia's torso, and Nathaniel was in a good mood, insisting that Dora needed another pair of shoes. The journeyman measured her feet as well, whereupon she showed him the white pair that had belonged to Cecilia and asked if he could blacken the leather and repair them. Even on December 13, when they were in deep trouble, Dora thought about her order and visited the shop, but not all the shoes were ready. As a result, all three pairs ended up in court.[24]

On the eleventh, the very day when dredgers fished Cecilia's head and arms from the shallow water, Donker received a letter from his mother-in-law. The neighboring woman who used to do her writing had posted it on the previous day. Since they were ignorant about the house at the water, she had addressed it to his former landlord, Deegens, whose wife passed it on. One can imagine the letter's content: Cecilia should have been home for six days and she would never prolong her stay in Amsterdam without informing her mother. Mrs. Steffens demanded an immediate explanation from her son-in-law. Donker replied immediately, still expecting that Dora's act of impersonation would work. He had personally accompanied her daughter to the barge station, he assured Mrs. Steffens. He had assumed her to be safely at home with their children for over a week. Now he was no less worried than his mother-in-law and awaited further news from her. To facilitate further correspondence, it would have been convenient if Donker had mentioned his current address, but he did not.[25]

As long as the Amsterdam court was ignorant about the identity of the corpse, the investigation focused on how it had reached the Stone Dam, on the assumption that this was not the location of the murder. The magistrates considered it likely that the killer had hired professional help to move the body parts to their dumping place. The court probably made inquiries with the various trades engaged in transport. According to Bicker Raye, the porter took the initiative to inform the judicial authorities, after hearing about the discovery of a corpse at the Stone Dam and visiting the hospital. There is no official document confirming this. Whoever first approached whom, porter Stalli directed the court's attention to the house at the water. The magistrates summoned the resident couple to appear in court on Friday, December 12. They only had to answer questions; it was no arrest. We might consider this an example of deferential treatment for a suspect of high standing, but quite likely the judges were unaware yet that such a person occupied that house. They simply had no proof; they only knew about a suspicious transport the residents had ordered.

If he was already nervous on his way to the courtroom, Nathaniel got truly frightened when he noticed that porter Stalli was also present. Dora, on the other hand, remained self-assured. She told the judges the story she had invented earlier. She confirmed that they had hired this porter to carry a big basket to the Haarlem Gate but explained that it contained the belongings of a certain Madam Sjoenis, who was to pick it up as she passed by in a coach. Madam Sjoenis had come later than expected, Dora continued, but eventually Donker had handed the basket over to her. The judges asked no further questions about the transport, but they inquired about the couple's status, which prompted Dora to say she was Nathaniel's wife. The judges then said they could go, under the obligation of appearing anew when summoned. On their way home, Nathaniel repeatedly expressed his anxiety, insisting that they should flee from the town, but as lighthearted as ever, Dora thought that the court had nothing much against them. Yet they realized the fact that Kaatje had bought the basket was inconsistent with the Sjoenis story. They emphatically demanded the girl to tell no one about it. If ever the court questioned her, she ought to say that two old women had brought the basket. Donker promised to wrap her in gold if she obliged.[26]

On the same day, The Owl, about whose intervention the porter had informed the judges, received an official visit. A deputy came to verify that the brothel keeper was the right person and, upon receiving confirmation, announced that he could expect a summons in court. Either from this official or from the gossip circuit, The Owl found out that Nathaniel and Dora had already appeared there. Once again, the brothel keeper worried about the rent he had advanced. When he visited them in the evening, he saw a peaceful scene: Nathaniel, Dora, and Verhoef were playing cards. After joining them for a game or two, The Owl came to the point, asking them what the judges had wanted to know. Dora said she had been stupid to claim she was Nathaniel's wife, but that reply failed to satisfy The Owl. He told the couple about his summons and repeated his question. Dora admitted it had been about the basket, whose transport he had stopped at Haarlem Square. The Owl looked surprised and exclaimed, "What, for heaven's sake, is the matter with that basket? Do they think it contained the body that has been fished from the water recently?" Dora denied this, repeating that the basket belonged to her acquaintance, Madam Sjoenis. When she seemed ready to add further details, Nathaniel stopped her by making a gesture with his finger on his mouth. Not knowing what else he could do to assure he would get his money back, the brothel keeper asked Nathaniel to correct the declaration of debt that he had signed with the name of Donk. Obligingly, Nathaniel added "er" to his last name.[27]

News that the court had summoned a couple to appear in relation to the murder case quickly reached the gossip circuit. Again we depend on Bicker Raye, who dated his entry December 12 but ended it with Donker's arrest on the evening of the fifteenth. Possibly, he wrote the whole item after the fifteenth. He began, "A further investigation has been done in the case of that murdered body and one has discovered that it is the wife of Mr. Nathaniel Donker, a lawyer, who has lived in The Hague or Voorburg, but last Summer he stayed in [a house near] the Park with a Whore named beautiful Dora and now since November he lives in a house at the water, near the Old Bridge. . . ." Some of the visitors in the hospital, Bicker Raye continued, had recognized Cecilia's head, whereupon the court had summoned Donker and "this Whore," who failed to show up after a second summons.[28] This passage illustrates how information about a person could circulate quickly and get distorted in the process. Obviously, gossip had been going around about Nathaniel's stay in Amsterdam with Dora. Some people knew that his brother, Pieter Gerbrand, practiced as a lawyer in the city. In Bicker Raye's diary the facts were mixed up to become a different story, with Nathaniel himself as the lawyer. That visitors to the hospital recognized Cecilia, a stranger in Amsterdam, is unlikely. According to the court records, the official identification took place only after Nathaniel's arrest.

Before the arrest, the criminal couple was in hiding, making plans to escape the town. On Saturday morning, December 13, even Dora no longer felt safe in the house at the water. They moved out in a hurry, leaving Verhoef and Kaatje behind. Under false names, they rented a room in an inn called The Crowned City of Elberfeld. Yet, Dora briefly returned to the house at the water on Sunday. She discovered that Verhoef had left—for good, as it turned out later—but Kaatje was still in. Dora gave her some money for turf and light and told her she would be back within three or four days. Afraid to stay there alone, however, the girl returned to her mother. On that same day, after they all had left, the court ordered a search of the house. Its servants found nothing that could help the investigation. Dora and Nathaniel had removed everything connected to the victim and they had thoroughly cleaned the room in which Dora had cut up Cecilia's body. Although the knife she had used for this and the iron bar with which she had smashed the victim's chest were still there, they failed to draw the court servants' attention. Nathaniel and Dora heard about the search the next day.[29]

Meanwhile, Nathaniel had approached a certain Clempien, an acquaintance of his brother, and asked him to speak to the latter. Nathaniel was in dire straits. He pretended that the court had summoned him in a financial matter, which had alerted his creditors in The Hague to his whereabouts. Returning from his mission, Clempien could do no more than report Pieter Gerbrand's annoyance. His younger brother, he had said, had always refused to follow his advice; only if Nathaniel promised to sail off to Indonesia for good was Pieter Gerbrand prepared to help him. It was the honorable lawyer's dearest wish never to hear about this black sheep again, so that none of his peers associated the one with the other.

To contribute to Nathaniel's worries, he received another letter from Cecilia's mother. Again, her neighbor had written it for the illiterate old lady. She had posted it on the twelfth, addressing it once more to Deegens, who was ignorant about the suspect's flight from the house at the water and was therefore unable to pass it on until Sunday night. Mrs. Steffens repeated she had no idea why her daughter had failed to return home. Nathaniel replied the next morning, but he indicated neither place nor date.

> Dearest and Respected Mother. I have received your letter of the 13th of this month in good order and I am writing to tell Your Hon. that you need not be concerned about my wife. We have to remain incognito here, so that no one finds out where we are staying, in order not to be discovered. We will be at Your Hon. place this Thursday or Friday. Therefore, don't worry and trust that all our affairs will be arranged well, so that we can enjoy an easy life with each other as before. Keep this to yourself and tell no one where we are. Count on it as I write that we will be at Your Hon. home on Friday at the latest. In confidence to find everything well with Your. Hon., I embrace Your Hon. and our dear children day and night in my thoughts and I pay all respect. I will write to Your Hon. on Thursday to tell the hour at which we will be home on Friday.[30]

Nathaniel hoped to exploit Mrs. Steffens's knowledge of his permanent troubles with creditors. These troubles obliged him and Cecilia to hide, he wanted her mother to believe. Obviously, this letter undermined the claim that he had accompanied Cecilia to the Haarlem barge on December 1. With so many indications of guilt against him already, Donker's only chance was to flee from the city as soon and as far away as he could. The letter was an effort to induce his mother-in-law to stay in The Hague and not come to identify the corpse before he had left Amsterdam.

Nathaniel had no other choice but to confront his respectable brother in person and confess what he had done. He and Dora lacked the cash necessary to leave Amsterdam for a safe place. It was Monday, December 15, two weeks after the murder, and they ought to flee from the town on this day at the latest.

In the morning Nathaniel left The Crowned City of Elberfeld to make his journey to Canossa. As he had no decent coat, the landlord lent him one. Pieter Gerbrand lived in a lodging house near the stock exchange. Upon hearing the news of his brother's awful crime, he turned pale and started to tremble. This was worse than his ugliest nightmares. He had been able to quench the scandal caused by Nathaniel's misconduct in the early 1750s by having him locked away in a private prison. No remedy was available now: for this murder even the most elevated person faced arrest and trial. The crime itself and the prospect that his brother might end his life publicly on a scaffold were the most serious blow to the family reputation imaginable. And who else was the family but Pieter Gerbrand alone? A scandal of this magnitude was a disaster even for the relatives of a respectable baker or shoemaker, let alone for a lawyer of upper-middle-class descent. As much as he hated his brother for it, Pieter Gerbrand's only option was to help him escape. Nathaniel proposed to flee to England, where he thought he could find employment as a bodyguard.

The knife fighters of a few generations ago often hid with family or friends when they had inadvertently stabbed an opponent to death. Usually, those providing shelter faced no prosecution for obstruction of justice. This was not only 1766, it was a homicide of an altogether exceptional category. Would the magistrates summon Pieter Gerbrand, if the murderer had escaped with his help? With the possible intention of implicating a third party, he decided to ask his friend Jan Gaubert, who had assisted him in tracing Nathaniel a decade earlier, to act as a mediator. Gaubert was a *makelaar* now. Pieter Gerbrand claimed he requested his help because of a lack of cash. With his hands still trembling, he wrote his friend a note: "Gaubert, in God's name, if possible, help N. further if you can, for he will reveal something terrible to you. I have no cash, but I promise to reimburse Your Hon. all that Your Hon. will procure him. Nothing should be neglected, my dear Gaubert, because the whole situation is desperate. I can go on no longer. I am Your Hon. affectionate P. G. Donker."[31]

Gaubert lived some fifteen minutes' walk away. Nathaniel personally presented his brother's note to the broker, and it said he should inform the latter about his crime. He bluntly stated that he had broken his wife's neck. These words, instead of shocking Gaubert, made him indignant. He had never trusted Nathaniel, and now he refused to believe him capable of murder. That rascal had made clever use of the talk of the town, the broker concluded, deluding Pieter Gerbrand into thinking the body found at the Stone Dam was Cecilia's. Having heard the rumors in the street, Gaubert was not so naïve: "Canaille, you are lying; it is a dirty trick to wring money from your brother, because they say that this murdered woman is a songstress." Nathaniel insisted: "No, it is the sincere truth; afterwards, you will find out that she is my wife."[32] Thereupon he burst into tears. Whether or not Gaubert believed him now, he gave him twenty-four guilders and one of his robes for a coat. Still crying, Nathaniel left the broker's home.

First, he returned to The Crowned City of Elberfeld, to give the landlord's coat back and pay the bill. It amounted to eight guilders and thirteen stivers, which left Nathaniel with fifteen guilders and seven stivers. He conferred with Dora about their escape. Pieter Gerbrand and Gaubert counted on him to take the barge to Rotterdam, where he was to embark on a ship to England. They did not expect Dora to accompany him. She and Nathaniel agreed to travel to Rotterdam separately, Dora by way of Utrecht and he by way of Gouda. They were to reunite in a Rotterdam lodging house, quite probably never intending to sail to England. It was all set, but Nathaniel realized he should say farewell to his brother. In the early afternoon he saw Pieter Gerbrand once more.

It was the final encounter, charged with conflicting emotions, between two men nearly the same age. Yet the one had recurrently played the other's mentor, without success most of the time. How divergent in character can two brothers be? The older one, almost thirty-eight now, was an honorable man and an established citizen. The younger brother, who had just turned thirty-six, clearly was not. Whereas Nathaniel constantly had made debts, contracted venereal disease, and now faced the prospect of becoming a fugitive, Pieter Gerbrand had obtained an academic degree, had been admitted to the bar, and practiced as a lawyer. A classic case of two brothers going separate ways! Even though brothers, their characters were Janus-faced. When viewed from the angle of social and cultural capital, the older brother continued a family tradition of economic success and bourgeois solidity. However, he was not in every way like their father. One of the few things we know about the father concerns the children he had with three Indonesian mistresses. Pieter Gerbrand lacked such a sexual appetite. As he lived in a lodging house, supposedly he was unmarried; none of the records mention a wife, and it is likely that any adventures he had were restricted to the period of his European tour. Seen from this perspective, Nathaniel was the real heir to their father. Geography made the crucial difference in outcome. What was socially permissible in colonial society, led to disreputability in the mother country.

While Nathaniel said goodbye to Pieter Gerbrand, Gaubert arrived. Understandably, he was surprised to meet the self-proclaimed murderer again: "Why haven't you left yet?" Nathaniel replied he could not possibly leave the country without saying goodbye to "such a tender brother." "Fellow, if it is true what you have told me, how dare you show your face in town any longer," the broker continued. The three agreed it was best if Nathaniel took the Rotterdam market boat immediately. He walked to the departure point, where he learned this boat was scheduled for 2:30 P.M.

This left him just enough time to inform Dora. She, however, thought there was no need to hurry. Even if they left right away, she argued, they would arrive in Rotterdam the following day, so they could easily postpone their departure until the evening. This is the crassest expression of the lightheartedness that had overtaken Dora ever since the murder. She managed to persuade Nathaniel, with fatal consequences for him.

Hearing that Donker had failed to catch the two-thirty boat, those interested in his disappearance took no further risk. In the early evening Gaubert and Clempien rode in a coach to The Crowned City of Elberfeld to pick him up. They were ignorant of the fact that Dora still stayed in the inn, ready to leave it after him. The two mediators first took their charge to the broker's home, where Gaubert gave him some extra money. Then the trio rode to the embarkment point of the Gouda barge. It was too late. When Nathaniel stepped out of the coach, a deputy and some court officials awaited him. They searched his pockets at the spot, finding the travel money and the two pistols he still carried. Proud of their catch, the deputy and his men took the suspect to the home of the city prosecutor, who ordered him taken to jail.[33] Booking him, the jail keeper had no hesitation in writing "for murder."[34]

Donker's prospects were bleak indeed. The following day, Cecilia's mother arrived in town. She had left home extremely worried, without waiting for a reply from her son-in-law. If news of a terrible murder had not reached her in The Hague already, she surely heard about the case upon her arrival in Amsterdam. Two deputies welcomed her. Mrs. Steffens told them that her daughter had a small scar near her mouth and a bald spot, the size of a five-and-a-half-stiver coin, on top of her head. This head had been transferred from the hospital to the jail in the meantime; presumably, they had buried the rest of the body. The deputies accompanied Mrs. Steffens to the jail, where they showed her Cecilia's head. Her emotions are not on record, but she positively identified it as her daughter's, indicating the very spots she had referred to before. Back in The Hague, she found Nathaniel's reply, which he had posted on the fifteenth. Although its contents had turned practically irrelevant, she took it to her neighbor, who read Nathaniel's latest lies to her aloud. The old lady asked her to write on the cover, "This is the last letter that my maid has received, yesterday morning when I was in Amsterdam." The maid and the wife of Mrs. Steffens's tailor now went to Amsterdam as well, identifying Cecilia on the nineteenth.[35]

On Monday night, just after Gaubert and Clempien had picked up Nathaniel from The Crowned City of Elberfeld, Dora left the inn with the landlord's son. He accompanied her to the Utrecht Gate, where the barge for Rotterdam lay ready. It was the eight o'clock boat, by way of Gouda, the one Nathaniel was supposed to take. At the departure point, she and the young man called each other cousins. None of the bystanders showed any suspicion. While her lover was on his way from Gaubert's home, she sat in the boat waiting for him. From a window she watched his arrest and the barge took off.[36]

What could she have done? Restlessly, she traveled the prearranged route to Rotterdam, but upon her arrival she decided she had better go to The Hague. She stopped in Delft, taking a cup of coffee in a tavern called The Rotterdam Gate, whose landlady she knew.[37] Her mind was fuzzy, and she grew worse. Dora had already imagined herself the new Cecilia; now she started to believe her own fiction.

The implausible story that she had invented for their boarder and repeated when summoned in court—about two old women who brought a basket destined for a coach that would pass by outside the Haarlem Gate—suggested that the mysterious Madam Sjoenis was an invention, too. Quite probably, Nathaniel himself had thought so. However, Madam Sjoenis really existed. Her maiden name was Johanna Le Boeuf, and she was the wife of Carel Otto de Jaunis, a former captain in a regiment of the Estates of Holland, who had been discharged dishonorably in 1757.[38] A year later he had disappeared, leaving his wife behind. She had stayed in The Hague, her native town, holding on to her husband's name. Around 1760 she had met Dora. She vaguely knew about the latter's relationship with Donker, but by 1766 she had not seen her for several years.

On December 17, to Johanna Jaunis's great surprise, Dora suddenly stood on her doorstep, dressed as a lady. Johanna boarded with Frans van der Star, a trader in mirrors. She invited Dora in, who told her she had lived in Amsterdam with Donker, who had reconciled with his brother. The latter had given him money to go to England, but two days ago, when Dora sat waiting in the barge, a deputy and his men had apprehended Donker. No doubt, this was because of Johanna's basket. Johanna had listened to this story with increasing disbelief. She interrupted Dora and asked, "What basket? What are you talking about?" Now Dora was surprised in her turn, or pretended to be: "Weren't you in Amsterdam two weeks ago?"[39] She had hoped to see Johanna again, she continued; that was the only reason to accept that basket, which Donker eventually handed over to her alone. Even more annoyed, Johanna protested that she had not left The Hague from October on and it was three years since she had last visited Amsterdam. She called upon Van der Star and his wife, who confirmed this. Dora seemed only a little dismayed, wondering who else could have owned the basket. She added she had consulted a lawyer in The Hague about the case. Dora spent the night in Van der Star's house and left the next morning, saying she had to see someone in Delft.

To all appearances, Dora had come to believe in her own invented story. Or else, she was incredibly naïve. For her mission to succeed, several miraculous things had to happen: She must somehow persuade this former acquaintance to cooperate and declare to the Amsterdam court that she had indeed received a basket from Donker outside the Haarlem Gate; the court would have to accept this testimony; and, finally, the magistrates had to be convinced that someone else had murdered Cecilia and dumped her body unnoticed.

On Thursday the eighteenth, between eight and nine P.M., someone reported at the mirror shop. Opening the door, Mrs. van der Star saw an ordinary woman wearing an apron and a jacket, her skirt reversed, a worsted cloth around head and shoulders, and a straw hat on top. Not recognizing her, the landlady called upstairs to Johanna, saying an old woman wished to see her. It was Dora again. She had left the pretty clothes she wore in the morning, most of them Cecilia's, with the landlady of The Rotterdam Gate in Delft and accepted ordinary women's apparel in return. Johanna was on her guard even without the change of clothes. Earlier that day, she had spoken to the lawyer whom Dora had consulted. He had confirmed that this woman had approached him with a story about a basket, but he had understood neither head nor tail of it. Johanna asked Dora if she was in trouble. She explained she had changed clothes because she feared to be committed to the women's prison for living with a married man. For the time being, Dora remained in Van der Star's house as a boarder.

The next morning an event occurred that deserves to be classified as a landmark in the history of popular culture. A street singer crossed The Hague, loudly advertising the new song he was to perform later that day. When he passed Van der Star's house, one could tell Dora's anxiety from her face. She longed to know what kind of song the man announced, but she was afraid to leave the house to find out. Johanna did and reported that it was about a murder in Amsterdam; the singer was selling the printed text, and she had bought a copy. She offered to read it to Dora. After a few lines, Dora interrupted Johanna impatiently, asking "Does it list the criminals' names?" Johanna read the last line stating that "the murderers or perpetrators are still unknown." After hearing the full text, Dora commented it was a terrible crime in which, she hoped, no "children of honest people" were implicated. When she said this, Johanna noticed tears in her eyes. This episode, it appears, is the only recorded instance in which a street singer confronted a killer with the story of her own crime.

It prompted Dora to consider alternative sources of information, a newspaper for example. The Amsterdam court, she suggested, might have particular suspects in mind and advertise their names—with the promise of a reward, she added, suddenly realizing this formed an incentive for her temporary hosts to betray her. But Van der Star refused to get her a newspaper. They were not in the habit of reading the gazette, he explained, so the bookseller might easily become suspicious if they bought one now. Although this eased Dora's fears that they would turn her in, her uncertainty about the actions of the Amsterdam court reinforced her state of agitation. She inspected the house for possible hiding places and found a sleeping place with empty space beneath, closed off by a small door. She asked Johanna if she could hide there, in case they might come looking for her, but Van der Star suggested that a closet upstairs was a safer place.

The host's refusal to buy a newspaper forms an instructive detail. The bookseller around the corner knew the habits of his neighbors, whether or not they were clients. Any sudden change in these habits was noteworthy, as a possible indication they had something to hide. This constitutes one more example of informal social control operating through the gossip circuit in the neighborhoods of preindustrial cities. Garrioch made similar observations for the neighborhoods of eighteenth-century Paris. When a domestic servant had left her master for a few weeks and then returned, people supposed she had borne a child. When a man suddenly had more money than usual or wore a new, expensive suit, surely he had been out stealing.[40] In The Hague, this was no different. If, for once, he bought a gazette, Van der Star realized, his neighbors would soon wonder what news he was interested in and why.

By this time, obviously, all three—Mr. and Mrs. van der Star and Johanna—were convinced that Donker and his mistress had killed his wife, which meant they gave shelter to a murderess. Knowing where to hear the latest news, Johanna visited The White Horse, in the center of The Hague, that afternoon. The landlord confirmed it was Donker's wife who had been found murdered in Amsterdam. When she returned home, Johanna asked Dora straightaway if she had assisted with the murder, but she denied any complicity. No doubt, her hosts thought this denial conflicted with her anxious search for a hiding place. We can interpret this contradiction in the light of our earlier supposition: Dora had convinced herself that nothing had happened and that she had merely transported a basket and had never seen Cecilia at all. This psychological denial made her weary of any evidence to the contrary. She literally closed herself off from it.[41]

For their part, the Amsterdam magistrates thought Dora smarter than she actually was. They imagined her further away than The Hague, where so many people knew her. On that very Friday, they sent a message to the judges and assessors of the town of Cleves: A certain Dorothea van Borstelman, alias German Dora, fled our town on December 15; we do not know where she went. She is the mistress of our prisoner, Nathaniel Donker, who is well acquainted with Cleves, because he lived there for several years. We suspect this woman of complicity in the murder of Donker's wife. Should you discover her, please arrest her immediately.

Believing that Dora might pass through Nijmegen, the Amsterdam magistrates sent a similar message to that town. Since they referred to the lawsuit of 1765, they possibly thought Dora still had something to gain there. The authorities in both places received a description of the fugitive. Quite likely, The Owl had provided it. Forced to reveal his occupation to the authorities, he was keen on obliging them, and he was angry at Dora, realizing he would never collect the ƒ125 she and her lover owed him. He estimated her age at about thirty, five years too old. The description concerned her body and looks, which we already know, and the clothes she supposedly wore.[42]

Dora's mission to The Hague was not entirely unsuccessful. Convinced that she had assisted her partner in his crime, her temporary hosts were afraid to be charged with obstruction of justice. They definitely wanted Dora to leave their home, so they were prepared to help her find another hiding place. Van der Star confided his predicament to an acquaintance, a paperhanger named Thomas Ernst. He knew the address of a farmer in the village of Voorburg who provided pregnant women a safe haven to give birth in secrecy. These women rarely arrived there in the apparel that Dora now wore. Thomas either was a very good friend of Van der Star or he owed something to him, since he spared no time or effort to help. First, the two men and Dora went to Delft on foot to recover the clothes she had left there. Because the landlady of The Rotterdam Gate warned them that a deputy had inquired about Dora a little earlier, they quickly left again. When they were back in The Hague, Johanna sold Dora's dress for two and a half guilders. On Saturday the twentieth, Thomas accompanied Dora to the farmer in Voorburg. They went on foot again, leaving between eight and nine in the evening. To avoid detection, they took a detour of one hour, which meant they arrived at their destination toward midnight. Thomas told Dora to introduce herself as the chambermaid of a certain gentleman. The farmer and his wife duly took her in.

Obviously, it was impossible for Dora to stay in her new hiding place for long. At the latest, she had to leave before her hosts realized she was not pregnant. She badly needed money. Her life as a penniless fugitive seemed a dead-end street. Her only chance was to forget about rescuing Nathaniel and take up her old trade in a town far away from Holland. When Johanna visited her on the twenty-third, Dora asked her to go to Rotterdam on her behalf. A Mennonite gentleman had maintained her for a while in that town, at the address of a music hall keeper nicknamed "Fatty." Hopefully, Fatty might persuade her former protector to provide her a sum large enough to escape the country. Given her interest in Dora's disappearance, Johanna was willing to help. She visited Fatty in Rotterdam just after Christmas. He seemed concerned about poor Dora. He was sure this gentleman would keep his purse closed, he said, but he himself gladly granted her twenty ducats. If Johanna revealed Dora's current address, he would give her the money personally. Impressed by the considerable sum Fatty promised, Johanna provided him with the Voorburg address in good faith.[43]

During Dora's stay in Voorburg, two events related to the case took place in Amsterdam. The first was a decision stemming from unbearable shame. We have seen Pieter Gerbrand Donker acting recurrently out of concern for the family honor. Twelve years earlier he had been able to salvage the Donkers' reputation by having his brother imprisoned in Delft. After Nathaniel's arrest, the irreparable dishonor for the family, for him, was public knowledge, discussed everywhere in the streets. A heinous murder like this rarely occurred in upper-middle-class circles. Nathaniel's stay in jail and the prospect of his execution anticipated further infamy. In this situation, Pieter Gerbrand's only means of refuge was to hide his own person from public view. By Christmas he was ready to leave the country. In a notarial act of December 24, he appointed a certain Nathanael Wilthuyzen as his representative. Apparently, this man's first name formed no objection. Pieter Gerbrand authorized Wilthuyzen to represent him in all legal matters, to sell his furniture and books, and to open letters arriving from Indonesia.[44] He would establish himself in Italy, the country he knew from his European tour.

Although Pieter Gerbrand's emigration was motivated primarily by shame, another factor probably played a part. After all, he had kept his brother's crime silent, even providing him money to escape. He had done so in the interest of family honor, just as he had been silent about his own age thirteen years earlier, when he became Nathaniel's guardian. But would the court pardon him? The magistrates might easily find him guilty of complicity or at least of obstructing justice. His departure, therefore, precluded the possibility of another great embarrassment. Later, when the court found out about his role on December 15, it only had Gaubert for questioning.

The second related event during Dora's stay in Voorburg was the court's seizure of the basket used for transporting Cecilia's body. Remember that Nathaniel had left it in an alley in the Jordaan quarter, where a grain carrier had stored it in his attic. Since this man attended service on a Wednesday evening, he probably was a religious devotee. This may explain his relative deafness to the talk of the town; presumably, he avoided gossip and refused to watch the performances of street singers. Only weeks later he realized he had an object related to a crime in his attic and informed the court. Between Christmas and New Year, a deputy picked up the basket from the finder's home. He noted that some earth stuck to the bottom outside.[45]

The police forces of various cities were looking for Dora, but it was a deputy of Rotterdam, her victim's native town, who tracked her down. No doubt, Fatty had tipped him. Good relations with the local court and its officials were always important for a music hall keeper. Fatty had traded Dora for a little goodwill. The Rotterdam deputy arrived in Voorburg on December 30, but only the local authorities were entitled to arrest Dora. Voorburg belonged to the bailiwick of Rijnland, whose court held its sessions in Leiden. On January 1, 1767, its clerk wrote in the register of prisoners "taken in: Doorettah Bosselman." The next day, the Amsterdam prosecutor sent a message to the Rijnland magistrates, congratulating them and their Rotterdam colleagues on the catch and announcing that a deputy would come to Leiden. He left Amsterdam on the third, while the Rijnland court was busy making an inventory of the goods found with Dora. On January 4 its clerk noted that the prisoner had been picked up and taken to Amsterdam. In the evening, the deputy delivered Dora there to be jailed.[46] It was exactly two years after Nathaniel had left his wife for her.

On New Year's Day, Bicker Raye, too, had heard about the discovery of Dora's hiding place. Satisfied, he wrote in his diary: "The news has come that this Whore of Nathaniel Donker has been grabbed by the neck in Voorburg." Next, he noted that she had been jailed in Amsterdam.[47] The two lovers were in each other's vicinity again, but not reunited.

5

Nathaniel's Ascension

They met each other for the last time on the morning of August 22, 1767. Outside the town hall the scaffold stood ready, while a large crowd eagerly waited on Dam Square. Two court officials led Dora into the interrogation room. Sternly, the assembled magistrates inquired if she persisted in denying complicity in the murder of Cecilia Klos, despite the repeated accusations from the victim's husband. Dora remained steadfast: "If she were guilty of this, she would not have let them inflict so much pain on her." Upon this statement, the magistrates ordered Nathaniel Donker, "standing ready to be punished by death within a few moments," to be brought into the room as well. He accused her once more, face to face: She had incited him to commit the crime time and again; she had provided assistance in the act of killing; she had always participated, in every way. "I am ready to die in peace on the veracity of this testimony, awaiting the judgment of the high and mighty God, in front of whom I am about to appear within a few moments." Again she denied the accusations. The court officials led Nathaniel out of the room, onto the scaffold, for his ascension to heaven.[1]

Before this event could take place, a great amount of judicial energy had been spent and a large quantity of ink inscribed on paper. Trials in Amsterdam differed with the location. The court tried serious offenders and everyone belonging to the floating population "downstairs," in detention in the dungeon under the town hall. Members of the settled population, unless their offenses were too serious, and everyone guilty of a minor transgression were summoned to appear "upstairs," where they remained free from detention.[2] The charges against Nathaniel and Dora were very serious, so their trial took place "downstairs." The procedure was inquisitorial, geared at obtaining a confession from the defendants, who had no lawyer and could be subjected to torture.

Yet the court was obliged to proceed carefully. Use of the rack, although permitted, was bound to strict legal rules. If a defendant denied in the face of testimonies from two or more witnesses, torture was lawful without a doubt. But the prosecutor had no witnesses to the crime itself. Permission from the judges to use the rack depended on the quality of the remaining criteria. Circumstantial evidence was good on the issue of transporting the victim's corpse, but hardly so on the murder itself. Consequently, the court had to obtain new evidence in endless interrogations. The magistrates ought to proceed in a tactical fashion, emphasizing the absurdity of some of the defendants' claims, trapping them into contradictory statements, trying to wring new admissions from them, and demonstrating that all actions they had already admitted to only made sense in a chain of events that included murder and covering it up. In all this, the interrogators had a definite agenda, not always transparent to us. For example, they showed the basket to Dora fairly quickly, leaving Donker ignorant about its discovery for months. We are not even sure if Donker knew that Dora, too, was in jail, until he was confronted with her on June 22. She knew he was there, because she had watched his arrest.

The most important magistrate in a trial like this was the *hoofdofficier*, a function usually abbreviated as HO in the records. The HO had the double function of chief of police and city prosecutor. He presided over the interrogations, assisted by two rotating members of the college of *schepenen*, the judges. When matters seemed to reach a climax, all judges were present. Their role can be compared to that of a present-day jury: They ought to know the relevant information at the end, but they need not witness all the "police work." Sooner or later they had to grant or deny torture to the prosecutor, and they were to determine the final sentence. The prosecutor was Mr. Isaac Sweers. Born in 1707, he was sixty years old during the trial. His office as HO lasted from 1763 to 1768, and he was a member of the city council from 1761 until his death in 1777. Sweers never married, an intriguing detail in a trial for killing a spouse.[3]

Before Dora arrived in jail, Mr. Sweers questioned Donker five times, the first time on the day after his arrest. The opening interrogation dealt in large part with his life history: the three marriages with Cecilia, the places where they had lived, his brother's guardianship. Asked when he had seen his wife for the last time, he duly related he had accompanied her to the seven o'clock barge on December 1 and that he had not even heard about her since. Then Sweers arrived at the day's climax. He ordered a court official to bring the victim's head into the interrogation room and asked the prisoner whether he knew whose head it was. Pretending to inspect it, he replied "that it resembled the head of his wife somewhat, but he cannot tell positively whether it is hers." Donker firmly said no to the last question, an invitation to confess that the basket about which he had been summoned earlier contained Cecilia's body, horribly murdered and truncated.[4]

After the interrogation of December 16, Sweers realized that patience was a cardinal virtue. His prisoner showed no inclination to admit anything voluntarily. At that point, moreover, Sweers could not count on capturing the prisoner's fugitive mistress. He first occupied himself with preparatory matters, such as the tracing of witnesses. On December 22 he questioned Donker again, continuing his interrogations on the two remaining days before Christmas. The focus was on the transport of the basket. While Donker clung to the story about Madam Sjoenis, Sweers tried to trap him: what did her coach look like; had he ever met her; how could he know she was in that coach if he had never met her? Donker's last interrogation before the new year was on December 29, when the magistrates confronted him with the four witnesses who had seen him leaving The Castle of Antwerp. In passing, they asked him through which gate he had re-entered the city on December 3, a question prompted by the fact, unrevealed to him, that they knew he had left the basket in the Jordaan quarter. Nathaniel lied, saying that it was the Haarlem Gate.

The new year brought the prosecutor luck. Dora's arrest meant a second suspect behind bars and a greater chance of directing the case to its desired end. But already at her first interrogation, on January 5, the iron lady showed herself even more resolute in evasion and denial than her accomplice. She said she never worked as a prostitute. She claimed to have been ignorant at first that Donker was a married man and that, when she knew, she no longer allowed him "to use her carnally." Hence, she was innocent of adultery. She admitted to having told the court on December 12 that she was Donker's wife, for which she humbly apologized. Whatever her view of the crime of adultery, Sweers objected, she had set up a household, in another town, with a man who had left his wife and children. Did she consider that an honorable way of life? She bluntly said yes, in discordance with the value system of nearly the entire population. During this first session, Sweers made no mention of the victim, nor did he question Dora about her role in the murder. His approach was rooted in the same traditional stereotypes about gender and honor that Bicker Raye had confided to his diary. Also for this prosecutor, Dora was first of all "Donker's whore" and only secondarily a murder suspect.[5]

Dora's role in the killing of Cecilia was an issue the following day. Sweers had ordered the victim's head to be brought from the hospital, where they had kept it in preservative liquid. It was thirty-six days since her death. This time, the interrogators refrained from working toward a climax. They first asked Dora whether she knew Cecilia. She replied she had met her only once and did not recall her looks. Then a court official came in with Cecilia's head. Dora persisted: Since she hardly knew Donker's wife, she could not possibly tell whether this head was hers. The prosecutor then asked the suspect about Madam Sjoenis, whom she identified as the wife of a military officer. She had last seen this woman two years ago, she maintained. If that were true, how could Sjoenis know Dora's Amsterdam address? She had no idea.[6] Her blunt denials originated from the fantasy world in which she lived, inducing her to believe that no murder had occurred. Cecilia had mysteriously disappeared, and Dora had rightfully taken her place.

Sweers wished Cecilia's mother to come over again to identify the victim's clothes, but the old lady was ill, probably from the shock of seeing her daughter's severed head. On January 8 she provided written information instead, expressing her regret that neither Donker nor "this woman" had confessed yet. Her health was improving, she added, and she hoped to care for "the two orphans" to the best of her abilities. Mrs. Steffens counted their father already among the dead![7]

It was not until his sixth interrogation, on January 9, that the prosecutor explicitly charged Nathaniel with a sexual offense. Asked why they had left the house at the water after their summons, he replied he was afraid that the court, finding out they "lived together as whore and rogue," might surprise them there. Tuning to this, Sweers asked him to confirm that he and Dora had lived as husband and wife and had had sexual intercourse until the day of his arrest. Donker answered with an unqualified yes. He was even glad to admit this, it seemed, hoping that his judges, unable to prove him a murderer, would be satisfied with condemning him and Dora for adultery. The standard sentence for that offense was a fifty-year banishment from the province, annoying when one had intended to stay in Holland, but highly preferable in their predicament.[8]

The correspondence between Donker and his mother-in-law formed the prosecutor's next target. The old lady had provided the court with the original letters he had sent to The Hague. On January 13, Sweers showed Donker his second letter, which stated he had gone into hiding with Cecilia and planned to return in a few days. He admitted that this was a lie, claiming his motive had been to prevent his mother-in-law from coming to Amsterdam and discovering that he and Dora lived as husband and wife. It was not until six days later that he was confronted with the first letter, which said he had accompanied Cecilia to the barge station and not seen her since. Again a day later, the prosecutor decided to point out that the second letter obviously contradicted the first. He did so in the form of a clever question: was the prisoner ready to admit that, when his mother-in-law received the second letter from him, she must have concluded that he "had written a gross lie to her in his letter of the 11th"? The prisoner replied "yes." This was a major breakthrough. Until then, Donker had only confessed that the second letter was untrue, not the first, since he maintained having accompanied Cecilia to the barge station. Now Sweers had made him say this was a lie. Satisfied, the prosecutor kept the statement in store for later, focusing the rest of the interrogation and the next one on minor issues.[9]

On February 11, the court confronted Dora with no less than five witnesses: the landlord of The Crowned City of Elberfeld, his son, the basket maker, its finder, and Kaatje. The defendant denied almost everything they said, in particular that she had ordered Kaatje to buy the basket. In addition, she warded off a renewed accusation of adultery with the claim that, although sharing a room with Donker in the inn, she had slept in a chair next to the bed.[10]

After this round of questioning, there was a lull in the investigation. The HO left Nathaniel undisturbed until May. During the interval he heard Dora on minor issues twice, in early March. At the second occasion, Mrs. Steffens's letter writer was present to identify as Cecilia's most of the clothes Dora had on or with her at her arrest. Although this woman had been in town the previous month to testify against Donker, only now did the court ask her to view Cecilia's head. She recognized it immediately. A notary took her official statement, which, befitting a writer of letters, she signed with a precise and regular hand.[11] Cecilia had been dead for more than three months. Did the magistrates order her head to be buried now? If it stayed in preservative liquid in the hospital, this curiosity disappeared at a later time.

Dora's condition was a factor in slowing down the pace of the trial. We know she was ill from the jail keeper's accounts. This official received nine stivers per day for each person entrusted to his care, and the court reimbursed him separately for expenses incurred for washing a prisoner's linen and bedclothes and the like. He presented his bill four times per fiscal year, which began on February 1. Over the period February–April 1767, the jail keeper charged six guilders extra for expenses during Dora's illness.[12] Although this illness prevented the court from questioning her, the prosecutor's trouble in finding his next witness constituted another reason for the interval in sessions. He heard vague rumors that a *makelaar* had helped Donker in his abortive escape, but it was difficult to discover this man's identity. At the end of April the court found out it was Jan Gaubert. He had kept the note that a desperate Pieter Gerbrand Donker had written to him.

Between May 13 and 29, the court questioned Donker four times, based largely on Gaubert's testimony. On the thirteenth, the broker was present in person. The crucial element, understandably, was Donker's admission to him that he had killed his wife. Donker denied having said this. Confronted with his brother's note to Gaubert, saying Nathaniel would reveal a terrible thing to him, the prisoner said this referred to some big fraud. During the third interrogation in this series, Sweers made Donker say that he never knew his wife was dead, until her head was shown to him in the courtroom. Sweers immediately picked this up. It meant, he explained, that the prisoner acknowledged that the head shown to him during his first interrogation was his wife's. Donker acquiesced, saying he was sure now. To have it on record unequivocally, they asked it again three days later, when Donker replied he had no doubts about it.[13]

The prosecutor thought that his prisoner was on the verge of breaking. On June 3 Sweers triumphantly held up the basket to him, nearly four months after he had shown it to Dora. First, Donker evasively declared it was the type of basket that he had handed over to Madam Sjoenis. Then Kaatje and the basket maker entered the interrogation room. The latter recognized the thing as a typical product of his shop, and he remembered Kaatje buying one. Hearing their statements, Donker admitted Dora had ordered the basket, but for the transport of Madam Sjoenis' things. He could not tell for sure, he added, whether the one shown to him was the same.

As part of his tactic, Sweers waited eight days before continuing. A lengthy session followed, in which he made Donker admit that several earlier statements related to the basket were untrue. For the first time porter Stalli was present as a witness. He recalled Donker asking him whether the persons holding up the basket were court officials, which

Donker denied. Sweers continued with the strange journey Donker had undertaken with his heavy load and came back to this point the next day, asking Donker why he had stood there in the cold, dark night, risking a fall into the water, for a total stranger. It was only because Dora had requested it, Donker insisted. A host of other questions, pointing at inconsistencies, followed. For the first time, Sweers spoke of "the so-called Madam Sjoenis." No doubt, he, too, had long believed she was a fictitious person.[14]

However, that same day Johanna Jaunis was in Amsterdam. We do not know when and why the magistrates began to think she might really exist. Dora had been silent in court about her visit to The Hague after her flight. Johanna had been in hiding with friends in Leiden for several months, afraid they suspected her of complicity. The prosecutor confronted her first with Dora, leaving Donker ignorant of her presence. The court finally had a reliable witness that the basket did not belong to the mysterious Madam Sjoenis: the no longer mysterious Johanna Jaunis herself. They pointed this out to Dora on three consecutive days, but she persisted in her statement that the basket had been brought on Johanna's behalf and that, when Donker told her he had handed it over to a woman in a coach, she believed him.[15]

On June 22 the magistrates questioned both Nathaniel and Dora, separately at first. They started by revealing to Donker they knew where he had left the basket, showing it to him with the earth still sticking to its bottom. Donker could only say he had no idea how the basket had ended up in the Jordaan quarter. This proved, Sweers concluded, that a certain Sjoenis could not possibly have accepted the basket. Without saying this woman had been in court, he asked Donker again if the basket contained Cecilia's corpse, which the defendant denied. A court official led him away and brought Dora in. She claimed that the basket they had transported was smaller and older. Then the servant brought Donker back, as a witness. They saw each other for the first time since December 15. What could have remained of their mutual love in this predicament, after six months of incarceration? If only the court clerk had recorded how they looked each other in the eyes. But he merely wrote down questions and answers. Did she persist in claiming she stopped having sex with Donker after she discovered he was married? She persisted; Donker stated the contrary. She clung to her statement, only admitting to have worked as a prostitute in The Hague. Donker said they had planned to keep girls of pleasure in the house at the water, which Dora denied. Donker explained he had already admitted that Kaatje had bought the basket for them, which the girl had confirmed. Dora denied. Whether or not Nathaniel and Dora had drifted apart with respect to the affection they felt for each other, they certainly had with respect to their attitude toward survival. The difference would soon become manifest.[16]

By now, the prosecutor thought the evidence against Nathaniel Donker sufficed to obtain permission for torture. The evidence included his own admissions so far and, unknown to him, Johanna Jaunis's statement that she never had anything to do with a basket. The session of July 10 was a long one. First, the secretary (the principal court clerk) read Donker's entire "confession," that is, the protocols of his previous interrogations, to him. When the secretary had finished, Sweers asked Donker the standard question "if he persisted in negation." He did. Another standard formula followed: "Mr. Isaac Sweers, hoofdofficier of this city, requests that the prisoner be placed in his hands in order to make him tell the truth through pain and irons." The secretary noted the judges' consent and continued: "the prisoner, brought in again undressed and placed on the bench and tied up with the shinscrews loose around his legs, without any pain inflicted on him yet, confesses that on December 1, 1766, with the help of his mistress, he violently took the life of his wife."[17]

During the remainder of the session, Nathaniel told all relevant details, from the first murder plans until his abortive flight. The magistrates heard few things they were not already convinced of. New elements included the pawning of some of Cecilia's goods and an explanation for the damage to the victim's ribs and liver. Donker also confirmed Jan Gaubert's testimony that the latter refused to believe him capable of killing, insisting that the victim was a songstress and that Nathaniel tried to trick his brother. This exonerated the broker from the charge of consciously assisting in a murderer's attempted escape. Donker finished with an apology for bothering the gentlemen with lies for so long. He had hoped to avoid a scandal for the sake of his children. If not for them, he would have told the truth much earlier. Dressed and taken into the interrogation room again, he confirmed his confession, adding that Dora had urged him to commit the murder at least three months before.[18]

To request a defendant to repeat his confession first made under torture or threat of torture was a legal obligation. The law said he must confirm it a second time on the following day, which he did. The prosecutor took that opportunity to complete his protocol, showing three objects to Donker. The first was the knife with which Dora had cut off the victim's head and arms. A deputy declared he had found it under the chimney in a back room. This was on April 22, when he and his men emptied the house at the water on the court's order. Donker immediately recognized the second object, the big handkerchief in which they had wrapped Cecilia's head. He confirmed they had used it for this purpose. Inspecting it anew at the spot, the magistrates observed it still contained a few black hairs. Finally, the iron bar with which Dora had smashed the victim's ribs was there. The deputy had looked for it the other night, after Donker's confession. He took the new resident of the house at the water with him to court, who declared he had found the iron bar in a chest in the front of the house.[19]

With satisfaction, Jacob Bicker Raye opened his diary that day, to write a new item in it: "for a long time, Nathaniel Donker has managed to mislead the gentlemen with lies, but finally they obtained enough evidence to have him tortured. He confessed before it came to that. The details will be known soon."[20]

Dora had admitted to no crime yet, but Nathaniel's confession was a powerful new testimony incriminating her. The prosecutor was in no hurry to request permission to place her on the rack as well. On July 13 he tried it once more by way of persuasion. In the form of questions, he went through Donker's entire protocol of the tenth, leaving her ignorant of the fact that he had confessed. She was bound to realize this, however, because of the details they asked her to confirm. Dora said no to every question, except for finally admitting she had asked Kaatje to buy the basket. But she still clung to the Sjoenis story. Then the magistrates brought Donker in. He accused her, face to face, of everything she had just been charged with. He awaited God's judgment with peace of mind, he added, knowing he had told the sincere truth. She remained silent.[21]

On the same day, the waitress at the wine bar, in which Dora had stayed as part of her act of impersonating Cecilia, was in court. Although she failed to recall Dora's looks, she did recognize her accent and the clothes she had worn. Visitors for the next day were the owners of the two depositor's shops, where Dora had taken most of Cecilia's belongings. The court had confiscated these from the municipal pawn shop. Donker inspected every item carefully, each time confirming it was Cecilia's. Dora, who had just received a new pair of stockings from the jail keeper, denied obstinately. On July 18, the court concluded the protocol of Nathaniel's interrogations. He signed it with NDonker, the N and D artistically woven into each other.[22]

Dora's ordeal had taken place the previous day, July 17. Amsterdam's custom concerning torture was unchanged since the early seventeenth century. There were three degrees, the application of which depended on the seriousness of the crime and the prisoner's perseverance. The latter factor also influenced the duration of a torture session. During the whole process, the magistrates repeatedly urged the suspect to confess, so that the ordeal could stop. This caused some defendants, like Donker, to admit to the crime before the actual torturing started. The first degree, reserved for somewhat lesser suspects, consisted of whipping only. Those who refused to confess while whipped got away with a lighter punishment. A person suspected of a major crime immediately suffered the second degree, the shinscrews. When screwed to the full, these caused considerable pain, unbearable to many of the men and the few women subjected to this treatment. The seventeenth-century judge Hans Bontemantel commented that it made the prisoner's calves look like wafers. When it failed to make him confess, the third degree started. The hangman tied weights of a hundred pounds each to the suspect's toes. With a rope tied around the wrists, he lifted the suspect from the floor, making him hang in the air with the weights swinging under the feet. Finally, if even this failed to produce the desired effect, the suspect was whipped while hanging in this way. By the middle of the eighteenth century, the court applied the second degree, if need be, followed by the third, two times a year on the average. About 20 percent of the suspects undergoing it were women.[23]

The task of providing this treatment fell to the so-called indoor executioner. The term had a literal meaning, since this man seldom worked in public. Throughout Holland, the application of torture as well as public punishment was the prerogative of the provincial executioner residing in Haarlem. When another town's prosecutor or a rural court needed his services, they warned him in advance. The Amsterdam HO did so when the magistrates had scheduled a justice day. In this populous city, however, the remaining tasks were far too numerous to depend solely on an official who lived twenty kilometers away. Amsterdam's indoor executioner took care of torture, the penalty of whipping indoors, and the bodily inspection of prisoners. In 1767 Carel Kleijne held this office.[24] After the judges had consented to Sweers' demand to question Dora under torture, he ordered Kleijne to begin.

First, she was led away for undressing, which presumably referred to her lower legs, back, and shoulders only. Back in the interrogation room, she took her position on the bench. Sweers asked her if she had assisted in the murder of Cecilia Klos. She said no. Kleijne turned the shinscrews a few times. Sweers asked the same question, followed by the same answer. This continued until the indoor executioner had turned the screws to the full. Her perseverance earned her the third degree. Kleijne tied the weights to her toes, and Sweers urged her once more to confess. She refused. Kleijne tied a rope around her wrists. She refused to confess. Kleijne lifted her until she dangled with the weights under her. Sweers asked her about the murder; she knew nothing about it, she said. It was time for the finale. Sweers ordered the indoor executioner to whip Dora, while she hung there with the weights. He took his rods and beat her on the bare back. Do you confess to helping Nathaniel Donker in killing his wife, the prosecutor asked for the last time. She replied with a firm no. The torture session was over; she had withstood the ordeal.[25]

Dora had suppressed her memory of the deed from the beginning. She had just taken Cecilia's place, she imagined, and nothing unlawful had happened. Nathaniel's first wife had miraculously disappeared at about the same time as when they had transported that basket with Madam Sjoenis' things. If only the court, too, had believed this, she and her lover would be happy together. Quite possibly, this psychological denial gave her the strength to bear the tortures inflicted on her. Bicker Raye betrayed no sign of astonishment, when he noted the event in his diary the next day, the same day on which Nathaniel signed his confession. "Donker's whore, beautiful Dora, has withstood the rack in all phases," he wrote. "She said she knew nothing of the case."[26]

Nathaniel Donker had arrived in Holland at age nine and became an orphan while an adolescent. His own actions caused his young sons to become orphans within a year: their mother murdered, their father on death row. One adult, not having many years to live, was left to care for the boys. The oldest person related to him wrote the very last petition the Court of Holland received regarding Nathaniel Donker. The justices dealt with it on August 11, 1767. Maria van der Linden, grandmother of Pieter Gerbrand Donker, aged ten, and of Nathaniel Jacob Donker, aged five, humbly requested a provision from the provincial court. By now, she knew her son-in-law had confessed and would soon die on the scaffold. She mentioned he was in jail in Amsterdam, but not what for. In the meantime, Visvliet had been sold, and the revenues were about to become available. Hence, the Court of Holland should appoint a solicitor to represent the children's interest. Hendrik van der Ven, Cecilia's former representative, was prepared to take this burden upon himself. His principal task consisted of finally laying hands on the ten thousand guilders legally reserved for Donker's children. In order to care for them properly, their grandmother needed this sum badly. The justices agreed, to the proposed trustee and his principal task.[27]

In Amsterdam, nothing happened for a while. When the prosecutor intended to demand capital punishment and he expected to get it, the formal conviction was planned as the opening part in a sequence of ceremonies. The judges pronounced their sentence two days before the execution, which sometimes meant long after closing the interrogations. The magistrates scheduled a justice day whenever they thought it convenient, customarily on a Saturday. Nathaniel Donker waited for his sentence during most of August. In this period of agony, he was ill for a number of days.[28] On Thursday, the twentieth, the HO announced his demand: that the prisoner be laid on a cross on the scaffold and broken alive from below; his body exposed on the scaffold for some time; then placed on a hurdle and dragged to the gallows field, on a peninsula at the other side of the harbor; exposed on a wheel there to be eaten by the birds and consumed by the air. As usual with a capital demand, one of the burgomasters was present as an advisor. The judges agreed with the HO for the most part, canceling the hurdle for the body's transport and, more important, granting the convict a grave, albeit an ignominious one. His body was to be laid in a coffin and buried under the stone gallows on the peninsula. This favor was probably his reward for testifying against Dora several times.[29]

Breaking on the wheel was the standard punishment for intentional murder in early modern Amsterdam. The origins of this penalty date back to the sixth century, when the convict was driven over by a heavily laden wagon. In later centuries, the executioner hit him to death with a big wheel, a variant still practiced in the early modern period in a number of German territories. When it is done that way, breaking *with* the wheel is the best term for it in English.[30] However, in countries such as the Netherlands and France, the procedure was further simplified. The executioner tied the convict on a wheel, proceeding to break his bones with an iron bar. In Amsterdam, a structure obliging the convict to stretch his arms and legs widely, called a cross, replaced the wheel. Occasionally, a sentence allowed the criminal to be broken from above (starting with the heart), which meant he was put to death before suffering the breaking of his bones. But most often the sentence was breaking from below (starting with the legs), while alive. In that case, the coup de grâce on the heart came last, after the eight blows smashing shin and thigh bones, and upper arms and forearms. When exposed at the peninsula opposite the harbor, the corpse of a convict who had suffered this punishment, sat on a wheel put up on a stake. Although nearly half of the criminals condemned to death in Amsterdam escaped exposure of their corpse at the gallows field, this was highly uncommon for a murderer broken on the wheel. Moreover, convicts whose body was "granted the earth" normally got a regular burial. Donker's burial under the gallows at the peninsula was an unusual mixture.

The series of rituals continued on Friday evening. HO Sweers, accompanied by two of the judges, visited the prisoner to urge him to prepare for death. This ceremony took place at the inner court of the town hall. Sweers began with the standard formula: "Nathaniel Donker, the reason why I have come to this place is to announce to you that you must die. I summon you to appear in the high tribunal tomorrow at nine to hear the sentence of death, which will be executed immediately." After this formal announcement, the HO made his customary speech, edifying as always and attuned to the person of the condemned.

> Thus you see, Donker, how Divine Providence watches over you, allowing the earthly judge to have you punished and get what you deserve. Not only this, but in a moment you will be summoned before an Almighty Judge whom you cannot deceive and to whom you will have to give account for everything you have done or failed to do. When you contemplate the Trinitarian God in his Holiness and Righteousness, it would appear there is no hope left for you, and you have to exclaim as Cain in desperation, "My sins are too grave to be pardoned." But believe in the great God who, in Jesus Christ his dear son, has conceived of a road toward reconciliation, through which he promises forgiveness to the most evil sinners and from whom you, too, can acquire forgiveness. So, go over yonder. Go over yonder, unfortunate sinner, plead on the merits of Christ Jesus. Fall at his feet and beg him to be your intercessor with the Father, causing you to become blessed. If there be streams of blood of the woman murdered by you calling for vengeance before God's throne, the sacrificial blood of Christ Jesus, which he has shed on the cross for all repentant sinners, has the power to smother this gloomy cry. Take refuge in Him, then, in order for you to be saved. Then your end will be blessed and your death a happy one. Amen.[31]

Reconciliation over vengeance, Christian repentance and forgiveness over retribution, Jesus' blood over Cecilia's: it exemplified the religious atmosphere of death penalty ceremonial. Capital executions were only partially secularized events. Surely, the eighteenth-century revolution in emotional standards made little imprint on these ancient traditions. Another traditional ritual concluded the day. Donker had his last meal with the jail keeper and a few servants. It cost the court twenty-five guilders. The total cost of keeping Donker in jail, from December to August, amounted to 178 guilders and eighteen stivers.[32] After his gallows meal, the prisoner received spiritual assistance from the Reverend Ten Brink. This minister was glad to report to the magistrates Donker's great remorse and sorrow over his horrible deed.[33]

Saturday, August 22, was the justice day. The scaffold had been erected the previous afternoon; since the late seventeenth century, removable wooden scaffolds had been the rule in Dutch towns.[34] In the morning, the city gates remained closed, to prevent nonresidents, for whom the ceremony was not meant, from streaming in. The authorities posted a military regiment in the town hall and another one in the weigh house on Dam Square. The soldiers saluted the HO and the judges when they arrived, wearing the traditional black tabards girded with a sash beset with Saint Andrew's crosses from the city's arms. Inside the town hall, the magistrates said a prayer together with the convicts and the preacher. It was common that a number of criminals received their punishment, for the majority only a corporal penalty, together. On this justice day, six criminals in all stood ready to mount the scaffold, of whom only Donker had been condemned to death. He had "number one," because it was customary to execute the sentence of the principal convict first. Number two was a man condemned to a whipping and an eternal banishment from Holland for smuggling eight bottles of wine. The others, two male and two female thieves, were to be whipped as well. The executioner was Jan van Aanhout.[35]

The ceremony continued with some more standard formulas, focusing on the capital convict. The HO loudly asked the judges and the one burgomaster present whether it was the right time to do justice according to the town's ancient customs. They all answered affirmatively. Then the judges declared Donker a child of death. The next event, his last confrontation with Dora, was an individual peculiarity rather than a standard part of the ceremony. Since it was not a success, the magistrates probably tried to forget about it quickly. Meanwhile, the soldiers played pipes and drums as usual, while the crowd outside produced an immense noise. According to one witness, the Reverend Ten Brink asked Donker if the drumming and the noise bothered him. He replied he did not even hear it, because his thoughts were "with Jesus at the cross, who prays for me now to His Father."³⁶ After these pious words, Donker joined the five criminals condemned to suffer a corporal punishment after him. The bell was tolled and the rod of justice put up. The HO and the judges, but not the burgomaster, took their seats in the windows of the gallery from which they had a view of the scaffold and the watching crowd.

The part visible to the spectators outside had come. First, the secretary recited the sentences of all six criminals, which included the tale of their misdeeds, to the crowd. The audience was chiefly interested in Donker's. His sentence opened with the charge that, legally married to Cecilia and having two children with her, he had indulged in shameful adultery with Dorothea Bosselman, a notorious whore from The Hague now in the city jail. This informed everyone that Dora's case was undecided yet. She had incited Donker toward the murder, the sentence continued. The details of his final confession followed, with third parties left anonymous. The notary Verhoef was "a certain gentleman," The Owl "a certain man who had advanced the rent to them." Donker's offenses, the sentence concluded, amounted to adultery, desertion of his family, and heinous murder, committed after previous deliberations and in cold blood against an unsuspecting person; the final charge was his assistance in the mutilation of the body and dumping it. The sentence closed with Donker's condemnation.³⁷ We may wonder whether the audience continued to listen carefully to the reading of the other sentences, or commented on Donker's crime in the meantime.

The magistrates, the criminals, and the preacher returned to the justice room once more, to say a final prayer. When the former took their seats anew, the actual execution began. Bicker Raye, who seldom missed a justice day until his death in 1772, saw it happen. When the executioner had fastened the convict to the cross, the latter sang a religious hymn together with the Reverend Ten Brink. Then the hangman placed a rope around Donker's neck and tightened it a little to silence him. Jan van Aanhout did not have his best day. He partly missed the convict's thigh bones, which remained unbroken. The blow meant for his heart landed too low, so that it failed to kill him instantaneously. Seeing this, Van Aanhout wanted to strangle him, but then the noose got loose. Nathaniel Donker had "a very hard and slow death," Bicker Raye concluded.³⁸ After this spectacle, the audience could watch the executioner administer a whipping to the smuggler and the four thieves. When he had finished, the magistrates withdrew from their seats and the rod of justice was taken in.

Despite his clumsy performance, Van Aanhout charged the usual sums for his various activities. The authorities of the early modern period paid their executioners relatively well, partly to compensate them for the low esteem they received from the populace and partly as a conscious strategy to raise their status. Breaking on the wheel proper was three guilders per blow, amounting to twenty-seven guilders. Strangling Donker was another six guilders and taking him from the cross three guilders. For the whole event, Van Aanhout additionally charged a per diem, money for his ropes, and the cost for travel as well as assistance, which amounted to twelve guilders; with six convicts in all, the share for Donker's execution was two guilders. Then Van Aanhout took the corpse to the gallows field, placed it in a coffin, and buried it, which amounted to twelve guilders. The transport across the harbor had taken place in the ferryboat for cows, for which its skipper received twenty-five guilders (and seven stivers for having a bridge opened). Thus, executing Donker's sentence cost the court a total of eighty-one guilders and seven stivers, almost three months' wages for a worker.[39]

The execution of a notorious criminal often was an occasion for publishing sermons, broadsides, or booklets. The literary production about Donker's case either was modest or little has survived.[40] The one work extant contains a transcript of the final confession Donker made under threat of torture, followed by the prosecutor's speech on the eve of his execution. This booklet mentions the full names of Verhoef and Gaubert and refers to Pieter Gerbrand as "his brother, the lawyer."[41] Whatever the quantity of printed material, the execution reactivated the gossip circuit, for which Bicker Raye is our source once more. A few days after the execution, he inserted a new passage into his diary. Probably, he had just read the booklet with Donker's confession, since he noted a few details such as his age and place of birth and rendered the entire speech of the prosecutor. Bicker Raye added one comment of his own: The perpetrator's brother, a decent man who also lived in Amsterdam, has moved abroad because of this sad occurrence; both brothers had inherited eighty thousand guilders, but Nathaniel was practically poor, having dissipated it all.[42]

Still another testimony to the notoriety of this crime appeared years afterward, although the author pretended it originated from before the murder. It concerns a prophecy ascribed to the famous healer and astrologist Ludeman, who had died in 1757. In the same year his self-proclaimed follower, the hack writer Kersteman, had published a semifictional biography. In a later edition, Kersteman added an illustration of his subject's cunning in forecasting the future. In old age, so we learn, Ludeman was no longer that keen on drawing horoscopes, but for some people he made an exception. Drawn by his fame, an adorable young maiden comes to Amsterdam. She has many pretenders but only one man she favors. While drawing this woman's horoscope, Ludeman is suddenly shocked: "The man you are about to marry will be your murderer within eleven years." Astonished, she replies, "This is impossible; Mr. D* is an honorable man and he loves me dearly." Yet, she, too, is a little worried, so she avoids his company for twelve weeks. When he finally asks why and hears about the prediction, he blames the astrologer for messing with their courtship. In anger, he travels to Amsterdam, visits Ludeman, and calls him a wizard and a quack. Undismayed, the old man makes another prediction: "You are on the verge of marrying someone whose murderer you will be within eleven years." Nathaniel says he is an old fool and leaves, as angry as he came.

Believe it or not, a few months later a third person knocks on Ludeman's door—an "ordinary citizen" with his twelve-year-old daughter. With an adorable face and charming graces, she is the little Dorothea B*M*. After drawing her horoscope, Ludeman stares into the room, bewildered. To her father, who has turned pale, he explains, "If you wish to save this girl from a great shame and a prison in which she will die, then send her abroad immediately, or else, after eleven years, she will cause and assist in a murder committed by an honest man on his true wife." Ludeman refuses the coins lying on the table, advising his client to leave as quickly as he can. All three prophecies came true ten years after Ludeman's death, Kersteman concluded, a sure proof of the astrologer's great gift. A footnote added that the case was extremely well known in Amsterdam.[43]

Whereas collective memory of the crime lingered on for years, the Donker family all but disappeared from official records after 1767. Nathaniel's mother-in-law was old, and we can only guess at the fate of the two boys.[44] If their uncle in Italy remained single, they possibly inherited from him in the end. The dossier in the Orphan Chamber's archive contains one more letter—the last official mention of the Donker family. It has been preserved with the original envelope, addressed to The Honorable Gentleman Mr. Jan van Loon, secretary of the Orphan Chamber at Amsterdam. The red seal on the back has been broken, so we know Mr. van Loon opened it. Pieter Gerbrand Donker wrote: "You know very well which awful misfortune has prompted me to leave Holland. From a friend, I learned that your Chamber still has a sum of ƒ5,120 belonging to me. You can hand it over, after deducing your costs, to my representative, N. Wilthuyzen. I trust your willingness to help a miserable person. Naples, November 29, 1774."[45]

Dora never had family in Holland, but she was allowed to live for more years. Because the inquisitorial procedure, according to which she and Nathaniel were tried, only recognized the defendant's confession as a basis for establishing guilt, a defendant who persisted in denial could not be condemned to a scaffold punishment, not even a mere public whipping. It was legal, however, to send such a person to prison because of remaining suspicion. On October 14, the court sentenced Dora to a term of fifty years in the spinhouse, followed by an eternal banishment from the city.[46] Of course, the news reached Bicker Raye soon. He thought the banishment was for twenty years, which made little difference in practice. Because of the torture and her long detention in jail, he added, her hands and feet were lame.[47] Indeed, the jail keeper reported her ill; he had been obliged to rent a bedpan for her. The total cost of her detention in jail, January–October, amounted to exactly f157. She arrived in the spinhouse on October 16.[48]

By the middle of the eighteenth century, imprisonment was a common penalty in most of Europe, but separate prisons for women were uncommon yet. Having opened its spinhouse in 1597, one year after the male prison or rasphouse, Amsterdam was a longtime exception. After about 1700 spinning was no longer profitable, so the inmates were occupied with sewing or knitting. Like their male counterparts, female convicts received a reduction of their original term if they behaved well or provided services to the court such as betraying escape attempts. Consequently, most inmates stayed for a considerably shorter period than their sentence stipulated. Visitors from the general public were admitted to see both the rasphouse and spinhouse, but each one had a "secret" ward as well. Originally, these sequestered parts of the institutions served to accommodate inmates confined at the request of respectable families, but in the eighteenth century private prisons had largely taken over that function. By then, the spinhouse's secret ward housed just a few women, who, as a consequence of its original purpose, had no right to reduction. According to a count in 1765, the institution as a whole housed sixty women. The great majority had been condemned by the city court, most of them for theft rather than prostitution. Still, visitors routinely referred to the inmates as whores. Many men made obscene remarks or insulted the women in other ways. The women often answered them in kind.[49]

Although Dora served her term for a crime—alleged but unconfessed—

Original gate of the spinhouse, where Dora was imprisoned. Photo: Pieter Spierenburg.

and her sentence mentioned the spinhouse without further qualification, the court placed her in the secret ward. The magistrates had a rather cynical motive for it. Opposition to judicial torture was mounting in this period, in the Netherlands as well as elsewhere in Europe. Some delicate persons shunned the sight of a tortured criminal, even if the crime was so heinous as in this case. And after all, the prisoner was not some beast of a man but a young woman. The judges knew very well she had come off the rack partly paralyzed. When placed in the spinhouse's public ward, they feared, she would complain to visitors that she had been maltreated. To Dora, the court's security measure was an additional disadvantage, since it kept her from the reduction list.[50] With a fifty-year term, she may not have realized the difference at first.

Mentally, the iron lady was unbroken. She recovered from her lameness and she contemplated regaining her freedom. This was toward the end of 1772. She shared the secret ward with one other woman then, a twenty-seven-year-old widow named Judith van der Vecht. The court had condemned her for swindle earlier that year, and her relatives had successfully petitioned to keep her away from public view. Dora and Judith made contact, because the latter found out she could open the lock of the door separating their cells with scissors. Dora had stayed in Judith's cell earlier, discovering it bordered on the street. She had thought about breaking out, but at that time she was far from being recovered, and even now she felt too weak to try an escape on her own. But they could work their way toward freedom together, Dora proposed. She had got hold of a knife some time ago. Judith objected there was a neighboring house behind that wall, but Dora convinced her it bordered on a small alley. They enlisted the help of a third prisoner, twenty-four-year-old Stijntje Sijpes. She sat in the spinhouse's public ward, but the warden's maid often left the door between the two sections open. This facilitated the transfer of instruments from one place to the other. Stijntje first brought them a little iron nail, which they found of no use. Subsequently, she came with a kitchen knife, a mason's jointer, a big iron pin, and a wooden block. Under Judith's bed they found big iron scissors, which they fastened to the wooden block. The two women also asked Stijntje to get them an axe, but she did not dare to take it. Afterward, the court reproached the warden and his staff for severe negligence, in leaving doors open and equipment unstored.

They started breaking at the beginning of December. Stijntje stood on guard most of the time. When she heard someone approach, they quickly removed the bed to cover the hole they had made. Judith did most of the work, because Dora still was weak and Stijntje's interest only marginal. Stijntje had been condemned, for theft, to a public whipping and a banishment only, so her stay in the spinhouse was provisional, until the justice day about to be scheduled. They doubted if they could finish the job before that date. Indeed, it was not quite done when the justice day came, on January 23, 1773. Released after her whipping, Stijntje was to inspect the alley; if she saw an iron fence, she would knock against the wall with a stick. But she forgot her promise. Dora and Judith went on, and a few days later they thought they were almost through. Dora had to keep stones from falling into the street. Judith cut their bedclothes into strips. The opposite wall, facing the secret ward's courtyard, had a window covered with iron bars, to which they intended to fasten the stripped bedclothes. Dora planned to go first, being in need of help because of her weakness.

At that point, so close to freedom, they were detected. Perhaps a few stones had already fallen into the alley, alarming the warden. The court interrogated all three, easily getting hold of Stijntje as she went through the city gate two days after her banishment had started. The judges condemned her to stay in the spinhouse for a year. The penalty for Judith and Dora consisted of a one-year prolongation of their confinement and a temporary removal from the reduction list. This made Dora's total term fifty-one years.⁵¹

Dora had failed to regain her freedom, but the incident alerted the magistrates to her long stay in the secret ward. They realized she had never been on the reduction list, so her "removal" from it was no more than a confirmation of an existing situation. Her original sentence, they noted, made no mention of any ward. A year later, when her term of "removal" from the reduction list had expired, the magistrates reconsidered her case. Sweers's successor as HO, Willem Dedel, posited that the 1767 college of judges had intended to keep Dora separate forever and grant her no reduction. The current college, save for one member, refused to go along with that point of view. The sentence had no such clause, they argued. The prisoner's sequestration had been a provisional measure because she was paralyzed as a consequence of the torture, but now she had recovered. Without the prospect of reduction, she would turn desperate. On January 24, 1774, seven years after her arrest, Dora was admitted to the spinhouse's public ward.⁵²

Now people could see her! Residents of Amsterdam as well as the surrounding countryside remembered the discovery of a mutilated body in the shallow moat and the display of the head and limbs in the city's hospital. Those too young at the time heard the story from their elders. They included Aafje Gijsen, a twenty-year-old daughter from a wealthy Mennonite family in Westzaandam. According to her diary, she loved visiting friends and making trips. On Friday, February 24, 1775, Aafje and her friends went to Amsterdam for a visit to the spinhouse. After a while, some wanted to leave, but "we went upstairs once more, because *juffrouw Fransie* was very eager finally to see Dora, Donker's whore. Toward one, we drove home again."⁵³

There she sat behind bars, known as Donker's whore, not as Cecilia's murderess. Yet Dora and Nathaniel had made plans and acted together in everything. That the words of another woman belied her active participation constitutes one more example of the tenacity of the image of women as men's passive associates. On the other hand, Dora herself had always denied complicity. Legally, she was not a convicted murderess. Only Nathaniel had confessed their joint misdeeds and urged her to do so likewise. This does not mean that the previous chapters are in need of revision. In a modern legal system, circumstantial evidence had severely incriminated her. Withstanding torture saved her life, but it is unlikely that she spoke the truth in court and that, by implication, her lover lied about her role. So she was a murderess. But it hardly mattered. HO Sweers had treated her first of all as the wanton woman leading Nathaniel astray and the public remembered her as Donker's whore. This reminds us once more that the eighteenth-century revolution in love primarily concerned marital affection. When that revolution extended to an illegitimate relationship, the whole thing shaded into its darker side and the relationship was perceived by the majority in terms of traditional stereotypes.

Dora never left the spinhouse alive; at least, it is implausible that she did. The registers of prisoners from 1731 until 1810 are missing, and in the latter year her name was not listed. It is also absent from Amsterdam's burial registers. According to the 1784 edition of Ludeman's biography, the one that included the "prediction," she had died in captivity a few years earlier. If the author was right, her death came around 1782: she lived just as long as the woman she once thought she had replaced.

The minimal conclusion the evidence allows is that Dora was up for view to curious visitors from early 1774 to early 1775. This was a hectic time, when hack writers vied with each other for the favor of Amsterdam's reading public. In this very period, an infamous infatuation arose, which evolved into a new story of fatal attraction. Ignorant of it yet, a host of Amsterdam residents was eager to take a look at the notorious female prisoner who had assisted Donker. Could it be that these residents included the man about to become the perpetrator in the next murder that would shake the city? Imagine Van Gogh on a rainy day in 1774. He has no urgent business, and he fancies a visit to the spinhouse. He strolls around the courtyard, along the cells of female thieves completely unfamiliar to him. Then he notices Dora, whose story he has heard upon his return from a voyage. Love, passion, and deceit surely were major motifs in the plays in which he once acted. And they dominate his private life. He stares at Dora for a minute, absorbing her looks and her figure. "I would never have fallen in love with her," he says to himself.

6

An Unsuccessful Career

Dressed in a white gown decorated with an embroidered purse, in his hand a fishing rod: thus he appeared the very first time the historical record mentions him. It was Tuesday, January 4, 1763. This was no drag queen but the same man whom we imagined walking in the spinhouse on a rainy day in 1774. Whether he really entered the spinhouse or not, far more consequential was a visit he made in January of the next year to a whorehouse. There he met, not Dora, but Annie—more about her later. First we must penetrate the mind of Annie's lover, a man of riddles.

Like Donker, Van Gogh failed to tell his exact age at his first interrogation. The court clerk noted that "by conjecture" he was thirty-eight or thirty-nine years old. That is the only similarity, apart from their ultimate fates, between these two defendants. Though both succumbed to fatal attraction, they greatly differed in character and presumably in social background as well. For the investigator inquiring into their lives, they differ with respect to the available information on family of origin and early years. As well informed as we are about Nathaniel Donker, we are to the same degree ignorant about Van Gogh.

The difficulty is this: According to the interrogation protocol, Johannes Bartholomeus Ferdinandus van Gogh was born in Amsterdam, a fact that the writer Nicolaas Hoefnagel confirmed by calling him an Amsterdamer; however, his name is absent from the city's baptism books.[1] In the baptismal as well as the marriage registers of Amsterdam, no Van Gogh appears whom we can link with any probability to our man or his relatives. Possibly his family had moved to the city in his early youth. The court made no effort to find out about it. Indeed, no one seemed to be interested in Van Gogh's family background. The published versions of his confession are literal copies of the interrogation protocol, repeating the conjecture about his age without comment. Prosecutor Dedel conspicuously demonstrated his lack of interest during the last appeal procedure, in his reply to Van Gogh's lawyer. The name of a witness for the defense was Johanna Barendina van Gogh, which prompted the prosecutor to cast doubt on her testimony, saying "she is probably someone from the defendant's family."[2] Apparently, Dedel had not even bothered to check whether his claim was true, let alone the exact family relationship! Finally, we are unsure in which form our man's friends addressed him. Authors writing about his case sometimes called him Jan. Many of their readers, however, knew him only by his last name, and Annie's neighbors also addressed him that way.

What do we know about him and his family? In 1775 his father was dead and his mother was living in Ouderkerk, near Amsterdam. A passage from a pamphlet by Hoefnagel suggests she was a midwife.[3] The Ouderkerk auction book lists a public sale of the goods of the deceased widow of Bartholomeus van Gogh on March 26, 1782. Ninety-one items were on sale, mostly kitchen utensils and porcelain, bringing in a total of just over seventy-five guilders. Presumably, she also had owned furniture, which was kept from the auction. This makes the widow neither wealthy nor really poor. The auction book lists all buyers by last name, sometimes with a first name or an initial added, save for one buyer, mentioned three times and just called Johanna.[4] It is reasonable to assume that the widow was Van Gogh's mother and Johanna her daughter, who testified in favor of her brother in 1775.[5] At the time his sister testified, she lived in the orphanage of the Collegiants, a small Protestant sect. Presumably, she worked there, but does this mean the whole family originally belonged to that sect? The Latin forms of Van Gogh's three Christian names rather suggest that the family was Catholic. He also had a brother, whose initials were J. D., living in Vreeland in 1775. That is all we know about this brother.[6] So, the quest into Van Gogh's family background leads to a dead end. On the assumption that the conjecture about his age was right, he was born about 1736–1737.

At his first appearance on stage, historically and literally, Van Gogh had reached his mid-twenties. According to a friend of his, he was under contract as a *figurant* at the Amsterdam theater from 1761 until 1763. In modern Dutch, *figurant* means extra, but the extras of those days did more

An Unsuccessful Career 119

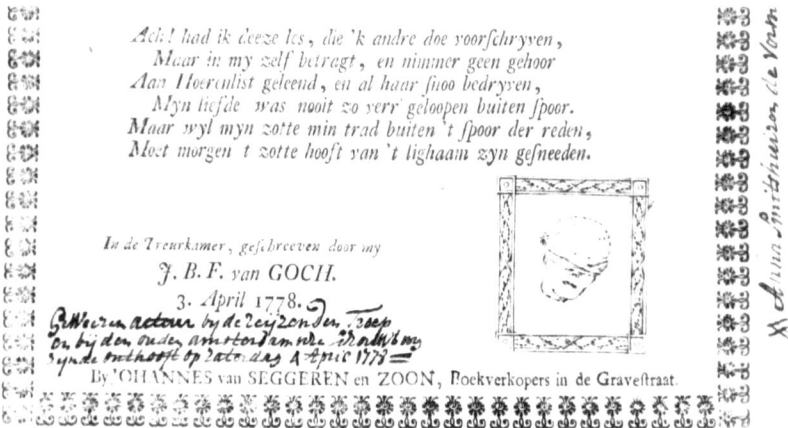

The only extant portrait of Van Gogh, on a leaflet published at the occasion of his execution. The original owner wrote on it that Van Gogh was a former actor. Photo: University Library Amsterdam.

than just serve as backdrop. They can be compared to the chorus line in a modern musical. Dancing and sometimes singing, they accompanied the principal characters. Van Gogh did just that in the play performed on January 4, 1763. That we know he had a role in it is a chance finding. The author of a review, published two weeks later, decided to list the whole cast, using the common *monsieur* for the male actors. Normally, if reviews contained actors' names at all, they only mentioned the principal roles. With an independent source about his contract available, there can be no doubt that Monsieur Van Gogh is our man.[7]

The play in which he acted had been written for a festive occasion. In 1763 the Amsterdam Theater celebrated its 125th anniversary. On January 4, the company of actors did the usual two performances, the first an adaptation of a French play by Corneille, and the second, the anniversary play, *De Juichende Schouwburg* (*The Jubilating Theater*) by Lucas Pater. It was an allegory, as revealed by the cast of characters: Apollo, Poetry, Theater, Melpomene, Thalia, Exercise, Amusement, Calliope, Terpsichore, Erato, Euterpe, Clio, Polyhymnia, Fame, Art of Singing, Art of Dancing, Diligence, Reason, Interest, Autumn, Winter, The Year, and Urania. The order is identical in the review and in the play's printed edition. Only the first seven roles were "speaking characters." The others were "singing and dancing characters," except Urania who was no more than a "silent character." The most celebrated actors of the time, Marten Corver and Jan

Punt, played the leading male roles of Apollo and Theater. Like Van Gogh's role, each character had its own prescribed outfit. Poetry, for example, played by Mrs. Brinkman, wore a laurel wreath on her head and a sky-blue dress decorated with silver stars. Monsieur van Gogh played Interest, so he was among the singing and dancing characters.

The play was short by our standards; declaiming the entire script probably took about half an hour. Throughout, Interest was merely a background figure. Near the end, Van Gogh had to perform a dance with four other men and five women from the chorus. The only lines spoken during that dance are a monologue by Theater. He opened with this stanza:

> O Batavians, who, within Amsterdam's vast walls,
> Enjoy an undisturbed peace and a free existence
> Who daily demonstrate that the Arts are pleasing thee
> Whenever thou payest them homage in this, their Citadel.

And he ended thus:

> May the war, through unlocking Janus's temple doors
> Never again close this joyful Chorus, as it did before.
> May the enjoyment of Peace always make you discover
> That your opulence is growing, shielded by the palm branches
> Strewn by Netherland's bride, the beautiful Freedom.
> Then, for the good of all, Art will flourish through Diligence.[8]

Jan Punt, the first Dutch actor whose biography would be published, declaimed this pompous verse while a man danced behind him who was to be remembered for stabbing his loved one to death.

Among the audience, opinions were divided. The play's reviewer echoed the criticism of some learned spectators who had noted that Apollo's part was at times incongruent with Greek mythology. The critics found two scenes outright "ridiculous." In the second of them, Apollo and The Year descended from the sky in a cloud, while Theater made a bombastic comment on this event. Theater's role in this scene reminded many spectators of a minstrel at a fair, who holds up a picture and then explains what it says.[9] Thus, the objection of the critics was that high culture looked too much like low culture here. Minstrels who frequented marketplaces and fairs customarily put up a sheet depicting the episodes of their story. A helper pointed with a stick to indicate which picture the singer was dealing with. He sang a ballad, for example, or revealed the details of a notorious robbery or murder. Remember that Dora heard a street singer announcing the tale of her own crime. Historians have debated the supposed withdrawal of the elites from popular culture in the eighteenth century. Some insist that the extent of this withdrawal has been exaggerated. Indeed, we can imagine that educated Amsterdamers occasionally stopped to listen to a street singer. Otherwise, how could they have known about this type of performance? But the educated wished the two cultural spheres to remain separate. When the companion of Apollo in the temple of the Muses resembled a market artist, it was an occasion for ridicule.

The critics may yet have left in a mild mood. Because of the jubilee, the theater's regents treated the public to cakes and tea with milk. Liveried servants continually served new plates. The rumor went that the regents had purchased one hundred pounds of cake and eighty liters of milk, and they had rented three hundred cups and saucers from a Jew. No disorder was reported, although some people said that a large part of the porcelain was broken, which obliged the regents to pay the owner an indemnity.[10]

The Jubilating Theater played nine times altogether, with the last performance on February 7.[11] About ten days later Van Gogh wrote a letter of resignation to the theater's regents.[12] It is almost as if his role in Pater's play made him weary of acting. His motives remain unrecorded. We also do not know whether he stopped immediately or his resignation was meant to be effective at the end of the season, in early May. Was he still present on Thursday, April 21, when all the women and men of the chorus line concluded the evening with a dance?[13] One more source provides a bit of information on Van Gogh's acting career. A poem attributed to him was published at the occasion of his execution. The anonymous owner of the copy that now survives in the Amsterdam University Library wrote on it with clear black ink: "former actor with the traveling troupe and at the old Amsterdam Theater."[14] Should we take this order of words to mean that Van Gogh played with a traveling company before the theater contracted him as a chorus player? If not, he may have continued acting after the spring of 1763. As we will see, in the fall of 1772 he was still consorting with actors.

More important than the length of Van Gogh's acting career was the influence of the social milieu of actors on his character formation. His tortuous life, his stormy love affairs, his excessive romanticism—no doubt, the roots lay in his years on stage. Although in the 1770s he was probably influenced by novels as well, the passionate atmosphere of the theater and the simple romanticism of some of the plays performed there made the original imprint on his personality. Even in 1775, several people noted his theatrical manner of speaking. And on that fatal evening, when he insisted that he read his passionate plea aloud to Annie and her neighbors, he imagined himself acting in a drama. Finally, his less than honorable status as the fiancé of a prostitute more or less matched the ambiguous social status of actors.

The status of actors partly depended on where they played. The Amsterdam Theater stood at the top in a hierarchy of playing sites. The Hague, Leiden, and Haarlem were the other cities in Holland with a theater, while Rotterdam would get one in the tumultuous years after the Amsterdam fire. Smaller places hosted traveling companies in barns or tents, or the performance took place in the open air if the weather allowed it. Some traveling companies consisted of foreigners; there were French, Italian, German, and English troupes who, like street singers, performed mostly during fairs and markets. But even actors under contract in Amsterdam traveled around, from mid-May until mid-August. Their wages covered the theater season only. Some actors, who had part-time work as engravers or booksellers, concentrated on these activities during the off-season period. The others constituted the summer company, traversing the country and usually playing the same repertoire as in Amsterdam.[15] The traveling troupe joined by Van Gogh may have been such a summer company.

A few actors, then, were semiprofessionals. An actor who owned a bookshop derived his social status primarily from his business. The status of those who lived fully by acting was lower the more their company traveled around. The proliferation of journals and almanacs devoted to theater, from the 1760s onward, points to a growing interest in acting as well as its increasing association with high culture.[16] As persons, however, actors became fully accepted only in the nineteenth century. Until then, though well-known figures, they were outsiders of a kind. A respectable middle-class family would never consider welcoming them into its inner circle of acquaintances.[17]

In part because of this social exclusion, actors constituted a close-knit group. In Amsterdam in the 1770s, two taverns had them as their principal clientele—and debtors.[18] Actors and actresses routinely intermarried. Mrs. Brinkman, who played the role of Poetry in *The Jubilating Theater*, was the wife of Gerrit Brinkman, actor and stage master, who perished in harness in the 1772 fire. If a play included a child's role, the young son or daughter of an acting couple appeared on stage. Such practices gave rise to actors' dynasties. According to one contemporary, they were nearly all interrelated.[19] The husband and wife also had an economic motive: a double income. As another contemporary remarked, an actor's wage hardly allowed one to live comfortably, in particular if you had to support a family on it.[20] Was it just calculation, then, when Monsieur Nieri, the ballet master, married the prima ballerina, Mademoiselle Monti, in May 1763? The marriage surprised many, since Nieri's friends said his feelings had been quite different a few months before.[21] Alternatively, this episode suggests that quickly switching passions was common in the milieu of actors. We will observe this as a characteristic of Van Gogh, as well.

Two contemporary works—the biography of the famous Jan Punt, published two years after his death, and the reaction to this book by his erstwhile colleague, Marten Corver—provide an impression of the life of actors in the 1760s and 1770s. Corver, the younger of the two, had left Amsterdam to become the chief director of The Hague's theater. Punt's biographer, Simon Styl, repeatedly emphasized that his protagonist's acting methods were far superior to those practiced in The Hague. This prompted Corver to publish a book refuting Styl's arguments.

One episode in particular gives us a glimpse of the emotional style linked to the world of acting and the theater. As Styl admired his protagonist, he wrote very movingly about the women in the latter's life. Jan Punt, born in 1711, first married the actress Anna Maria de Bruin. She died in 1744, when two of their children were still alive. Punt's second wife, whom he married in 1748, was the daughter of an art dealer. All of their children died young, and in 1771 their mother followed them. Punt observed a period of mourning, and on April 5, 1772, the actress Catharina Elizabeth Fokke became his third wife. We are definitely in a romantic age now. A few days after the wedding, bridegroom and bride appeared on stage as Pedro and Agnes in *The Crowned One after Her Death*. The audience was moved to tears: Love had bestowed youth on the newlyweds. He looked as if in his prime, and she reminded many of the graceful Anna Maria de Bruin. Classically oriented spectators saw, rather than Pedro and Agnes, Orpheus bringing back Eurydice from the valley of shadows. Alas, the flames of May 11 would soon destroy their happiness.[22]

The skeptical Corver refused to be moved in retrospect. He had stayed in The Hague, ignorant of the play and the audience's ecstasy, but "Orpheus and Eurydice—ridiculous! Punt was sixty-two at the time and his third wife forty-five."[23] The spectators who recalled Anna Maria de Bruin, it should be added, were at least middle-aged themselves. Van Gogh had no remembrance of Punt's first wife, since he was a child when she died. If he was among the audience, the parallel with Orpheus and Eurydice eluded him. But he would have felt at home in the romantic atmosphere surrounding him. His own infatuations were magnified versions of the scene that moved the theater's audience to tears. It is very likely that Van Gogh developed his romantic state of mind during the years he played on stage. The acting milieu was Janus-faced. Connected to high culture, it was yet unable to shake off the traditional association with wanderlust and libertinage. It bordered on the sphere of dishonor, which shaded off into the world of prostitution. At the same time, actors embodied the cultural revolution going on, in so far as they embraced the sentimentalism and romanticism that were the new fashions of the age. Van Gogh represented both sides of the Janus medal.

Nevertheless, Van Gogh started another career, that of surgeon. Perhaps he was already preparing for it while he acted in the theater. The registers of the surgeons guild mention a Jan van Gogh from Amsterdam, who started his apprenticeship in November 1760 and became a journeyman with the same master two years later.[24] We cannot be sure, though, that this Jan is our man. If he is, his registration as a surgeon's apprentice was actually his first mention in the historical record. Either way, it does raise the question of Van Gogh's education, about which little information is available. He knew enough German and French to do translation work. But his Latin was awful; the opening lines of his blood letter to Annie would make a schoolmaster panic. Among sailors, however, there was no need for correct Latin. Van Gogh's second career took him to the sea. It remains undocumented where he went and when. We only know that he made several voyages as a ship's surgeon from the middle of the 1760s onward. Quite likely, he was away when Donker and Dora were the talk of the town. Van Gogh settled down again in Amsterdam in the course of 1771.

Back in town, Van Gogh continued to practice surgery. If he was the same man who worked as a journeyman surgeon earlier, this had failed to earn him an official license. In that case he had probably left his boss before finishing his term of training. In the 1770s he worked, in his own words, as an interloper.[25] Even licensed surgeons were a group with an ambiguous social status. They had professional contacts with academic doctors, but they performed low-esteemed medical tasks such as cleaning wounds and laying bandages. Traditionally, their work also included haircuts and shaves, which meant that some of them were simply barbers. This situation and the inability to live from his cures prompted Van Gogh to look for still other jobs. Early in 1772 he worked as the clerk or personal assistant of a certain Willem Ockers. For him he translated German and French texts. This job introduced him to a new milieu, that of the lesser known epigones of hack writers like Weyerman and Kersteman.

Partly, the hack writers of the 1760s and 1770s are themselves to blame for our ignorance about their persons. They had the habit of often publishing anonymously. Next to books, they produced pamphlets in abundance and contributed to periodicals. Hundreds of titles survive in libraries, without an author listed in the catalogue. These pamphlets and periodicals contributed a considerable part to bookseller earnings. The risk of a governmental prohibition and subsequent prosecution was one reason why writers often preferred to leave their names from title pages. But they also had a taste for mystification. Notably, hacks loved to attack each other in print without revealing their true identity to their opponent. Van Gogh's patron, Ockers, was involved in such a polemic with a colleague, Nicolaas Hoefnagel. The conflict between them eventually led to the appearance of pamphlets that affected the relationship of Van Gogh and his fiancée.

Hence, both hack writers are involved in our story. Who were they? The first, Willem Ockers, is the more shadowy of the two. His name is absent from repertories or textbooks dealing with the literature of the period. The only work extant in Dutch libraries with Willem Ockers on the title page—a booklet with miscellaneous stories and verses, published in 1784—may have been written by a namesake, and if not, it takes us far from the polemics of the early 1770s. Many considered Ockers an enemy of religion. Yet, he does not appear in Margaret Jacob's *The Radical Enlightenment* nor in a later article by her on radicalism in the Dutch Enlightenment.[26] Perhaps he deserves no place there. We want to know more about this man nonetheless, if only because of the accusation that he imbued Van Gogh with irreligious ideas. Luckily, we know Ockers is the author of several works published anonymously.

According to his adversaries, Ockers had borrowed the radical ideas they despised from the French *philosophe* and physician Julien Offray de la Mettrie.[27] Ockers referred to this *philosophe* sympathetically indeed.[28] In the 1770s, viewed from a European perspective, La Mettrie was one of the lesser representatives of the Enlightenment. Among the educated public in Holland, however, his name probably was better known than in some other countries. People remembered the commotion raised by the publication and prohibition of his *L'Homme-Machine* two decades earlier. In view of his influence on Ockers, one element in La Mettrie's philosophy deserves greater emphasis than previous students of his work have given it. He refused to draw a sharp line between humans and animals. According to him, all creatures showed unmistaken signs of emotion. Among animals as well as humans, these emotions were expressed, not primarily in language, but in behavior such as crying, fleeing, caressing, or singing. In other words, La Mettrie extended the new recognition of emotions, visible in European culture by midcentury, to other species. His philosophy, in contrast to the prevailing theory of Descartes's, provided support for a more positive view of animals.[29] That is precisely the use that Willem Ockers appears to have made of La Mettrie's work.

Animals played the leading role in Ockers's first book, *Amsterdams Honden-Mirakel* (*Amsterdam Dog Miracle*), published in 1766.[30] The owner of the copy that now survives in the library of the city archive wrote with a pen on the front page: "The author is Willem Ockers, a person living in Amsterdam, of very bad conduct, who is known as a Deist." One wonders why this owner bought it in the first place; maybe the title had misled him. The title page announced that the book was a dialogue among five dogs, serving to expose human frailties in a comical manner. It was dedicated to "Signor Magito," who directed a dog circus in a tent at the Amsterdam Butter Market. In comparison with humans, animals do well, the dedication stated. Although animals are our inferiors when it comes to civility, foresight, and knowledge, Ockers continued, they are burdened less by troubles, concerns, and sorrows. These were arguments La Mettrie could have agreed with.

Another book, although published anonymously as well, got Ockers into trouble three years later. He had cleverly exploited the name of a well-known contemporary, the popular poet Lucretia van Merken. In her *David* she had presented a biography of the biblical king in almost four hundred pages of bombastic verse. That book was sufficiently well received for a second edition to appear in 1768.[31] A year later, *De Waare Held* (*The True Hero*) appeared, with van Merken's name printed conspicuously on the title page. It purported to be a poem written to congratulate her on the second edition of her *David*, but its principal theme was an investigation as to whether the king truly deserved to be called a hero.[32] There can be no doubt about its author's identity, since both Hoefnagel and an informant of the Court of Holland named the same man, in the latter's words "a certain Willem Ockers, living in Amsterdam, a dangerous person."[33] Characterizing *The True Hero* as blasphemous, evil, and a desecration of the Bible, the Court of Holland issued a prohibition of this book.

What was blasphemous about Ockers's work? In fact, his only source was the Bible itself, and he scrupulously cited the chapters and verses in question. His appreciation of David, however, was in no way pleasing to Christians. Instead of presenting the king's actions as necessary steps in the history of salvation, Ockers announced he would judge him "in the

Court of Reason." That judgment was negative indeed: David had subjugated defenseless nations, even killing women and children; his military expeditions were motivated not by a love for his people, but by a longing for blood and honor; he had more than one wife. And so on. Moreover, supernatural and unbelievable events, such as slaying a lion and a bear at age thirteen, should have no place in the story of the king's life. Ockers argued all this in an extensive prose introduction. The actual poem followed, every stanza ending with the rhetorical question "is that heroic courage?" Not according to reason was the explicit answer on the last page. His own century, Ockers continued, had made a modest beginning with delimiting the power of church and state. He ended with a call for peace among nations. The obvious conclusion is that this man was a genuine representative of the radical Enlightenment.

It is harder to pin a label on the second hack, whose pen would prove fatal to Van Gogh. Nicolaas François Hoefnagel was an opportunistic man. A later generation remembered him as a political writer, because he championed the cause of the Patriots, who opposed the Prince of Orange, from 1781 on. Although he hardly wrote about politics before that date, he was no less controversial then. Born in the small town of Monnikendam in 1735, he was of the same generation as Van Gogh. Like Ockers, Hoefnagel published his first works in the late 1760s. Having lived in various places, he moved to Amsterdam with his wife and two children in 1770. That was the right step for someone who wished to make money by writing, but soon the city brought him sorrow. In August 1771 his nearly five-year-old son fell from the window of his house and died.[34]

Hoefnagel realized that writing only books would never earn him enough money to support his family. On November 1, 1770, the first issue of *Neerlandsch Echo*, a weekly magazine, appeared. The name betrayed his admiration for Weyerman, the godfather of hack writers, who had published a periodical named *Echo of the World*. Gossip sold well. In a manner similar to modern tabloids, Hoefnagel's *Echo* portrayed well-known and lesser-known Amsterdamers, in particular their vices. Rumors about real or alleged lapses of conduct were Hoefnagel's principal source. Had someone seen this irreproachable husband entering a brothel? Did that ostensibly honest merchant cheat on his clients? Such questions were the subject of each "discourse" as the weekly issues were called, somewhat exaltedly. Of course Hoefnagel carefully omitted the names of his targets, but informed readers knew whom he meant. One of his sympathizers later characterized the *Echo* as a satirical magazine, which exposed unchaste married and unmarried persons, drunkards, and usurers. No one, he said, had ever sued the author, which proved his credibility.[35] The city fathers were less amused. Probably because of the commotion the *Echo* caused, they prohibited it in November 1771.[36] Undismayed, Hoefnagel continued the periodical under a new name and later under yet another name.

Exposing the vices of seemingly respectable citizens was a sure way of making enemies. One wonders who was angrier: those who felt unjustly accused or those who, deep in their heart, knew the charges were true. There was a market in turn for pamphlets pro and contra Hoefnagel and his magazines. Both sides in this polemic refused to reveal their names, while calling each other thieves of honor. One anti-Hoefnagel verse ended bluntly: "So you, libeler, finally get what you deserve. You, who did not mend your ways after the deadly fall of your son."[37] This verse as well as a pro-Hoefnagel one was printed in placard format, thus meant to be posted up, in taverns for example. Depending on the preferences of his clientele, a landlord could take his pick. An especially severe attack on Hoefnagel came from a pamphlet writer who called himself a gentleman from North Holland, pretending to live in his target's native town. In fact, this anonymous author was Willem Ockers.

A pamphlet war now started, into which Van Gogh was drawn later. Information about the activities of our main protagonists comes from these very pamphlets, which complicates the matter a little. We are constantly faced with accusations and counteraccusations, first between Ockers and Hoefnagel, then between Hoefnagel and Van Gogh. With one man's word against the other, it is often hard to reconstruct a plausible course of events. The easiest way out is to regard every source as a mere "text," to be analyzed as a narrative and nothing else. We must resist that temptation. After all, these sources with their unmistaken biases reported about animosities that eventually led to homicide. The web of events that ended so tragically has to be carefully untangled.

Ostensibly, Hoefnagel's magazine had offended Ockers by unfavorably portraying a relative of his, but professional jealousy undoubtedly played a part in his attack. The *Echo*, the gentleman from North Holland prophesied, would soon serve to pack cheese and smoked meat. Although the great Weyerman, in his similarly named magazine, had equally made fun of people, he at least had brains. The brunt of Ockers's attack was personal. He claimed that Hoefnagel had tried several trades without success and finally became a writer of the lowest kind. His aim was to make a living by destroying the reputations of decent people. He is married "in his way," Ockers continued, and his wife is a little crazy, especially in summer. Their little son has dropped dead from the window, which was best for the child anyway. Here Ockers was competing in bluntness with the poet just cited, unless he had written that verse as well.³⁸

Hoefnagel reacted with the publication of a twenty-two-page "Defense."³⁹ He acknowledged his authorship of the *Echo* and admonished his various opponents to reveal their names as well. Ignorant yet about the identity of the gentleman from North Holland, Hoefnagel scornfully rejected the incriminations against his person and his family. Did "married in his way" mean living with a whore? If so, it was a scandalous allegation. He and his wife lived together in happiness, and their marriage was perfectly legal. All Hoefnagel's opponents were infamous hacks themselves. Not he but they robbed another man of his honor out of lust for money. In this pamphlet war, honor had become a cheap commodity, to be mutually stolen on each occasion. In the last paragraph of the "Defense," Hoefnagel suddenly turned against the "monsters who write irreligious works, attempting to persuade their readers to become atheists." Apparently, he had a hunch who his adversary was, but he lacked complete certainty.

March 1772 brought good news for Hoefnagel's enemies. They learned that night watchmen had arrested him for making trouble in a tavern. He had broken a lot of glasses, and the watchmen had kept him in custody until dawn. This was a hot subject for another libel, possibly written by Ockers again. He accused Hoefnagel of frequenting bars and sometimes brothels, too. And this hypocrite chided other married men for the same things! He was reminded once more of his son's tragic death. Hoefnagel published a reply in April. His enemies had arranged for the incident to happen, he claimed. Someone had stealthily put heavy liquor into his wine. Occasionally, he went out for merriment with a few companions, he continued, which his wife found all right. More than that, she had done her best to have him released from the watch house.⁴⁰

Later that year Hoefnagel found out that the gentleman from North Holland was Willem Ockers. He revealed his knowledge in September with the publication of a voluminous attack on this "vermin of the Bible and cancer of religion." He received the news about Ockers's authorship from an informant. The informant was Van Gogh.

When Hoefnagel first met Van Gogh, the latter still acted as his patron's faithful servant. In fact, Van Gogh visited Hoefnagel at Ockers's request. This was shortly after the publication of the "Defense." Ockers had noticed that this pamphlet concluded with a condemnation of godless writers. He sent two spokesmen, Van Gogh and a German named Peter Weber, to question the author. We have to be content with Hoefnagel's own account of the incident. He came home with a friend in the early evening, saw the two persons at his door, and invited them into his house. Weber spoke first: "Mr. Hoefnagel, I bring you the compliments of Mr. Willem Ockers. He would like to know to whom you refer in your 'Defense' when you say you despise atheist writers." The reply: "I have no obligation to reveal this to you. Anyway, why doesn't Mr. Ockers come and inquire personally?" Van Gogh: "He has a sore leg." Hoefnagel: "Well, I have thrown a stick for anyone who wants to pick it up." Weber was content to leave it at that, but Van Gogh insisted that Hoefnagel disclose whether or not he had had Ockers in mind. When Hoefnagel refused, the disagreement escalated. Van Gogh even tried to slap Hoefnagel's face, but the latter's friend and Weber intervened. These two and Hoefnagel's wife finally managed to reconcile the contestants. They sealed the peace by drinking a cup of coffee and smoking a pipe together. Van Gogh and Weber left without the information they had come for.[41]

What caused Van Gogh to turn against Ockers a little later? Again our information is one-sided, coming this time from one of Hoefnagel's supporters during the 1780s. According to this supporter, a "well-known writer" had employed Van Gogh and paid him well. However, the two drifted apart because of a conflict of opinion. The result was that the writer dismissed his clerk. Van Gogh brooded on revenge. Of course he knew that his former patron had written the pamphlets that attacked Hoefnagel and that the latter still was eager for a confirmation. It was an easy opportunity for revenge, so Van Gogh visited Hoefnagel anew to betray his one-time patron.[42]

The confirmation of his suspicions inspired Hoefnagel to write a frontal attack on Ockers. He wished all the world to know that his adversary was an enemy of religion and mankind. For a modern reader, the most remarkable feature of the tract is that it fails to meet its stated purpose of proving that Ockers is an atheist. There is no philosophical or theological debate, no discussion of specific arguments put forward by the opponent. Hoefnagel "proves" that Ockers is a godless writer by constantly invoking public opinion: Many people consider him an enemy of religion. For the rest, a considerable part of the tract is devoted to Ockers's alleged bad treatment of other people, in particular a bookseller who had first agreed and then declined to publish his attack on King David.[43]

Surprisingly perhaps, Hoefnagel wrote with sympathy about Van Gogh, forgiving him for his rude behavior on the evening they first met. He had acted as his master's faithful servant, which befitted a man of honor. He was a good assistant, but his patron had done him wrong. Worst of all, Ockers had attempted to infect his clerk, raised in the fear of God by virtuous parents, with the pernicious ideas of La Mettrie. This accusation may refer to the conflict of opinion between Ockers and Van Gogh. During his employment Van Gogh had often protected his patron, Hoefnagel's claims continued, when Ockers's bad temper got him into trouble. Not keen on paying his rent, he allegedly had quarreled with two successive landlords and even beaten the first. The second had called for night watchmen once, but Van Gogh had persuaded him, with Ockers already handcuffed, to drop the charges. Afterward Van Gogh had searched the whole town to find someone willing to rent a room to his patron. On recent occasions when Hoefnagel and Ockers met and had a debate, Van Gogh had intervened when he thought his patron talked nonsense. This was all over now: Van Gogh told all honest people that he no longer worked for Ockers. The Almighty had saved the misled clerk at the last moment from accepting his patron's damned philosophy. Hoefnagel was glad for Van Gogh, wishing him never again to have such a master.[44] In September 1772, Hoefnagel could not foresee that a mistress rather than a master would cause Van Gogh's downfall.

Why did Hoefnagel write sympathetically about someone who, after all, had been the assistant of his archenemy? He could have thanked Van Gogh for betraying his master and then dropped him. Of course the sympathetic depiction of Van Gogh served a literary purpose. The portrayal of his own clerk as the innocent victim of his whims underlined Ockers's wickedness. Moreover, as one of Hoefnagel's Patriot supporters explained later, he hoped that his informant would tell him more about Ockers. So for a while Hoefnagel pretended to be Van Gogh's friend. When Hoefnagel expected no further disclosures, he promptly ended the friendship.[45]

Temporary as Hoefnagel's avowed sympathy for Van Gogh had been, the idea that the two were friends proved tenacious. Or perhaps it was revived by Hoefnagel's political opponents in the 1780s. The pamphlet written by his supporter was a reply to an attack, a book from the Prince of Orange's party. In the book, written in the form of a discussion in a barge, the crucial passage has one of the passengers, a citizen of The Hague, suddenly hearing a familiar name. He says: "Hoefnagel, you say Hoefnagel, Mister; I have heard that name more often. . . . Hasn't he been a friend of that Van Gogh who was jailed in our town for a long time? I remember that, whenever there was talk of this fellow, Hoefnagel's name was mentioned too." Another passenger, an Amsterdamer, adds: "Certainly, yes, Van Gogh who has been executed in Amsterdam for killing a girl; that man used to be his bosom friend. . . . Later the two guys went separate ways. They were both hack writers of a kind. The printing press has produced several pieces of trash by these two Seigneurs, which are not worth reading."[46]

That Van Gogh was also a hack writer is an exaggeration. He wrote poems in private and may have published pamphlets against Hoefnagel, but nothing has survived with his name as author on it. For his part, Ockers left the scene after 1772. No one mentioned him any longer in connection with our main protagonist. From now on, the enmity between Van Gogh and Hoefnagel sets the tone for our story.

The process of estrangement between Hoefnagel and Van Gogh probably took some time. A writer (the author of "Truthfull Message," analyzed in a later chapter) sympathetic to Van Gogh mentioned various sources of irritation, at least one of which is a well-attested event. It concerns the collection of money for a widow, whose husband, Pieter Zuiderhout, was the third actor to die within six months after the Amsterdam Theater had burnt down. He was buried on November 11, 1772, aged nearly twenty-six. The collection at his funeral was organized primarily out of sympathy for his widow, the actress Catharina Tithoff. Originating from Corver's troupe in The Hague, Zuiderhout had played in Amsterdam for just one season, and he was unpopular. Van Gogh agreed to collect the money. Nineteen persons contributed, including two regents of the theater, making the total eighty-four guilders. On November 13 Van Gogh handed over the money to the widow in the presence of seven witnesses, among whom were Hoefnagel and his wife.[47] Since Hoefnagel wrote many plays, it is no surprise to meet him among actors. The episode proves that Van Gogh, too, consorted with them, although we do not know if he himself still played as an extra.

The collection's aftermath made Hoefnagel and Van Gogh drift further apart, but to see how, we depend once more on the partisan account by Van Gogh's sympathizer. According to him, Hoefnagel managed with cunning to borrow from Catharina Tithoff almost the entire sum collected for her. Of course he declined to pay it back. In dire straits, Catharina complained to Van Gogh, who wrote a letter in her name and delivered it personally at Hoefnagel's home. He and his wife were furious and still kept the money. Despite this, Hoefnagel managed with sweet words to win over Catharina to his side. Henceforth she preferred his friendship over Van Gogh's. She even denied he had written the letter at her request. For his part Hoefnagel spread the rumor that Van Gogh had somehow benefited from the collection.[48] From this account Hoefnagel emerges as the great villain. Whatever happened exactly, the important effect was that it fostered the enmity between him and Van Gogh.

The year 1773 is a complete blank in the documentation of our principal character. During the next year he was in love. The object of his love was not yet Annie. In view of his passionate devotion to her some months later, the 1774 affair is intriguing. In Van Gogh's romantic mind passion could switch easily from one person to another. Possibly, he had also been attracted to the widowed actress. He was influenced by the transformation in emotional standards going on around him, but he gave it his own peculiar twist.

He had been engaged earlier, some time in the 1760s. Of this episode we only know that either he or his fiancée made a break.[49] The 1774 affair is attested by three independent sources.[50] Of course Van Gogh's sympathizer produced a flattering account. He identified his protagonist's fiancée as Lizette de G., widow of FJN and daughter of a catechist from The Hague. She had misled Van Gogh into believing she was an honorable woman, but he found out that she had served as a high priestess of Venus for no less than twenty-two years. Her sister Eva had been a prostitute, too. The Amsterdam court had committed her to the spinhouse, and now she exploited a brothel in The Hague together with her husband. Disappointed, Van Gogh broke off the engagement with Lizette.[51] Linking this story with the judicial records lends it credibility. A certain Eva de Groot from The Hague, whose sister also lived in Amsterdam, was banished for prostitution in 1760 and condemned to a term in the spinhouse for breaking her banishment in 1762. Born in 1736, she was of Van Gogh's age.[52] Lizette was probably the sister of this Eva, who passed on her dubious reputation to her sibling.

Both Hoefnagel and Annie's biographer claim that Van Gogh defamed his former fiancée after the break. Recalling the affair a year later, Hoefnagel suggestively spoke of "the person you wanted to marry" and of "those you thought were preventing you from doing so."[53] The latter phrase is ominous, in view of Van Gogh's conviction in June 1775 that Annie's neighbors conspired to induce her to dump him. In 1774 he aimed his revenge, still according to Hoefnagel, at his fiancée's advisors, by posting defamatory notes onto bridges and lanterns. Worse, some of the advisors had packets of human excrement delivered to their home. The whole world was convinced that the stinking presents came from Van Gogh. Admittedly, he too had received a packet with excrement and some of the posted notes injured his person, but that was only a clever ruse to divert suspicion away from him. The handwriting on the notes clearly was Van Gogh's, and they were written with red ink, a favorite substance of his. This last remark is again intriguing.

The contrasting accounts of the affair and its aftermath make it difficult to establish Van Gogh's state of mind at the time and, consequently, to evaluate his position vis-à-vis the revolution in love. His sympathizer, who in turn accused Lizette of spreading slander about Van Gogh and his family, made him act according to traditional notions of gender and honor. When he discovered that the woman he courted—or only her sister—had worked as a prostitute, he no longer wanted to have anything to do with her. This is hard to believe. We must assume that within a year he completely reversed his position about courting a dishonorable woman. If, however, we assume that she broke off the engagement because she was tired of his overly romantic attitude, his behavior becomes more consistent over time. In that case, the revenge against Lizette's friends stemmed from deeply felt frustration after a period of romantic infatuation.

Meanwhile, Van Gogh worked for a new patron, an engraver whom we only know by the initials C. P. J. Z. There is no information on the character of the job, except that Van Gogh traveled to Rotterdam for this patron early in 1774. Later that year Hoefnagel published a libel slandering both of them. We know its title ("Voluntary Auction of Some Stately Ladies of Venus"), but unfortunately no copies survive in Dutch libraries. Hoefnagel portrayed the engraver as king of the pygmies and called him "little fellow of seven stone." Apparently, he was a small person. The slander directed at Van Gogh was possibly related to his marriage plans with Lizette.[54]

Finally, 1774 was the year in which Amsterdam opened its newly built theater near the Leiden Gate. Both Van Gogh and Hoefnagel were involved, albeit very indirectly. Hoefnagel revealed his interest in theater in 1774 by publishing a magazine that parodied a well-known journal that reviewed plays.[55] Van Gogh probably still consorted with actors, since Annie's biographer was to introduce an actor as the person who knew him best. The actress Catharina Tithoff, for whom he had collected money, belonged to the company under contract at the new theater. She had remarried shortly before the opening. The entire company consisted of nineteen actors, thirteen actresses, and seventeen musicians and singers. It counted many new faces. In a move that was one of the first manifestations of rivalry between Rotterdam and Amsterdam, the former town's magistrates had decided to build a theater, too, and had invited Jan Punt to become its chief director. Most of his colleagues, temporarily without work, had followed him. They first performed in a provisional accommodation, but in August 1774 the Rotterdam Theater opened its doors.[56]

The Amsterdam opening night was September 15, 1774. The new company performed an allegorical play and a tragedy, while the staff kept a basin with water and a fire extinguisher ready behind the stage. It is unlikely that either Van Gogh or Hoefnagel saw the opening, but several people

An Unsuccessful Career   135

were present, or otherwise involved, who figure in our story. Of course, Catharina Tithoff stood on stage. Lucas Pater, the author of the 1763 play in which Van Gogh had acted, had written an ode for the occasion. Lucretia van Merken, the poet who had inspired Ockers in his attack on King David, was the author of the tragedy performed. She was absent, although invited with her husband and stepchildren. Foremost among the guests of honor were many of the city's magistrates. They included chief prosecutor Dedel who, within a year, was to preside over Van Gogh's trial.[57]

How does the milieu of Amsterdam hack writers compare to its Parisian counterpart as studied by Robert Darnton? A conclusion based mainly on two writers must be preliminary. A few observations are striking nevertheless. Like their French colleagues, Dutch hacks were "poor devils." Hoefnagel and Ockers did reasonably well, but those less successful had to struggle to make a decent living. They probably depended on other sources of income besides writing. Like La Senne or Brissot, the Amsterdam writers operated in semilegality, always facing the risk of prohibition of their books or magazines. Yet the differences between prerevolutionary Paris and prerevolutionary Amsterdam are more conspicuous than the similarities. Although the Republic's rulers grew more intolerant of dissent during the eighteenth century, they never set up a real machinery of control. In particular, they eschewed an active policy of censorship. An author might sell a sizeable number of copies before his book was forbidden. There was no need to print books across the border and smuggle them into the country. When the Amsterdam magistrates prohibited the *Echo*, Hoefnagel smiled and continued his magazine under another name. Both Hoefnagel's and Ockers's arrests by night watchmen were for trivial incidents unrelated to their writing. Darnton emphasizes the intense hatred that French hacks developed for "the system," the established church and the absolute monarchy with its censorship, privileges, and police meddling in writers' private lives. The Dutch Republic had no such system.

Consequently, Grub Street in Amsterdam was a more relaxed place than Grub Street in Paris. Dutch hacks did not automatically acquire an antiestablishment attitude. Radical writers like Ockers restricted themselves to religious and philosophical issues. Until about 1780, hacks showed no particular interest in politics. This attitude changed dramatically during the Patriot movement that followed, when representatives of each party could work safely in their local niche. So instead of writing about the decadence of nobles and bishops, Dutch hacks of the 1760s and 1770s thrived on gossip and the alleged misconduct of middle-class people. Whereas a Parisian writer delighted in venereal disease at court, his Amsterdam colleague looked for fellow citizens who had contracted it. Pornography, which elsewhere served to desanctify church and court, was practically absent from Dutch literature.[58] Nor was the term "philosophical books"—to denote the ensemble of pornographic and radical works—current in the Netherlands. Another favorite pastime of Dutch hacks was to defame each other in print, a habit in which their French counterparts indulged mostly in private letters to their publisher.[59] For their part, the Amsterdam police had no interest in writers' private lives. Hence, they lacked the opportunity of becoming spies, unless they were intimately acquainted with burglars and robbers.

A final difference lies in the importance of honor, to which Dutch hacks were especially sensitive. The word constantly recurs in their writings. Representatives of the French literary underworld, suffering from a psychology of failure and feeling that the system had corrupted them, often deliberately placed themselves beyond the fringe of respectability. They knew they were just canaille. Dutch hack writers, who loved to call others canaille, always claimed honor for themselves. In this, deists and traditional believers converged. Hacks made a living by exposing persons who failed to live up to the ideal of honor. By revealing their secrets, the writers tried to cast them from the domain of respectability. Because hacks were competitors in an uncertain market, their mutual envy and hatred comes as no surprise. Paradoxically, this hatred led each one to accuse the other of plying his trade. One's colleague was always a "thief of honor," wrecking the reputations of his fellow men for his own financial gain. Thus, while each individual writer considered himself honorable, the group of hacks collectively denounced themselves as dishonorable.

The model of honor they cherished was rather conservative: the unblemished husband who supported his family with legal means. That is why swindlers and married men visiting brothels were favorite targets. This housefather ideal gave Hoefnagel an advantage over his two enemies. Ockers was probably unmarried, and we know Van Gogh was. No wonder that Ockers attempted to discredit Hoefnagel with negative stories about his wife and children. As in Paris, less successful hacks constantly feared slipping into the lower reaches of Grub Street. That would mean dishonor for them. Van Gogh surely lived on the edge. If he ever published pamphlets, they cannot have earned him much. His supplementary income from surgery was insufficient also. Moreover, he was acquainted with prostitutes, which made him vulnerable to further public attacks on his reputation. If anyone suffered from a psychology of failure, he did, soon with fatal consequences.

We approach 1775, finding Hoefnagel in a mild mood. For New Year's Day he published a booklet with miscellaneous funny stories, without alluding to concrete affairs this time. Hoefnagel wished all Amsterdamers a happy 1775.[60]

7

An Infamous Infatuation

Anna Smitshuizen was baptized on March 28, 1751, in the Reformed Church of Alkmaar, a small town some forty kilometers northwest of Amsterdam. As only one family with that surname appears in Alkmaar's population records in the relevant period, we are sure it is hers. The fact that her parents had two Annas baptized poses a slight problem. They had conferred the same name on their first child, in February 1744. Their second was a son, born in April 1745. The "child of Gerrit Smitshuizen," mentioned in the burial register on December 14, 1745, must either be the boy or the first Anna. It is reasonable to assume it was the daughter, which led the parents to use the name Anna again in 1751.[1] Moreover, had the later murder victim been born in 1744, it is less likely that she thought Van Gogh too old for her or that her neighbors in 1775 referred to her as a girl. In Amsterdam everyone called her Annaatje, a diminutive for Anna. This conveyed the same sense as Annie in modern English, which will be her name here.

The lower Rhineland was the original home of Annie's parents. Her father, Gerrit Smitshuizen, was born in Xanten, her mother, Jannetje Kluiten, in Meurs. They had followed the footsteps of thousands of migrants who traveled to Holland each year from the western and northern parts of the Empire in search of work. Among them were many young women, looking for employment in domestic service. Jannetje was probably such a lone migrant. She brought no witnesses to the publication of the banns; the record mentioned that her mother lived in Meurs. Bride as well as bridegroom listed an address in Alkmaar, where Jannetje possibly worked as a servant girl. We can easily imagine the young man and woman meeting in this provincial town and, with their shared regional background, becoming attracted to each other. Since Gerrit's father lived in Amsterdam at the time, it means that the bridegroom, too, was independent at an early age. They married in Amsterdam on February 17, 1743, but they remained residents of Alkmaar. Gerrit was twenty-three and Jannetje twenty, a young couple by early modern standards. Apart from the three children already mentioned, they had a daughter in December 1746 and a son in July 1754. On October 18, 1757, Jannetje Kluiten was buried at age thirty-four. Annie was six then.

Whereas Annie's parents occupied the lower edge of the statistical curve of marriage ages, her father was a conformist with respect to another preindustrial custom. It was common for widows and widowers, especially for widowers, to remarry rather quickly. Among the lower-middle classes, family, household, and workshop overlapped. The death of a husband or wife left a vacancy for which the surviving partner had to find a solution. A long period of mourning was a luxury. These economic concerns overrode possible feelings of affection or loyalty to the first partner. Gerrit Smitshuizen was in such a situation. We know he had a wig maker's shop in the 1770s, and he probably worked in that occupation at the time of his wife's death. In any case, he had four young children to care for. Gerrit's second wife was an Alkmaar maiden, Catharina Cramer. They published the banns on December 25, 1757, and married on January 8 of the next year. Catharina's fertility outdid Jannetje's. She bore eight children in all, including two sets of twins. According to the records, only two of her offspring died young. Unless the registration of child burials was incomplete, the Smitshuizens were a large family. Catharina died in childbed after giving birth to the second set of twins, in February 1766. Four months later Annie's father took Bes Pieters van Slooten, a maiden from Hoorn, as his third wife. This marriage remained childless. Bes either was infertile or she successfully persuaded her husband to use contraceptive techniques.[2]

From almost age seven, Annie lived with a stepmother. Soon the latter had her own little children demanding most of her attention. As Annie grew up, Catharina undoubtedly entrusted minor tasks in the household to her. It was a source of irritation now and then. Some said Catharina was too severe on Annie; according to others, Annie was a little slow, which led Catharina, out of parental duty, to admonish her to act more diligently. Contemporaries agreed that children rarely were content with a stepfather or stepmother; the "sympathy of the blood" was lacking. The saying was that a mother would beat her child for a fault, whereas a stepmother would merely chide her child with words; however, the chiding of the second gave more offense than the beating of the first. In this view, the stepparents, dutiful and conscientious, carried no blame, but the stepchildren had a critical attitude. The reality, as revealed in court records, could be different. If a family had children from two beds, this was often a source of marital conflict. For example, a husband reproached his wife that she gave the best food to the child from her first marriage. Annie was a daughter from her father's first marriage. Possibly, her stepmother reproached him for being too lenient toward his daughter. Such conflicts were bound to influence her character development. Perhaps they implanted the idea that she could get her way by setting up people against each other.

Annie got another stepmother when she was fifteen. With her she had less frequent contact, because at a young age she became a domestic servant in the house of an apothecary, close to her parental home. With so many mouths to feed, it is understandable that her father let her go, and she still lived nearby. Getting bored in Alkmaar, however, Annie tried her luck in Amsterdam. She arrived there shortly before her twentieth birthday.[3]

We have moved now beyond the information contained in Alkmaar's population records. As it happens, an anonymous author published Annie's biography about a year after her violent death. It is a fictional account, in the popular form of a conversation in a barge, where several passengers piece together the story of Annie's life. A brief evaluation is necessary. Can we identify its author and, more important, is there any truth in this biography?

In the preface, the author explained his motive for writing the book. Van Gogh, he said, is widely known, due to his extravagant way of life and the extraordinarily long procedures in his case, but hardly anyone knows who Annie Smitshuizen was. The author wished to fill that gap.[4] Attention to the victim set the tone. Without fully condoning her behavior, let alone prostitution, the biography was sympathetic to Annie. It mentioned Van Gogh a few times only, with a negative tenor, which took away all doubts his sympathizer might have had: Hoefnagel had written the biography. Of Van Gogh's enemies, he was the only one diabolic and clever enough to accomplish this. He knew at least something about Annie, because he had spoken to her several times in the spring of 1775. Moreover, he had lived in Alkmaar for some time, and his wife was from there. In the biography, the two most distinguished passengers in the barge were an Amsterdam couple calling each other Frans (or Fransje) and Elisabeth. Although Frans was merely Hoefnagel's second Christian name and his wife was

An Infamous Infatuation 141

called Jannetje, Van Gogh's sympathizer identified the fictional couple as the notorious hack writer and his wife.[5]

Another contemporary source, however, denies Hoefnagel's authorship of the biography. According to this source, the hack writer was away on a trip at the time. After Annie's death he had published nothing about her or Van Gogh's case, even though Van Gogh thought so.[6] With two conflicting voices, it is hard to tell. Some elements in the biography remind the reader of Hoefnagel: the opening, with a condescending depiction of two female Jewish beggars; the mimicking of outlandish speech; the introduction of an atheist, whom Annie despises. For the rest, the book's style is different from Hoefnagel's pamphlets. Possibly he wrote this biography, but we cannot tell for sure.

In a repertory of crime books, Buijnsters, a specialist of Dutch eighteenth-century literature, ascribes Annie's biography to an even more famous hack writer: Franciscus Lievens Kersteman.[7] The basis for this is the book's last page, where passenger Frans says his initials are FLK.[8] It seems to fit perfectly, even though Kersteman's wife was not called Elisabeth. However, his authorship is simply impossible. Annie's biography appeared when Van Gogh was still in jail, thus before April 1778, when he was executed. Kersteman had been imprisoned in Rotterdam early in 1773, and it was only in November 1778 that he was allowed to earn his income with translating work. For five and a half years he had had no pen in his hand.[9] The initials FLK were a mystification by our unknown author. Such mystifications were common. Take, for example, a pamphlet that appeared in the fall of 1773, commenting on the contract some Amsterdam actors had signed in Rotterdam. Its title began with "Rare Dream Dreamt by Master Franciscus," and it identified this man as the heir of the famous astrologer Ludeman. Kersteman was widely known as Master Franciscus and the follower and biographer of Ludeman. As late as 1792, the year of Kersteman's death, the author of a comic almanac found the combination of Master Franciscus and Ludeman attractive enough to put it on the front page.[10] If it was so common to abuse Kersteman's alias, the initials on the last page of Annie's biography have no particular significance. Either Hoefnagel wrote the book or a third hack writer did.

Did the author simply invent Annie's life? At least one firsthand source, Van Gogh's published confession, was available to him and all his contemporaries. The author had a barge passenger occasionally refer to this confession, which made the whole account sound more authentic. He also had information about some events in Annie's life in late 1774 and in 1775, not mentioned in Van Gogh's confession. The latter's sympathizer, while quibbling about the details, confirms that these events took place. For example, both authors agree that Annie had a grandfather living in the old men's home in Amsterdam and that he died a natural death shortly before her violent one.[11] Annie's biographer knew that she grew up with a stepmother, but he was wrong in assuming that her father still lived with his second wife. That is about all. Annie's supposed experiences from her arrival in Amsterdam until she met Van Gogh are unconfirmed by other sources, and they convey the impression of literary invention. In particular, one very long passage about a gentleman who tried to seduce her appears as a figment of the imagination, inserted to give body to the story. Essentially, Annie's biography is a work of fiction.

As long as we realize it is fiction, there is no problem. We can take the story of Annie's years in Amsterdam as an account of how her life might have been, beginning with a statement true for all young women who migrated from a provincial town to the metropolis.

According to Annie's fictional biography, she did not come to Amsterdam with a firm intention of earning her income as a prostitute. To continue in her former occupation was a logical start, and she had hopes of doing better soon. During her first domestic service she lived in the home of her employer, but when the contract expired she looked for another arrangement. The days of traditional, paternalistic relations between masters and mistresses and domestic servants were over in Holland. Many journeymen, too, lived apart from their bosses. Enterprising women specialized in mediating between domestic personnel and potential employers. Female servants often stayed with such a broker woman, going to their place of work in the morning and returning at night. Many girls preferred this arrangement, even though the broker's dwelling was a more humble place than their employer's residence. They enjoyed the freedom. Artisans and other young men frequented the home of the broker woman, which meant ample opportunities for courtship. Although not procuresses, these broker women were of low repute. They encouraged the girls to steal from their masters or mistresses, people said, and on Sundays, when the servant allegedly went to church, she visited her patroness to discuss new intrigues. One of these women contracted Annie, after which one job quickly followed another. The rent she owed to the broker woman was high, however, and she had to take more and more of her linen to the pawn shop.

Annie realized she should leave the mediation circuit, but this was difficult. Precisely because she lacked her own chest of linen, no respectable master or mistress would hire her. It was a catch-22. With dishonorable activities she could earn enough money to retrieve her goods from the pawn shop, but with a dishonorable reputation she was unwelcome in a respectable household. Her neighbors thought her a virtuous girl yet, but already she knew people who cared little about chastity. Hesitatingly, she made her first steps into night life. Shame always diminishes over time, especially if one remains poor. The only way out was to find a procuress who introduced her to a house where girls of pleasure worked. She found such a woman and entered one of the city's secret brothels. Called The English Haystack, it was ostensibly a tavern serving punch, but in the back rooms the clients could take their pick. Annie had the choice of becoming a "young lady" or a "maid." The former type had to be available to everyone, including Walloons, Frenchmen, and Jews. She refused to lower herself that much, so she became a maid. Also to her credit was her sober attitude. She liked brandy now and then, but she only got intoxicated when clients offered her too many drinks. As a "maid," she received no fine clothes from the house, but in simple dress she looked better than many a "young lady." Several clients preferred her over these dressed-up puppets. It caused irritation with the madam, who attempted to win her over to become a young lady after all, in vain. After six months, Annie left the house.

Now Annie had definitely started on a career of prostitution. She traversed the whole city, staying in one house of ill repute after another. These were not classy brothels, so her earnings remained meager. Only occasionally, she had the luck to pick up a strayed libertine, who spent money more lavishly. Poverty diminished her scruples. Soon she offered her services also on Sundays and in houses frequented by Jews. Sometimes, however, she was able to supplement her income with honorable work such as washing or cleaning. Once, she managed to get a job as a domestic servant again, at the outskirts of the city near the Leiden Gate. Unfortunately, the family who hired her found out she had been a prostitute, whereupon they promptly dismissed her. The passengers in the barge, still busy telling this story, understood perfectly the catch-22 situation. The citizen of Alkmaar: "By expelling her, these people cast her back onto the road of vice. I would never have done that; I would have given her a chance, because otherwise I would have felt guilty about her later fate." The gentleman from Amsterdam: "I really don't think so; you would have dismissed her immediately after discovering her previous conduct." The skipper: "That is certainly the most sensible course of action. If otherwise, what would the people in Alkmaar say, Sir, if you had a lady of pleasure in your house?" In late-eighteenth-century Holland, middle-class men were allowed to have sentimental feelings, hoping that a fallen girl might find rescue, but the prevalent code of honor, with its strict demarcations, prevented them from putting their feelings into practice.

During her life of vice, Annie met an older woman from her native town. She had also been a prostitute, but now, approaching fifty, she worked as a charwoman. She had managed to seduce a younger man, a journeyman tailor named Samuel, into marrying her. Samuel had consented out of laziness, hoping his wife could earn a double income. Although also a native of Alkmaar, he spoke with a strange, childish accent. Because the couple was unable to live from her charring, the man had to take up tailoring work. This changed when his wife introduced Annie to their home. From then on Annie stayed with them, adding her income to the ménage à trois. At night, the tailor's wife acted as procuress, praising Annie's charms to interested men. During the day, the wife continued as a charwoman. Samuel could indulge in his laziness now. The three shared the only bed in the room, and when the wife left for work in the morning, you can guess what happened. The tailor's wife pretended ignorance, especially since Annie's earnings started to improve. She could afford nicer clothes now, had several steady clients, and her looks became ever prettier. Even without blanching her face, thus giving it a lighter color, she looked more graceful than ever before. The trio moved to a nicer room in the same house, and they bought a new bed and some furniture. This allowed Annie to receive clients of a slightly better sort. It appeared as if the house would soon become a renowned "pricking place."

Just when business was thriving, discord tore the threesome apart. The tailor's wife no longer concealed her jealousy of her husband's affair with Annie. For his part, Samuel was jealous of Annie's clients. He fell ever more in love with her and resented seeing her receive men in their home. He blamed his wife for the situation. More than once, he threatened to kick her from the room, along with the clients she recruited. Annie gradually took his side, which caused the business to slow down. Regretting this, the tailor's wife scolded her husband and Annie, who retaliated with violence. Samuel swore that, if his lover had to leave, he would go with her. Annie left indeed. For a moment, she thought of trying her luck in domestic service again, but she was too well known as a prostitute to find employment other than in a brothel. Meanwhile, the tailor and his wife got into heavier quarrels, whereupon he finally left her. He rented a room in the Jordaan quarter, where Annie soon joined him. From then on, Annie and Samuel lived together as if they were husband and wife.

As before, it was her task to supply the household's income. Annie alternated offering her services in brothels and visiting a few wealthy clients in

Annie's portrait, from her biography. The artist had probably seen her body displayed in the hospital. Photo: University Library Amsterdam.

their homes. The latter included a wine merchant and a glazier. The tailor, still too lazy to work, had no option but to acquiesce in the situation again. Sometimes, he acted as her pimp. As Annie had started her career in vice as a simply dressed girl, this remained her image until the end. Her whore's name was "Anna the Maid."[12]

This fictional story can be concluded with a look at Annie's portrait, at the frontispiece of her biography. She is dressed like a servant girl indeed, wearing a decent cap, but a portion of her neck is nude. Her face is somewhat chubby. The caption reads: "Anna Smitshuizen, former lover of J. B. F. van Gogh, born in Alkmaar." Perhaps the engraver, like other curious visitors, had seen Annie's body when it was publicly displayed in the hospital before the autopsy. Alternatively, he invented her looks. It is time to return to confirmed events.

A few things are certain. Annie worked as a prostitute during most of her stay in Amsterdam. After The English Haystack, she lived for a time with the widow Sluiter, alias Mother Jeys, a madam from the Jordaan quarter. Annie's relationship with the journeyman tailor is beyond doubt. All sources mention the same address that they shared and the fact that he was married to another woman. Confirming that he and his wife came from Alkmaar, Van Gogh's sympathizer had Annie and the tailor cohabitating since 1774; according to Annie's biographer she met the tailor and his wife as early as 1772. The man appeared in Van Gogh's written and printed confessions simply as "the journeyman tailor." In a letter to his lawyer, Van Gogh once referred to him as Samuel van Beek. Van Gogh's sympathizer mentioned his name twice, calling him Samuel Ramsbeek.[13] This journeyman tailor remains a shadowy figure. Strangely enough, the court never questioned him as a witness, even though he played a key role in the events leading to Annie's death. Was the apparatus of justice unable to trace him? Did they find him unimportant after all? It is one of the mysteries in our case.

When Van Gogh woke up on the morning of Thursday, January 12, 1775, it seemed just another day. Since business was lax, there was no need to rise early. He had some surgery to perform later that day. Van Gogh lived in a simple room in the house of Barend Moreu, near the Rokin in the city center. An artisan who made felt slippers, Moreu was a man of modest means. His wife was illiterate. The couple could use the extra money they obtained by keeping a boarder, and they had empty space available since their three children had left the parental home.[14] Moreu and his wife occasionally did minor favors for Van Gogh, like passing on messages, a common thing to do for boarders. In a sense, the couple acted as surrogate parents. It gave Van Gogh pause for thought: Now that he was approaching forty, what had life brought him? After two unsuccessful courtships, he still lived as a bachelor. His acting career had been abortive, his jobs as a clerk temporary, his surgery without a license. Since he was an unofficial practitioner, procurers and prostitutes constituted a prominent part of his clientele. The appointment he had later that day was in a brothel. Located on a canal called the Oudezijds Achterburgwal, near the Old Men's Home, the brothel was run by a certain Geertruyd van Kesteren, widow of Thomas Wolters, whom everyone knew as Black Truy. The hairdresser, who combed the hair of the beautiful ladies of the house, had recommended Van Gogh to her. He was to give the whores a regular checkup, and sometimes he wrote letters for the madam.

Annie worked for Black Truy from late 1774 onward. She was present in the house that day, probably because she, too, needed a checkup. When she caught Van Gogh's eye, his heart stood still for a moment. Never before, he thought, had he seen such a beautiful young woman. Immediately, irresistably, and totally, he fell in love with her.[15]

In love at first sight—those were his own words. What did it mean to Van Gogh when he said he was in love with Annie? Exactly to feel what he felt, to penetrate his innermost thoughts and emotions, is impossible. We do know his subsequent conduct. He had nothing but Annie on his mind; he did everything only to be in her company. Whenever she seemed to back off, he was sad. He wrote poems for her, of which only a few lines have survived. And he wrote a passionate plea with his own blood to persuade her to marry him. It is obvious that he wanted her and no one else. But if he ever confided his view of true love to paper, it has not come down to us. We depend on contextual evidence about the emotional standards of his day. Contemporary writers defined love as consisting of four elements: the conviction that another person has certain merits; a desire to possess the object of one's love; a feeling of benevolence that causes the lover to do good to the loved one; a longing to unite oneself with the loved one. This was a very intellectual definition and a middle-class one at that. The writers who made it warned that a marriage based on physical attraction alone was doomed to failure. Pure lust led to jealousy and, worse, to crime. The writers favored a "soft passion," agreeing that a stable love thrived on a "chaste flame in the heart."[16] All this sounds much more Biedermeier-like than the heavy and intense passion experienced by Van Gogh. But then, no one is simply the product of his cultural environment. Undoubtedly, Van Gogh was influenced by the emotional standards available to him, but they blended with his personal life experience. Deep down, his feelings of love remain elusive.

We do know that Van Gogh linked love and marriage. He intended to propose to Annie, but he first made inquiries with her colleagues in the brothel. Had he only been aware of the well-known solidarity among whores, a contemporary remarked. They wished Annie the best, so they painted an overly flattering picture of her. Obviously, she worked in the house, but she was a newcomer to vice, they said. A gentleman kept her as a courtesan but on a meager allowance, which obliged her occasionally to supplement her earnings. Believing this, Van Gogh proposed to Annie. He offered to pay her debts to the madam, so that she could leave the brothel and marry him. However, if she decided to consider his proposal, she had to admit that she lived with Samuel. She did and consented on the condition that she would continue to live with Samuel in their room in the Jordaan quarter until May. It was impossible to separate from him at an earlier date, she claimed. Many men would have backed away at this condition, but Van Gogh agreed. To the madam he paid the amount Annie owed her for clothing and rent. At nearly twenty-four, Annie's prospects for raising her social status looked bright.

For his part, Van Gogh realized he had proposed to a prostitute. This step took him to the edge of the domain of respectability. He hoped he could persuade her to lead a decent life. To his own conscience, Van Gogh rationalized his dubious step with reference to his past. Twice he had been deceived by women he thought virtuous. This time, deception was out of the question, since he already knew that his loved one was a whore. To the rest of the world, he was able to claim respectability because he had bought Annie's "freedom" and intended to make her a proper wife. He gave her a written promise of marriage, with a seal of twelve stivers.[17]

Annie's motives to consent to Van Gogh's proposal are more elusive. None of our sources even hints that she immediately requited his love. Possibly, she was motivated by the prospect of becoming a respectable married woman. But was she ever sincere about that? Her insistence on staying with the tailor until May invites suspicion. Was it really so difficult to separate from him right away? On the other hand, Van Gogh had little to offer her instead. Quite probably, paying her debts had already strained his finances. He had no money left to pay her rent if she moved to another place. His own room was too small for two persons, and moreover, living together before marriage meant a bad start on the road toward respectability. It was not simple naïveté, then, which made Van Gogh agree to Annie's condition. Soon, however, he had every reason to worry.

On a day in early March, when Van Gogh was with his fiancée, they heard a knock on the door. Her former madam appeared, accompanied by two big fellows, demanding back two guilders from Annie. She had kept them the other day, Black Truy said, but they belonged to her. The madam had come deliberately at a time when she expected Van Gogh to be in, which was why she had the bodyguards with her. Annie claimed she had taken these two guilders as compensation for a French cap of hers, which got lost in the brothel, but in the end she returned the money. Mad at her former madam, she made Van Gogh promise he would no longer practice surgery in that brothel. For his part, he had to conclude that she, too, had recently been there, but he kept quiet. Later that month, Annie disappeared for three days. Upon her return, she admitted to having stayed in another brothel, called The Rotterdam Purse. To her fiancé, she insisted she had only helped the madam with washing, starching, and ironing.[18] These incidents make us wonder whether Annie ever intended to alter her life course. The tailor was the man she really wanted, which obliged her to keep on earning an income as a prostitute. She had simply been contented to take advantage of Van Gogh in January when he offered to pay her debts to Black Truy, but she did not intend to do a favor in return. Or she used him as a decoy, to ease her family in Alkmaar into believing she was finally returning to the path of virtue.[19] This interpretation makes Annie a rather callous person.

An alternative interpretation is that Annie, although acting primarily from economic motives, was sincere after all. Van Gogh had made her believe he was a man of some substance and dignity, a boon to her. Subsequently, when she discovered this to be a false image, she began to have doubts. Her biographer suggests it happened that way. If we want to believe him once more, it was the tailor, understandably jealous, who opened her eyes. Van Gogh's fine clothes, his self-assured appearance, and his commanding voice had impressed the simple artisan at first. When Van Gogh increased the frequency of his visits to their room, the tailor began to feel uncomfortable. He made inquiries around town, and one day he came home all excited, shouting to Annie, "You thought you were to marry a gentleman? I know him now; he is the man who courted that Lizette last year, a rogue and a naked dog." Supposedly, Annie answered, "He may be a naked dog, but he wants to marry me, while you are keeping me as a whore." That settled the matter for the moment. The tailor kept a low profile once more, because Van Gogh threatened to denounce him to the court as an adulterer.[20] Meanwhile, Annie had celebrated her twenty fourth birthday.

The odd engagement was bound to generate serious trouble sooner or later. When exactly Van Gogh and Annie had their first quarrel is unrecorded. In his words, they drifted apart now and then, but he made peace with her each time, hoping she would mend her ways. While still living with the tailor, she had promised to have no sexual relations with him, but Van Gogh received reports to the contrary. On what intimate knowledge, we may wonder, were these reports based, since everyone knew they shared a room in the first place? In May, when Annie finally left the tailor, the situation failed to improve. She first moved in with a friend, a certain Roelofje Cornelisse, and later with Mother Jeys. Van Gogh did not know that Roelofje was also a prostitute, nor that mother Jeys had kept a brothel. He soon discovered that both were active in the vice trade. Annie simply refused to change her lifestyle, it seemed. Her fiancé reproached her anew; repeated quarrels and reconciliations followed. Van Gogh's suspicions only increased, while his obsession for Annie rose to unprecedented heights. He began spying on her.

On Sunday afternoon, May 21, Van Gogh knocked on Annie's door in vain. She had promised to accompany her fiancé on a tea visit to his cousin. Rather than visiting his cousin alone, Van Gogh waited for Annie until 11:30 at night. The next morning she showed up at his place when his mother was there, so he could only reproach her later. Meanwhile he had ordered a porter to take a fake message to Mother Jeys, that the lady of the house where Annie had been the previous night requested her to be there again at 2:30 in the afternoon. The ruse seemed to work. While Van Gogh was hiding in a bar close to Annie's place, he saw her passing by, dressed up nicely. He followed her at a distance and, indeed, she went straight to that notorious brothel, The Rotterdam Purse in Nes Street. In a small pub at the corner, Van Gogh found another hiding place. He inquired with a few customers if they knew the girl in the white jacket and the red lacey skirt, who had just entered the house at the opposite side. To explain his interest, he pretended to be her cousin, on a mission on behalf of the family acting upon negative rumors about her conduct. Faithfully, some customers replied they had often seen her entering that place but rarely leaving it. To see her leave, in the company of one or more clients, was precisely what Van Gogh was waiting for. As on the previous day, his patience was put to a severe test. At eight P.M. he still stood at his watch post, leaning over the pub's lower door, when an acquaintance happened to pass by. The acquaintance was no less than his inveterate enemy, Nicolaas Hoefnagel.

The writer had decided to take a walk after dinner. He spotted Van Gogh from a distance, while the latter had his attention focused completely on the house on the other side of the street. Van Gogh did not recognize his enemy until he stood right in front of him, and it was too late to turn around. An unpleasant conversation ensued, in which Hoefnagel accused Van Gogh of being the author of a recent libel. He denied this, trying to look past his opponent's face, at the door of The Rotterdam Purse. It was no use. The heated conversation had caused commotion in the pub, and Van Gogh felt obliged to leave his watch post. Once more, he had failed to collect definite proof that his fiancée was continuing in her horizontal profession. When he saw her later, she denied it as usual.[21]

In the same week, the tables suddenly turned. Until then, it had always been Annie's conduct that lay at the root of their quarrels. She had nothing to reproach him for, except that he had pretended to be wealthy. Now his name was all over town. The libel to which Hoefnagel had alluded opened with a dedication to "the myopic lover from the cave of Gog Magog." It was clear to every insider whom this dedication was mocking: "Excuse me, Sir, how did it come about that your third girl already gave you the sack; you know, this Annie, who went with this tailor before. Good for you that you are a quack, because of your blue shin, which you have bumped so blue three times that it can hardly be cured. That happens when you play the great pretender. But may I advise you, if you take another sweetheart, you better confess right away who you are; perhaps she takes you out of pity then."[22] Annie was astonished. It was the first time she realized that her fiancé was a notorious man, and now her name was in print along with his. Annie felt ashamed. She definitely wanted to do what the pamphlet supposed she had already done, but she lacked the nerve to confront her fiancé in person. On Wednesday, May 24, she wrote him a note saying "thank you, but it's over."[23]

As expected, Van Gogh refused to accept the sack. Directly upon receiving the note, he rushed out to see Annie and found her home. He succeeded in softening her heart. The note, she now said, had been a means of testing his devotion to her. That was the kind of quasi-religious language that Van Gogh understood. He saw Annie as a supreme goddess who subjected him to severe ordeals at times.[24] As long as he survived the ordeals, he came out for the better. The next day, Ascension Day, they paid a visit to his mother in the village of Ouderkerk, a few miles from Amsterdam along the Amstel river. To her they formally announced their wedding plans.

The phrase about testing his devotion had its own peculiar meaning in the context of the 1770s. Words like these equally fit into the context of courtly romance, taking us several centuries back. In a courtly novel a noble lady might give an assignment, as a test, to the knight who loved her. But as already explained, for such a knight love did not mean constantly being in the company of the woman he adored. To the contrary, the assignment would often be to fight an enemy of the castle where the lady resided. The knights of courtly romance conformed to the homosocial pattern of life, prevalent for so long. With Van Gogh this was entirely different. Although he had reluctantly consented to Annie's temporary stay with the tailor, he wanted to be in her company as frequently and as long as he could. This was something new—love meant romantic devotion to one's beloved and to do various things together. The observing writers of midcentury had advocated this same kind of love, but expressed in marriage. Novelists, too, were writing about it and the trouble it might cause if there was no prospect of marriage. Van Gogh expressed the new kind of love in a tortuous courtship. That is, he now thought that he and Annie definitely were to become husband and wife.

After the visit to his mother, Van Gogh took the initiative to find a new room for Annie. He needed less time than three years earlier, when he did the same for his patron, Ockers. Already on the 26th he got word about a widow who planned to move to the countryside for a while. He immediately went to see her, accompanied by Annie. When the widow learned that the couple was to marry soon, she promised to make her room available. Later that day, Annie heard that her grandfather had died.[25] This caused a delay in making further arrangements for the room, in one way or the other. Some said that Annie sincerely mourned her grandfather. According to others, she cared little about him and welcomed his death as an excuse. Supposedly, she went straight to The Rotterdam Purse, wearing rented mourning clothes during the intervals when she was not working.

She and Van Gogh had an appointment with the widow on Sunday, the 28th, to set a date for moving into the room. When he came to pick her up at Mother Jeys's, she was not in, which obliged him to see the widow alone. The widow served him a cup of tea, and as they waited for Annie, Van Gogh became confiding. Unfortunately, he explained, his fiancée let him down too often, making him seem a fool. However, he was delighted that she could move into this room. Until now, she had lived with bad people, who set her up against him. Those days were over. Hearing these words, the widow had every reason to be skeptical. After three hours, without Annie appearing, Van Gogh left in distress.[26] Soon he arrived at The Rotterdam Purse for another round of spying. Shortly after midnight he thought he saw Annie leaving the place with three men, but it was too dark to be sure. The next day Annie claimed she had been in the old men's home, to make arrangements for her grandfather's funeral.[27]

On the same day they got word that another acrimonious libel against Van Gogh had appeared. Understandably, it made Annie even more anxious about her fiancé's notoriety. Upon her suggestion or his own initiative, they agreed to refrain from seeing each other for a while. Van Gogh went off to see his brother, who lived in the village of Vreeland, some twenty kilometers to the southeast of Amsterdam, just across the Utrecht border. He promised Annie to stay there for two weeks. Delighting in her freedom, she turned milder toward him, as evidenced by two letters that have survived. The first, dated June 2, opened with "dear friend." She promised to write again, instructing him to address his letters to the room at Barend Moreu's, where she would pick them up. "Don't worry, everything will turn out right," she wrote, referring, no doubt, to the commotion the pamphlets had caused. The heading of the second letter, dated June 6, was "dear lover, J. B. van Gogh." She announced she would soon move into the widow's room "and then I will at once tell you my heart, because I bring over much with me." The words, from the pen of a young woman with little education, sound ambivalent. "I cannot write it to you," she continued, "but trust my word. . . . The note you have sent to be inserted in the newspaper, I like it that you defend yourself, because the whole town is full of it. But the printer cannot do it without a note from the HO. . . . I remain, with respect, your faithful lover."[28]

The pamphlets that had so upset Annie numbered three in all, dated May 10, 19, and 26, 1775. Unfortunately, the first has not survived.[29] From the second, we know that the one of May 10 was a belated reply by Hoefnagel to four "thieves of honor" who had attacked him the previous November. Whatever caused the delay in replying, it had given him the opportunity to change his mind about the engraver whom he had called king of the Pygmies in an earlier libel and for whom Van Gogh had worked in 1774. The engraver suddenly had become an honest citizen, in whose house Van Gogh had shamelessly shown his "calimanco face." Calimanco was a cloth fabric often used to make men's underwear.[30] That is all we know about the first pamphlet's contents. Its appearance probably passed unnoticed by Annie and her fiancé.[31]

The second pamphlet was an anonymous "letter" addressed to Hoefnagel but preceded by the dedication already cited. Obviously, the author knew both Hoefnagel and Van Gogh. They were enemies now, he wrote, but they had been friends and they could become friends again, as soon as it was to their mutual advantage. Strangely enough, the enemies accused each other of having written the pamphlet. According to Hoefnagel, Van Gogh had deliberately mocked himself, in order to make the readers believe the author was someone else. He had performed the same trick with the packets of excrement sent around the previous year. This argument by analogy is hard to accept. Can we imagine Van Gogh so masochistic as to publicly mock his own person and his love for Annie? Moreover, had he been the author, he could have masked this more conveniently by omitting any reference to himself.

Neither is Hoefnagel a likely candidate for the authorship of this libel since it threw nothing but dirt at him. The libel exposed him as a corrupt writer, who first threatened to publish ugly rumors about people and then accepted money for refraining from it—an accusation echoing Weyerman's case. The anonymous author ridiculed Hoefnagel and his pretensions in every possible way. Among other things, he alluded to an ambition that many people knew the writer had cherished: When Jan Wagenaar, the official historian of Amsterdam, died in 1773, Hoefnagel had expected the city fathers to appoint him to this function. His enemies considered it a convincing proof of his megalomania. The libel closed with a verse, calling its target a coward, a rascal, a lunatic, and a host of similar words. Van Gogh never read this pamphlet carefully, obsessed as he was with the opening dedication. Otherwise it is inexplicable that he referred to the whole series of pamphlets simply as Hoefnagel's libels.

The authorship of the pamphlet of May 26 is plain. Its heading read, in large capitals, "reply by Nicolaas Hoefnagel to the baron from the cave of Gog." A long series of epithets followed, referring to past events in Van Gogh's life and, for want of information, mostly unintelligible to us. We do understand fired actor, runner of messages, traitor, slanderer, misshaped cuckold, and presumed dealer of dung. Thinking his enemy had written the libel of May 19, Hoefnagel threw his entire supply of venom at him. He admitted he had always despised Van Gogh, from the moment this man entered his house to betray his patron. With success Hoefnagel managed to outdo the author of the earlier libel in mocking Van Gogh's affair with Annie: "He asks himself how it came about that his third girl gave him the sack. Well, I know the answer to that. I don't believe you can find anywhere in Europe such a dirty Venus nymph who has a soul lowly enough to marry the slanderous Doctor Cobbler. I even trust that the most vulgar shivering ladies, who cruise the streets on a Winter night with a little fire pot under their cotton dresses, consider themselves too good to mingle with this mender of old trousers."[32]

The libel further dealt with the various allegations made in the preceding one. Hoefnagel denied them all. He was angry in particular at the suggestion that he extorted money from people under threat of publishing about them. Van Gogh hoped to become a writer, Hoefnagel continued, but he would never succeed. In vain, he had tried to get some poems published. Other passages referred to episodes in Van Gogh's past, in particular one during his period as a ship's surgeon: On the isle of Curaçao they had falsely taken him for a murderer; the scaffold had been erected already when everything turned out to be a great mistake. The court there would have done the Republic a great service, Hoefnagel added, if they had ordered Van Gogh broken on the wheel. As yet, the hack writer was ignorant of just how ominous his words were.

The series of libels had dealt a serious blow to Van Gogh's reputation. In the idiom of honor, he stood on the wrong side of the line now. Until May 1775, Amsterdamers knew him as a clerk for hack writers and minor artists, while they remembered his affair with the notorious Lizette. From now on, they associated him fully with the infamous world of prostitution. He had willingly proposed to a prostitute, and she had only made a fool of him. Even the ugliest whores scorned him—such a vivid message caught on. Furthermore, he was an impecunious interloper, a bungling amateur in several occupations. His desperate attempts to become a poet or writer were doomed to failure. It was a highly unfavorable image, and Van Gogh did little to improve it. There is no indication that he ever managed to publish a defense. Although Hoefnagel's other enemies were less inclined to share his view of Van Gogh, a large part of the public adopted the negative image. Most important, his public humiliation fueled Annie's doubts about the engagement.

The break was not final yet. On June 8, Annie moved into the room that her fiancé had arranged for her. The address was along a canal, the Herengracht, an unlikely place for an ordinary girl. Although eighteenth-century Amsterdam knew no segregation into class-based neighborhoods, the Herengracht was inhabited chiefly by rich burghers and patricians. It contrasted markedly with the Jordaan quarter, where Annie had lived with the tailor. However, although she moved to a better place, she did not live far above her rank. Each part of an Amsterdam house had its own status. The ground floor, a meter or so above street level with a stone stair leading to the main door, was the "front stage." As one moved up to the attic, the apartments increasingly had a "backstage" character. Many upper floors were divided into sections, with whole families crowding into one small room. Annie moved to such an upstairs room. The house stood at the corner of an alley, with a shoemaker occupying the first floor. Annie's room was on the front side of the attic, which also had a back room. In between lay a small corridor leading to the stairway. There was a door between the attic and the stairway, which could be locked from the inside. Incidentally, the house was only a few blocks from the site of the old theater in which Van Gogh had acted.

156   Chapter 7

House in which Annie's attic room was. Eighteenth-century Amsterdam had no house numbers, but this is the most likely site. The house was rebuilt in the early nineteenth century. Photo: Pieter Spierenburg.

Paradoxically, in this house selected as a safe haven, Annie and Van Gogh drifted further apart. In that process, her neighbors played a crucial role, which calls for a brief introduction. The only man among them was Teunis Jansen, a porter. He will be called by his first name, a typically lower-class variant of Anthony. Next, there was his sister, Maria Jansen, widow of Willem Jager. Teunis and his sister shared the back room opposite to Annie's, being the oldest occupants of the attic. The third person was Truy, in full Geertruy Elisabeth Muller, widow of Pieter van der Loos. She lived around the corner and worked as a charwoman, which brought her to Annie's room almost daily. Her adolescent daughter, Johanna Helena van der Loos, often assisted her. So we have Teunis, his sister, the charwoman and her daughter, and . . . the widow who had occupied Annie's room. Already on June 23, she returned to the city. The records do not disclose where in the countryside she had been, but clearly she was dissatisfied with the place. With her former room taken by Annie, she moved in with Teunis and his sister in the back room. Her full name was Dina Eykens, widow of Dirk Stroom. She will be referred to as the widow, which the court clerk did as well, even though two of the other women shared that status. She, the charwoman, and Teunis were able to write their names, although the latter signed somewhat clumsily. Teunis's sister and the charwoman's daughter were illiterate.[33]

Van Gogh had promised to stay with his brother in Vreeland for two weeks. During this period, Annie moved into the room at the Herengracht. There is an ambiguity in the records as to the date of her fiancé's return to Amsterdam. A statement by his landlady suggests it was rather soon. She was talking to Van Gogh in his room some time after Pentecost, she said. When she saw a knife with a white bone handle lying on a chair, she recognized it as one of the sharp knives with which her husband cut felt. Asked why it lay in his room, Van Gogh replied he had permission to take it. He had lost his own knife while traveling to Vreeland. Ever since he had been at sea, he was accustomed, like a sailor, to always having a knife with him. From then on, Van Gogh carried the felt cutting tool in his pocket, ignorant yet about its final use.[34] Pentecost was on June 4, so the landlady's dating suggests he returned to Amsterdam shortly after Annie moved to the Herengracht. Van Gogh himself, on the other hand, said he returned from Vreeland on June 24. Significantly, all events in and around Annie's room for which we have exact dates occurred from the 24th onward. The number of undated incidents, however, suggests Van Gogh also was in Amsterdam in mid-June. Probably, his return on the 24th was from a second visit to his brother.

While living at the Herengracht, Annie continued to see her former lover, the tailor. Self-assuredly he visited her in the room where her fiancé thought her safe. It was a source of repeated conflicts. Sometimes the tailor appeared when Van Gogh was there or vice versa. When the two rivals stumbled upon each other, they always quarreled. Twice, Van Gogh beat the tailor. It was of little help, since Annie obviously still favored him. She even managed to make her fiancé agree to a peculiar solution. They drilled a little hole in the door of her room, into which they put a small wedge. Whenever Van Gogh came upstairs, he removed the wedge to see if the tailor was there. If he noticed a man in the room, he was to back off. It was an ingenious idea from Annie, since it facilitated receiving other men as well. She continued working as a prostitute, for which Van Gogh, suspecting this, reproached her time and again.[35] How else could she have paid her rent and the charwoman? There are no indications that Van Gogh paid it. He was even more upset when he noticed that Annie's neighbors started to side with her. They prevented him from contacting her, usually saying she was out.

Annie's relationship with Teunis and his sister remained distanced for a while. They were often away, he in his porter's station and she doing washing and starching in other people's homes. Annie first confided in Truy, the charwoman, who came to clean her room every day. Truy could not help noticing that the engaged couple often had words, especially when she wanted him to leave and he refused. After one of their quarrels, when he had finally left, Annie talked to the charwoman. She admitted she disliked the idea of marrying Van Gogh, for which she gave three reasons. He was a little too old for her, he lacked a proper job, and he had a bad name. With the last she referred to his tarnished reputation as a consequence of Hoefnagel's libels. There was little Van Gogh could do to change it. He could do nothing about his age, fifteen years older than she, but never mentioning it, he refused to see it as a problem. To the question of how to earn a proper income, they had found an answer. The idea was to move to Alkmaar, where Van Gogh would assist Annie's father, now fifty-five, with wig making. That is, Van Gogh thought they had agreed on this; he even envisaged them eventually taking over the shop. Given her attitude, it is unlikely that Annie ever intended this seriously.[36]

On Saturday, June 24, Van Gogh returned from a visit to his brother, entering the town with the opening of the gates. Because he thought it too early to visit Annie himself, he asked his landlady to go ahead. When she arrived at eight, she found Annie sitting at the coffee table in her nightgown, with a "caddishly clad fellow" beside her. Although Annie tried to make the man understand he should leave, he was still there when Van Gogh arrived half an hour later. Incidents now quickly followed each other. The next Monday morning Annie and Van Gogh, reconciled once more, went out shopping together, while the charwoman cleaned her room. Just as they returned, the tailor walked down the attic stairs. Van Gogh immediately seized him by his coat, asking him what business he had up there. He replied he had wanted to speak to the young lady. Annie preferred to flee to the street, while her fiancé started another fight with his rival. With his hands or with words, he persuaded the tailor to leave. Then Van Gogh vented his anger on the charwoman, who first refused to open Annie's door and, when her daughter did, allegedly hurled at him, "I shit on you." While mother and daughter attempted to push Van Gogh out of the room, Annie returned. Of course she succeeded in softening his heart again.[37]

Not for long. In the afternoon of the following day, Tuesday, June 27, the widow sat alone in the back room. Half asleep, she suddenly woke up from a loud noise. She heard yelling and furniture tumbling in the front room and went over to see what happened. First, Van Gogh caught her eye, moaning and crying. Annie had said a thousand awful things to him, he complained, and then she had severely beaten him with tongs. He had done nothing to her. The widow's entrance only encouraged Annie to continue scolding her fiancé, challenging him to beat her with the tongs in turn. He refused. Instead, he requested the widow to plead for him with Annie. As the widow had no idea what to say, it was again Van Gogh himself who tried to hush her up with sweet words.

It was simply a bad day for him. A little later, with the widow still present, someone knocked on the door. The widow noticed Annie shuddering, and indeed it was the tailor. He walked straight to Van Gogh, knocked him on the chest and asked, "Do you want to come with me?" Interpreting the invitation as a challenge to some kind of duel, Van Gogh replied this did not suit a man of his standing. He ordered the tailor to leave the room, but the latter refused to back off so easily. It was time for another plea to the widow: "Madam, please, take my side, for this is a married man; his presence here is improper." Without a reaction from her, another fight between Van Gogh and the tailor ensued. As they were wrestling, Annie slapped Van Gogh in the face. Then the widow finally intervened and persuaded the rivals to stop fighting. To seal the peace, all four of them drank a cup of tea together.[38] This was a respectable imitation of the reconciliation ritual common among knife fighters, who instead of tea shared a jug of beer or wine in a tavern. Van Gogh, though he had a knife, was no knife fighter.

From the various incidents recorded, the widow emerges as the most neutral person vis-à-vis the quarrelling couple. This is understandable, since she was around for less than a week. The charwoman and her daughter were the first to side with Annie in trying to rebuff Van Gogh. Teunis and his sister, not fully in the picture yet, were to confront Van Gogh on the fateful day of June 29. No doubt, the quintet was motivated by their understanding of neighborly assistance. They had concluded that Annie was unhappy with Van Gogh, so they wished to help her in keeping him out of her way. They sided with their neighbor against an outsider, as millions of preindustrial villagers and city dwellers had done before them.

Perhaps Van Gogh, as a modern individualist, was ignorant about traditional neighborly assistance. He experienced the quintet's actions as a deliberate conspiracy. He thought that, deep in her heart, Annie really wanted to marry him, but that her neighbors incited her to the contrary. His naïveté was plain already, but we have to conclude that he was also a little paranoid.

Van Gogh's sympathizer, who wrote about his case later, faithfully adopted the idea of a conspiracy, referring to the quintet as "the *cabale*." He added a number of unsubstantiated accusations. Teunis, for example, supposedly wanted beautiful Annie for himself. He got hold of copies of the libels, about which he made jokes in her presence, which increased her dislike for Van Gogh.[39]

Van Gogh was more than just naive; he was a naive romantic. He voiced his romanticism most tellingly in the document he wrote with his own blood on the night of June 28, with which this book began. The likely source of his attitude to love and life—his experience with the world of actors—has also been discussed. Yet, still another source has to be taken into consideration. Van Gogh's romantic longings inevitably remind us of the literature of his day—not the work of the hack writers he knew, with all their cynicism and ultimate respect for bourgeois values, but the sentimental novels that were the new fashion of the age. English writers, such as Richardson and Sterne, enjoyed great popularity in the Netherlands. Two Germans, Goethe and the Reverend Johann Martin Miller, would soon take the lead. The latter's sentimental novels, published between 1776 and 1780, came too late to inspire Van Gogh's love for Annie. What about Young Werther?

No probate account of Van Gogh has survived and, in any case, probate accounts seldom specified the titles of books. We can only speculate about Van Gogh's reading habits. Possibly, he was familiar with Richardson's novels. *Clarissa* was well known in Dutch translation. The publisher of the Dutch translation of Goethe's *Werther* advertised the book as an enjoyment for tender hearts, comparable to *Clarissa*.[40] The Dutch edition of *Werther* appeared in 1776, and it took a few years before the book became popular in the Netherlands. Van Gogh can only have read *Werther* in the original German edition, which came out in the fall of 1774. He knew German well enough. Without a craze yet to draw his attention to the book, he possibly discovered it out of an interest in this type of novel. His romantic personality makes such an interest plausible. Later critics of *Werther* complained that sentimental readers completely identified with the main character. No doubt, Van Gogh conformed with their view. Like Werther, he felt an intense and pure love, impossible— although for other reasons—to come to fruition. In his blood letter he spoke of the sentence of life or death, proclaiming his wish to die if Annie no longer wanted him.

The observing writers from the middle class, guardians of respectability, espoused an ambivalent attitude toward sentimental novels. They wavered between admiration and concern. Since the 1760s they positively valued tears and expressions of sentiment, in their own peculiar variant though. The philanthropist, moved by compassion for the miserable, was their true hero. They advocated a responsible and restrained sensibility, that of the mature man who ultimately controlled his passions. The cult of sentiment inspired by contemporary novels, these moralist writers warned, could easily lead to excess. Sensibility might degenerate into malady. Although women were particularly susceptible to this danger, the malady caught young men, too. They developed an unhealthful preoccupation with writing love letters or composing sentimental poems about nature and death, they lost all sense of reality, they firmly intended to commit suicide when their love had turned hopeless, and all the while they did nothing to assist the really needy. That was the wrong type of sensibility. As a source of such excesses, moralists condemned *Werther* in particular. Its protagonist failed to control his love feelings, and he indeed killed himself in the end.[41]

Van Gogh was no longer a young man. When they thought of excesses, the observing writers never had someone like him in mind. Van Gogh was one individual among his contemporaries. The uniqueness of his case lies in the peculiar combination of old and new elements. He partook of the new sentimentalism of his day, which meant that he embraced cultural modernity. The object of his unconditional love, however, was a prostitute. This linked his case to traditional notions of honor and respectability, certainly in the eyes of average Amsterdamers. Whereas the newest literature was a source of inspiration for his love, his crime would generate the usual, age-old warnings about whores leading men onto the road of vice. For their part, sentimental novelists avoided this peculiar combination of old and new. Their heroes and heroines, however strong their passions and however abundant their tears, remained gentlemen and ladies.[42] We have to return to the world of actors to find sentimental persons of a less elevated standing.

One more intriguing parallel exists between Werther's love and Van Gogh's love. Werther and Lotte, his friend's wife, obviously had no sexual relationship. About sex between Annie and Van Gogh the records are equally silent. As her sincerity about the engagement is doubtful, we may also doubt whether she ever wished to sleep with her fiancé. They never lived together, whereas she was living with another man during most of the time they were engaged. In June, according to the testimony of Teunis and his sister, Van Gogh visited Annie almost daily, but the two neighbors always saw him leave at night.[43] To his mother and his landlady, he introduced her as a decent girl, which to them meant a virgin. The possibility remains that, while keeping up appearances, Van Gogh secretly had sex with Annie a couple of times. The only allusion to sexual contact is the passage in his blood letter stating his conviction that she was pregnant with his child. The court ignored this passage, and he himself never raised the issue again. Annie's autopsy report mentions nothing about a pregnancy. Quite probably, it was just a fantasy he indulged in on the night he wrote the letter.

Van Gogh had a medical reason to be reticent with pressing for sexual contact. He suffered from a condition that contemporaries loosely denoted as a *breuk* (rupture). They meant a kind of hernia, a rupture of tissue in the abdomen or groin, from which men suffered in particular. An operation was very risky, and physicians as well as surgeons shrank from it. Only self-styled masters in this art offered their services at fairs. Even a successful operation had its consequences, as the author of a textbook published in 1733, made clear. He proudly described his technique for treating a rupture without removing the testicles. In some cases, however, castration was unavoidable. Without a successful operation, his condition caused the patient no less trouble. Because of the malfunctioning of the tissue, the bowels tended to sink, pressing down the scrotum, which sometimes hung on the patient's knees.[44] Obviously, this disease was a severe handicap to sexual intercourse. Van Gogh had incurred two such ruptures during his last voyage. They had robbed him of three-quarters of his former strength, obliging him to avoid any exertion.[45] In June he lay ill for a few days, because "both his ruptures had opened up."[46] When Annie heard about it, she rushed to his bedside to comfort him: an easy opportunity to be nice without having him meddle in her affairs.

On Thursday, June 29, 1775, Van Gogh got up early in the morning. He had gone through a sleepless night. His eyes were fixed on the drawer containing the letter he had written with his blood. The moment of truth had come. Now he must read the letter to Annie and hear her pronounce either the decision to spare his life or his death sentence. He had no idea it would take him the whole day.

At 8:30 in the morning Van Gogh arrived at the house on the Herengracht for the first time that day. Finding the front door open as usual, he hesitated for a moment. Then he went inside. When he climbed the stairs to the attic, Teunis and his sister awaited him, saying Annie was out. They took Van Gogh into their own room, where he insisted on waiting for her. At nine o'clock another person came upstairs, a woman named Johanna Leeman. She owed money to the widow, who occasionally made caps for her, and she had some business with Annie. Let us consider the next events from Johanna's point of view. As she approached the door of the back room, she glimpsed a hand closing it from the inside. When she identified herself, the person opened the door again and, to her surprise, Van Gogh let her in. She inquired into the whereabouts of the widow and if they knew Annie was in. They were both out, Teunis and his sister replied. The sister made a quick signal indicating she should wait. Then Van Gogh left. A little later, someone opened the door of the front room slightly, and a voice asked, "Is he gone?" Now they admitted Johanna into the front room, where she met the widow, Annie, the charwoman, and her daughter. When Johanna started to argue with the widow about the price of the caps, Teunis's sister admonished them to be quiet, because Van Gogh might come back. They continued their negotiations in the back room, where the two other occupants joined them.

Later that morning Van Gogh returned. He walked straight to Annie's door and removed the wedge from the hole in it. Thinking he wanted to force his way in, the watchful Teunis approached him. He warned Van Gogh to refrain from using force, or else he would have to throw him out of the house. Van Gogh explained about the hole and the wedge, adding this was with Annie's permission, but Teunis was unimpressed: "I don't care; if you don't stay away from that door, I will kick you down the stairs." Johanna, still present, heard Van Gogh wail back, "My dear man, if you knew how close I was to this woman, you would pity me with all your soul." It only made Teunis angrier: "That is none of my business; you can make anything good with your mouth." Johanna decided to intervene with an admonition of her own: "If you consort with whores, you get what you deserve." With two people hostile toward him, Van Gogh left the house for the second time.

A final scene Johanna witnessed appears rather mysterious. A while after Van Gogh had left, a gentleman, dressed in black, arrived in the back room. To the widow he handed over a paper sack with a few ducats, ordering her to give it to a certain young gentleman and to tell him it came from his mother. The man in black exchanged a few words with the widow, and then he read a poem. Teunis filled a glass and offered it to him.[47] None of the others ever referred to this incident, and Johanna's purpose in reporting it remains unclear. It conveys the impression of a scene from a novel. Already, Johanna had couched Van Gogh's plea to Teunis in language reminiscent of sentimental literature: he had spoken with tears in his eyes and in a moving tone. Like a minor character in a novel, Johanna disappeared again.

How many visits did Van Gogh pay to Annie's place in vain that day, being told each time she was out? He himself said he went there often, claiming he had spotted Annie in the window once.[48] Since it was about five minutes on foot from his room to hers, he probably walked up and down. He arrived again at four in the afternoon, when Teunis and his sister were drinking tea together in their room. This time, Annie really was out. As the two siblings had their own door wide open, they heard the visitor coming upstairs and saw him knocking on Annie's door. For once, Teunis could say in truth: "Van Gogh, Annie is not home." He replied that he had to speak to her and suggested that Teunis or his sister should ask Annie at what time she was ready to see him. Van Gogh left once more, soon followed by Teunis going to his porter's station. His sister passed on the message when Annie came home at five. Surprisingly, Annie asked her to tell Van Gogh that she expected him at nine that night. Did the two women consider nine P.M. a safe time, because he would have to leave soon? Were they in a mild mood for a moment? Or had Annie finally decided to tell him it was over for good?

A little later, Teunis's sister went out for some business, taking the opportunity to pass by her brother's porter's station. She reported what Annie had said. Again a little later, Van Gogh arrived at the porter's station. Of course he promised to be at the Herengracht house at nine o'clock sharp. Glad at finally having an appointment, he stated his purpose: He wanted to read a letter to Annie, so he hoped that Teunis, his sister, and the widow would be there, too. Teunis replied he wished to stay out of their quarrels, but Van Gogh insisted on his presence. If Teunis refused to come, Van Gogh would pick him up from his room. Did he realize he was collecting witnesses to his own crime?

The tormented lover punctually arrived at nine P.M. at the home of the woman he adored. If he had taken dinner in the meantime, his appetite had probably been less than ever. Annie was in her room as promised, alone. Since they had agreed on the time, he refrained from the ritual with the wedge and knocked on her door. She let him in. He explained he had something very important to tell her, that he had written it down, that he intended to read it to her, and that he wanted the neighbors to hear it too. In other words, he had been deadly serious when he told Teunis a few hours earlier they should be present. There can be no mistake: Van Gogh wanted an audience. He had been an inconspicuous extra when he played in the theater in the 1760s. This was his finest hour. Now he would be the principal actor in the drama of his own life. He himself had written the script for the first act. If only the play would end well! Together, Annie and Van Gogh went to the back room to collect the audience. The widow, Teunis, and his sister followed them to the front room. They saw him take a piece of paper from his pocket, and he started to read. Imagining himself on stage with thousands of spectators, he declaimed the entire text in a loud voice—from "in nomen . . . adorable object of my purest love," through "pronounce . . . the final sentence," to "beloved soul guardian, your tender loving lover."

If the widow, Teunis, and his sister were familiar at all with sentimental literature or plays, this piece of writing failed to touch them. At least, their later reaction sounded rather ironic. They were not sure they had completely understood the text, they said, but the gist of it was that he wished to persuade her to lead a decent life and to marry him. Annie's immediate reaction was worse. She knew his style of writing, but she hated it ever more. Absolutely not, she declared; marriage was out of the question, and she no longer wanted to have anything to do with him.

It had been, according to his own statement, his ultimate attempt to win her over, and she had pronounced the sentence of death. But even now, Van Gogh refused to accept it was true. As so often before, he started to plead with her. The others' presence, on which he himself had insisted, served to sustain his paranoia. In his perception, Annie went against her heart, and her neighbors were the wicked advisers. He heard them say all kind of things: Annie ought to reject a man who caused so much trouble every day; if she wanted a decent income, why didn't she take up domestic service again? And so on. Teunis, on the other hand, later claimed he had asked her to think it over and see if they could make it up. That sounds strange, too, in view of his wish, expressed a few hours earlier, to stay out of their conflict. What matters is that Annie had made up her mind, whatever the neighbors said. She wanted a complete break. To Van Gogh she proposed an exchange of notes setting each other free. Desperately, he tried to dissuade her from the idea, all the while hearing the other three screaming, "do it, do it." Then he wrote:

> I, the undersigned, confess that, *vi coactus*, I must violate my heart, and in spite of its tender feelings, I surrender the object that I swear, in spite of all opposition, to love forever, but that I have to leave now. June 29, 1775. J. B. van Gogh.

He had intentionally used an ambiguous formulation. In particular, the insertion of the Latin clause *vi coactus* (coerced by force) was essential. It meant he considered the document null and void. With this idea he signed it, waiting for Annie to proceed with her note. Saying she was inexperienced at writing, she asked Van Gogh to do it for her. Indignantly, he refused to compose his own death sentence. He suggested instead that he would leave for a quarter of an hour, during which Annie could think it over once more. He entrusted his note to Teunis and went downstairs for a glass of beer. When he returned, Annie was as determined as ever. In her own simple words she had written her note.

> Van Gogh: I, the undersigned, request in or out directly not to bother me, be it the one or the other, for I renounce you completely, where I am. June 29, 1775. Anna Smitshuizen. Nothing can be changed about this.[49]

Again, Van Gogh hesitated, although Teunis had given him back his note. Annie acted decidedly. "Here is mine; now give me yours," she said. As they exchanged the notes, Van Gogh exclaimed: "Annie, Annie, think about it, realize what you are doing." And she: "There is nothing to think about; the thing is finished." Renewed pleas followed and, although Annie insisted he should leave, Van Gogh took a pipe from his pocket, put tobacco in it, lit it, and started to smoke. Meanwhile, the three neighbors went back and forth from Annie's room to theirs. While smoking his pipe, Van Gogh wrote another note: "Cruel woman, shortly you will be released from me. Only a few moments of life have I left, and then you will witness my last gasp of breath. I die then, true lover until death of Anna Smitshuizen."[50] To Annie, he explained the note's essence: If it was really over, he would kill himself before her eyes. Teunis, present again, intervened. Van Gogh's words, he assured Annie, were as hollow as the wind, only meant to blackmail her. To her suitor he added that it was ten-thirty now; he had to close the door to the stairway and, if need be, he would batter the unwanted visitor down the stairs. At just that point, the charwoman arrived upstairs to bring Annie her washed linen. Van Gogh's audience had increased to four.

The moment had come to inflict upon himself the death sentence that Annie had pronounced.[51] He took the felt cutting knife from his pocket, proclaiming with a theatrical voice that he was ready to thrust it into his chest. His beloved should watch the scene from close by. With firm steps he walked up to Annie, who stood in front of a chair close to the wall. The charwoman, who had missed the previous acts of the play and failed to notice he had a weapon, thought he wanted to kiss her. Annie looked at the knife in his right hand. Without saying a word, she gently took his left hand. Van Gogh held the knife in a "contrary" way, not protruding as duelists did but pointed downward. One turn of his arm sufficed for the final act. Van Gogh was in a state of trance, feeling as if he had left the world already. He raised the knife and stabbed, but where? Within a second he felt warm blood flowing over his hand and wrist— Annie's blood. The knife had penetrated her heart. Without realizing what he had done, he pulled it from her chest and threw it away. Annie first sat down on the chair, rose again and stumbled to the door. She fell to the floor in the corridor. Teunis jumped on Van Gogh, knocked him down, and dealt him a couple of blows. Then the charwoman screamed: "Oh my Lord Jesus, don't bother with him, Teunis, care for her; she is bathing in her blood." There was nothing he or the others could do. On the floor of the corridor, her head over the threshold of the back room, Annie had bled to death.

The neighbors stood perplexed for a while, unable to act. The charwoman's daughter also had arrived, completing the quintet. According to her own testimony, she came just in time to see Annie die. Then her mother ran outside to look for night watchmen. Van Gogh just sat waiting in the corner of the room, half-conscious. He oscillated between realizing what he had done and sinking back into a trance of ignorance. He vaguely heard the others say Annie had died and exclaimed: "Annie, are you dead, that is good; if you are not for me, then another won't have you either, certainly not a married pimp."[52] Did he want to implicate the tailor as coresponsible? His words shocked the neighbors. He wished to appear before a competent judge, Van Gogh continued, and die publicly for Annie. Meanwhile, the charwoman called out on the Herengracht for night watchmen. Three responded, whom she told to follow her to an attic where a girl had been stabbed. When the men arrived upstairs, they asked the people assembled in the corridor whom they should arrest. All five pointed to the front room: there is your murderer!

When the watchmen entered the room, Van Gogh slowly rose. He meekly obeyed, as they took him by the shoulder and told him to come with them. They led him through the door, into the corridor. Something, someone was lying there, he noticed. Focusing his gaze more sharply, he recognized her. For the first time, clearly, he saw Annie's lifeless body. "Is she really dead?" he exclaimed in a tone of surprise, "then allow me to give her a kiss before I have to leave." The watchmen rejected his request. Teunis was indignant: "What is it that you wanted to do?" And to the watchmen: "Just drag him away." The charwoman snarled at Van Gogh: "Yeah, you, go away now; we will strike back at you." The three men took the murder suspect out of the house and locked him up in the Amstel quarter's watch house.

The improvised script had taken a fatal turn. The play featuring Annie and Van Gogh as the leading actors finished as a tragedy with an unhappy end. An infamous ending, perhaps, because not Werther but Lotte paid with her life. As notorious as the case was to become throughout the country, news of it probably never reached Goethe's Weimar. And had he known about the case, it is a wild guess as to the nature of his reaction. It is easier to imagine the reaction of Dutch Calvinists at such plays gone wrong. They had always inveighed against luxury, extravagance, idle entertainment in general, and the theater in particular. A tragedy or a comedy, on stage or in real life, acting was sinful in itself. In Calvinist thought, acting was pretending you are a person different from who you really are. It was a form of cheating, invented by the master of deceit, the devil. Moreover, if you pretend to be someone else, who is accountable for your actions?

Thus, the Calvinist theory of acting comes close to the modern medico-legal notion of diminished responsibility or temporary insanity in criminal matters. In a modern court, Van Gogh probably would have received a less than maximum sentence on such grounds. Certainly, his attorney would have made a plea to that effect. Van Gogh had committed the act in a trance, agitated and full of conflicting emotions. Without realizing it, he put the Calvinist theory into practice. He pretended to be someone else, not the man struck by so many deceptions but a triumphant poet and lover. He had the principal role, but he suddenly found himself in the wrong play. Imperceptibly, it had changed from a romantic drama into a crime thriller.

8
Honor, Shame, and Notoriety

> Here abides a martyr of the tenderest love of all
> Anna Smitshuizen was the one who made him turn and fall
> She robbed him of his heart, pretended her affection
> With a vile madam she conspired, with unabashed complexion
> Falsely she misled the one, whom she took away the light
> Since he could not withstand the fate that was his plight
> You, ignorant passerby, pay heed to his sorrowful lore
> And never put your trust in the cunning of a whore.[1]

The words, translated after 225 years, come from the pen of a self-styled poet. They sound a little more individualistic than the moralizing verses, ascribed to the convict, which were usually peddled during an execution ceremony. The author of these eight lines is Van Gogh indeed, but he wrote them during Annie's lifetime. There was some confusion whether he did so on the day of the murder or earlier; most likely, he composed the poem during one of the temporary breaks in the odd engagement. According to Van Gogh himself, he read it to his loved one when she made up again. She vented her dissatisfaction with one word in particular, the last.[2]

Even though she worked as a professional prostitute, Annie took offense at being called a whore. It exemplifies the negative power of this word, connoting a state of dishonor rather than a low-esteemed commercial activity. What prompted Van Gogh to use it? His opening, a typically romantic lamentation about his lost love, would fit very well in a sentimental novel. But the tone became more accusatory in the next lines, incriminating Annie as a deceitful woman. This finally led him to the classical insult hurled at women, by men and other women, for ages. If even this sentimental individualist drifted back to the traditional idiom of honor and shame, the more so would most of his contemporaries. The literary reactions to Van Gogh's deed were ambivalent, wavering between a fascination with his person and a moralistic stance that condemned the behavior of killer and victim alike.

His association with hack writers and the recent pamphlet war had already made Van Gogh a public figure. As soon as people heard that he had stabbed his sweetheart to death, after reading to her a letter written with his own blood, his notoriety increased markedly. The public, eager for intimate details, hardly had its patience tested, since the Amsterdam court finished the interrogations six weeks after the fatal deed. As in Donker's case, the protocol became available in print. Because the defendant had amply spoken about his relationship with Annie, the printed confession essentially was a piece of autobiography. For us, knowing the story already, its principal interest lies in what is included and excluded. For example, the editor kept the full information that the madam of the brothel in which Van Gogh had first met Annie was Geertruy van Kesteren, widow of Thomas Wolters, alias Black Truy. Most of the other persons mentioned in the protocol had their names listed with initials. Hoefnagel just became H. The letters and notes that the court had confiscated, including the famous one written with blood, increased the attractiveness of this edition; the announcement "copy of his letter to Annie Smitshuizen" figured prominently on the title page. The editor incorrectly dated the last interrogation on August 19, so the booklet was published after that date.[3] Later, another edition appeared, without the letters and notes. A footnote explained that these were published already and "in everyone's hands." This remark definitely suggests great sales for the transcripts from Van Gogh's trial.[4]

With these editions, the literary market concerning Van Gogh and Annie was far from exhausted. Two works, both cited earlier, deserve closer scrutiny because they exemplify the debate going on: Annie's fictional biography and the reply to Van Gogh's critics by his sympathizer. They will be called by the English translation of their main titles, *Remarkable Life* and *Truthful Message*, respectively. As explained, the author of the former book had adopted the formula of a conversation in a barge, making several passengers comment on Annie's life story. This was a realistic genre; in actual life people loved to chat in barges, in particular those traveling first class on the upper deck.[5] The travelers on *Remarkable Life*'s upper deck were more sympathetic to Annie than to her lover. *Truthful Message*, on the other hand, praised Van Gogh's noble character throughout. Writing in 1777, the author was convinced of his friend's ultimate legal victory; as soon as a higher court released him, he would mercilessly attack his enemies in print. In *Remarkable Life* as well as *Truthful Message*, two issues stand out—religion and, even more prominently, honor.

Honor was a self-evident motif, relating to killer and victim alike. Incarceration, especially for stabbing a defenseless woman to death, surely made one infamous. In her turn, this defenseless woman had the disreputable status of a prostitute. Unconditional condemnation from respectable citizens, it seemed, was the only possible outcome. So how could *Remarkable Life* convey sympathy for Annie? Its method was based on subtle distinctions, akin to those prostitutes drew among themselves. The latter considered a "married men's whore" as the most abject of their colleagues. The author of *Remarkable Life* discriminated from the angle of personal attitudes: Although Annie exercised a disreputable profession, she still had some sense of honor and decency left. Often, this meant playing a virtuous girl in the presence of people unacquainted with her. Unsympathetic observers might consider this a proof of her dishonesty instead, but to her biographer it meant she was not entirely corrupted. As a consequence, *Remarkable Life* offers details about how honor governs women's lives that are rarely found in archival records.

A typical passage has Annie walking near the harbor one day. A boat passes by, taking a group of East India men to their ship, accompanied by two musicians. As she stops to watch the scene, she gets into a conversation with an older couple. Seeing her nice dress, this couple takes her for a decent servant girl or a citizen's daughter. The man reproaches the sailors for their merriment: They should rather pray to heaven for a safe voyage. Then a gentleman carrying a sword, who thinks Annie is the couple's daughter, joins their company. When Annie leaves alone a little later, this gentleman follows her from a distance. He is still convinced that she is an honorable maiden, not only because of her decent clothes but also because of her way of walking. The author then elaborates on two ways in which young women may walk the streets. When an honorable girl has to deliver a message, she never looks around, refusing to be distracted by any movement or sound. She does not react when she hears someone coughing or scraping the pavement with a walking stick. These counted as tricks, obviously, to draw a woman's attention. Above all, a decent girl never gives a man a friendly look, but she turns down her eyes when he passes.[6]

Women who wished to try their luck with a man, on the other hand, always did the contrary. They returned his gaze and, with subtle gestures, they indicated their desire to become acquainted with him. An experienced woman had an elaborate repertoire of signs at hand, to indicate that a man should follow her. In the barge, the actor assumed his fellow passengers to be ignorant of this, adding it was not to his credit that he knew. As it happened, the sword-carrying gentleman in the story was equally familiar with the sign language. Not honest himself, he pretended to court Annie and persuaded her to leave the tailor (the story is situated around 1773–1774). This character belonged to the shady zone of men of standing who kept a courtesan, a custom still half-accepted. In such a milieu, one knew another's worth. In the words of the actor, the gentleman persuaded Annie "that she was too precious a little horse to be ridden by a journeyman tailor."[7]

Refusing to look up versus subtle signs of interest: in this dichotomous picture, a middle road was unavailable. Women either wanted nothing to do with a man they met or they traded their body for money or favors.

Women bent on preserving their honor not only had to mind their clothing and way of walking in the streets, they had to anticipate the thoughts of others in all kinds of situations. Certain activities, even when completely innocent, could imbue a third party with the wrong ideas. Caution was even more in order when one was not quite virtuous but pretended to be. This applied in a complicated way to Annie and the gentleman, who mutually concealed their true character. The latter offered her a place to hide from the tailor in the home of an aged couple who worked for him. When Annie arrived, the gentleman told the couple she was a distant cousin of his; he had to discuss family business with her each night, for which he needed their back room. The narrator of the story slightly doubted whether the old man and woman really believed this, but dependent as they were on the gentleman, they refrained from further questions. The next evening Annie visited their home again, staying in the back room with the gentleman until one at night. The passengers in the barge had no doubt about it: so late! Surely, the couple must sense now that something was wrong and suspect that no family affairs were discussed in that room. The narrator excused them: perhaps, but they were simple folk. Moreover, Annie and the gentleman left the door open; they asked the couple to bring them coffee and wine all the time; and the gentleman behaved as a friend, not as a lover. The old couple's patron, the narrator continued, explained to them that his "cousin" stayed with another relative, an uncle who continually barked at her, which made her disinclined to return to his place before he had gone to bed.[8]

On still another occasion, the gentleman took Annie with a ruse into a disreputable wine bar. Now they started hugging and kissing, while emptying no less than three bottles of wine. This quantity comes as a surprise, given Annie's sober drinking habits, but she trusted the gentleman. Each time when he invited her to take a sip, she politely refused, whereupon he insisted there was no harm in it. She was in the hands of an honorable man. The wine stimulated the circulation of her blood, he added, necessary after the commotion she had experienced with the tailor. "But what will your servant and his wife say," she worried, "when they see me in such an excited state?" The gentleman replied they must pretend to have visited family of hers, who had treated her lavishly in the hope of making her forget her past sorrows.[9] To return a little drunk and excited from a family visit, we can conclude, was all right. The biographer did hold men responsible for a woman's reputation in the eyes of third parties. The old man and woman were the gentleman's dependents, but if they had realized what really went on, they would have refused to let him use their home.

We are far away here from the notion that seducing women adds to the reputation of a man of honor. In the eighteenth century, respectable circles held both the man and the woman responsible for the situation they were in. For those operating on the edge, the obligation, each time, was to prevent activation of the gossip circuit. That often required foresight and meticulous calculation. Whereas, for an earlier generation of knife fighters, the maintenance of an honorable reputation was compatible with impulsive behavior and violence, the author—and the readers—of *Remarkable Life* associated honor with careful planning, by women and men.

Although different in tone, *Truthful Message* was equally bound to the idiom of honor. Forced to admit that Van Gogh was in love with a prostitute, the author insisted on the sincerity of his protagonist's motives: He had an honest marriage in mind, but she cheated on him all the way. To convince his readers, the author had to blacken Annie, making her not only infamous but unsympathetic as well. She was violent at times, he claimed. When in a bad temper, she beat men with her ring of keys, which all whores carried with them. *Truthful Message* agreed with *Remarkable Life* about Annie's cleverness in appearing decent, but with a reversed judgment. Whereas the author of the latter work, for whom appearance was all that mattered, thought it a positive trait, the author of *Truthful Message*, to whom a person's inner state counted most, found it negative. It was no more than a common whore's trick. Tears, in particular, served to soften the hearts of men, and Annie excelled in weeping. Van Gogh simply lacked the strength to resist this. The author concluded that, whereas a prostitute mastered the art of playing a chaste woman, a truly respectable person was decent because of inner virtue.[10]

Religion was an important theme not only in Van Gogh's case. Contemporaries found it self-evident to discuss murder in religious terms. Murder, like many crimes, counted as a sin. Sins could be forgiven. Killers awaiting decapitation, no less than burglars sentenced to hanging, displayed their repentance on the scaffold, catering to a common expectation. They were criminals all right, but as repentant sinners they also were religious propagandists. Van Gogh, on the other hand, acquired the reputation of an enemy of religion. No doubt, his association with the freethinker Ockers, a few years earlier, contributed to this. As long as Van Gogh stayed in jail, it was easy to attribute writings to him, which nourished the speculation about his religious attitudes.

Both Annie's biographer and his critic mentioned the first of two pamphlets no longer extant: a "letter from Van Gogh, sent from his jail in The Hague, to a friend in Amsterdam." *Remarkable Life* denounced it as the fake product of someone hoping to earn money quickly—another example of a hack writer chiding a colleague for plying their common trade. The "letter" contained a critical discussion of all Christian denominations and Judaism, with Van Gogh concluding that he preferred to belong to none of them. *Truthful Message* agreed that this pamphlet was a hoax. The author also knew a "quasi-refutation"—a half-hearted defense that he easily saw through. He denounced both pamphlets, along with *Remarkable Life*, as libels, assuming that all three originated from Hoefnagel's circles.[11]

Without dwelling on the content of the two pamphlets, *Truthful Message* went at length to prove that Van Gogh was no freethinker. Poems and tracts, which he supposedly had written during his detention, served to demonstrate his religiosity. The poems expressed his trust in the Trinity to help him prove his innocence. The tracts testified to his true and sincere Christian beliefs. Although Van Gogh refused to align himself with a particular denomination, his ideas came closest to the Reformed doctrine, but he rejected the idea of an irreversible predestination. The accusation of freethinking, the author concluded, was an ugly piece of slander from his enemies. Lacking concrete incriminations, they hoped to discredit his beliefs, which they did with success, since many people now thought Van Gogh espoused a pernicious philosophy. The author knew the required procedure all too well. Every rabble-rouser intent on throwing mud at an honorable man had three words at hand: swindler, atheist, and sodomite. The third charge, however, was too dangerous (presumably because it suggested the accuser's own familiarity with the milieu of sodomites). The first could get one into legal trouble. So the choice fell on the second, easily believable and leaving the accuser unimplicated.

In fact, *Truthful Message* continued, one could find many hypocrites who externally appeared pious, no less than covert sodomites. Conversely, many persons hated for their unorthodox views were essentially virtuous. As in the discussion of chastity, virtue was the key word. It constituted a sure mark of true religion; religion without virtue equaled no religion. One should judge a pious person by his deeds, not his words. Ethically minded people deserved greater esteem than those externally observing religious prescripts but possessing no inner merits.[12] Here we get to the core of the difference between *Remarkable Life* and *Truthful Message*. The latter work propagated a culture of guilt, whereas the former, in its obsession with keeping up appearances, represented a culture of shame. Or, to put it differently, the author of *Truthful Message* adopted a position in the forefront of the spiritualization of honor, firmly linking honor to individual virtue.[13] That enabled him to confer honor even upon a man on trial for murder.

From a philosophical viewpoint, the author of *Truthful Message* positioned Van Gogh on the conservative side of the moderate Enlightenment. He rejected religious fanaticism and criticized the doctrine of predestination. He advocated a personal form of Christianity, overstepping denominational boundaries. This tuned in to the outlook of a large part, if not the majority, of the reading public. The author's preference for personal virtue, within the context of a guilt culture, likewise fitted into the moderate Enlightenment. But we cannot equate all this with Van Gogh's personal philosophy, about which the archival record remains silent.

For its part, *Remarkable Life* intended to demonstrate that its own protagonist had not altogether strayed from the path of virtue and awe for God. The author accomplished this by a detour. Annie's adventure with the sword-carrying gentleman culminates in a scene in which the gentleman betrays himself as an atheist. Although he has sworn a solemn oath that he has an honorable courtship in mind, his real intent is to have her once and dump her. By piling up cunning ruses, he finally sits alone with her in a separate room in a notorious brothel, where they consume a large quantity of wine again. The gentleman kisses and caresses her, but he makes no "dishonorable move." Suddenly, however, he loses his prudence, touching her "in the most shameless and disrespectful way." Although the wine has made Annie merry and, professionally, she has often been in such a situation, she immediately jumps up. Her lover is on the verge of breaking his oath. "You can only do such things after we are married; don't you fear God's punishment?" He just laughs and proclaims his disbelief in tales of instant punishment upon breaking an oath. "No, my dear child, the season of miracles is over, and the world is a little more enlightened than in past years." He pleads his case, but Annie is inexorable: "I'd rather die than marry you, because I absolutely refuse a perjurious atheist for my husband," and after another attempt to woo her: "Don't touch me, atheist, I despise you; I would always be afraid that God, whose judgment you provoke, will punish me along with you." Then Annie runs out of the room, never to see the gentleman again.[14]

The quoted sentence by the gentleman literally refers to the doctrine of the cessation of miracles, which the Church of England developed after 1660 in response to enthusiastic sects.[15] The Anglicans meant that, although miracles were possible, God had refused to let them happen after the age of the Apostles. *Remarkable Life* put the idea into the mouth of a representative of the radical Enlightenment who ridiculed the "superstition" of past ages. If Hoefnagel was its author, he possibly modeled the atheist gentleman on his former enemy, Willem Ockers. Alternatively, the author had Van Gogh in mind. In the cited passage, the gentleman called Annie the guardian of his soul, echoing the final address to her in the blood letter, which was "in everyone's hands." Moreover, the gentleman's oath paralleled Van Gogh's, which called for his own damnation should his love prove insincere. He never meant that seriously, so the implicit suggestion. Interpreted in this way, Van Gogh's oath became another source of the belief that he was a freethinker.

Finally, *Remarkable Life* refers, in an indirect manner, to the eighteenth-century revolution in love. Remember that the highest-class passengers in the barge are an Amsterdam couple, Frans and Elisabeth. As the only woman on the upper deck, Elisabeth accompanies her husband on a leisure trip. In this, they conform to the new romantic ideal that husband and wife spend much time together. Frans and Elisabeth address each other by their first names, usually with a diminutive, or they use sweet words. They tease each other sometimes, but only for fun. She comes up with a picnic basket, because she cares for her "little child," whereupon he calls his dearest "a woman in a million." The sweet word they employ most often, mutually, is *hondje* (doggy). Incidentally, this was also a favorite expression of streetwalkers to lure potential customers and, when uttered without the diminutive, it was a serious insult.[16] Even though this fashionable couple is of upper-bourgeois status, they show no aloofness. When they leave the company during a stop, the actor wonders about the identity of "this gentleman and lady from Amsterdam, who have such status and means and yet consort with their inferiors so politely and without pride."[17]

That phrase betrays the author's positive attitude toward this modern, romantic couple. Less sympathetic readers, on the other hand, could easily take their sweet words for a satire on the exaggerated affection fashionable in higher circles. Thus, the adopted formula ensured a wide market for the book. The presence of the tender husband and wife in the barge is significant nonetheless. Obviously, they were interested in Annie and Van Gogh, but they condemned his way of life and his passion for a prostitute. Frans and Elisabeth wanted to be together all the time, but theirs was no fatal attraction. While partaking of the revolution in love, they were impervious to its darker side.

So much for images and representation. The period from the middle of 1775 to early 1778 was marked no less by concrete events. These were largely of a judicial nature.

On June 30, 1775, between one and two A.M., Casper Pieters and Simon Smit, employees of the city hospital, picked up Annie's lifeless body from the attic at the Herengracht.[18] The hospital's staff put her on display the next morning. As with Cecilia's corpse eight and a half years earlier, curious visitors abounded. They included the author of *Truthful Message* and an acquaintance of the gentleman from *Remarkable Life*. For the former, it was the only time he saw Annie. The latter reported to his friend about her beauty. The actor, who had known her personally, specified her looks: a round and healthy face, red cheeks, black hair and eyebrows, bright white teeth, a small mouth, a well-proportioned bosom, a slim waist but fleshy for the rest, small hands and feet.[19]

Unlike Cecilia's case, the visitors came for romantic empathy rather than horror. This young woman, with one stigma of red blood at the place of her heart, offered no ghastly sight. The interest Amsterdamers showed in looking at Annie in 1775 prefigured the high romanticism of the early 1800s, with its exaltation over the fair complexion of women on their deathbeds. In France, Chateaubriand's novel *Atala*, about a pretty, young Amerindian woman, who took poison after an unhappy love affair, occasioned a craze. Visual artists vied with each other in romantically depicting scenes from Atala's life and her tragic death. Images of Atala even adorned vases and clocks.[20] Although no picture of the dead Annie survives, the fascination with the beauty of her lifeless body reminds us of Chateaubriand's female Indian. She, however, was no prostitute but a recent convert to Christianity. And in the nineteenth century, actual bodies no longer were on public display.

The autopsy report of June 30 sounded more prosaic. In the hospital the committee of sworn experts had inspected the body of an adult female. They observed a wound at the front left side of her chest, between the fourth and fifth rib from above, with a cut in the cartilage of the fourth. When they opened the chest, they found the entire left cavity filled with coagulated blood and serum. The wound went through the pericardium, well into the right cavity of the heart. "We declare this wound absolutely lethal. Signed: Andreas Bonn, Abraham Titsing, Adriaan van der Duyn and Pieter Jas."[21] The first was the city's anatomy professor, who now has a street named after him just outside the eighteenth-century town. The others were surgeons. The record does not reveal whether they knew that the suspect practiced surgery as an interloper.

On the same day, the court interrogated the suspect, transported from the watch house to jail, for the first time. Since 1769 the HO was Mr. Willem Gerrit Dedel Salomonsz. Born in 1734, he was of Van Gogh's generation, but he had a decidedly less tortuous love life. At age thirty, he had married the daughter of a Haarlem burgomaster. As council member, Dedel survived the Patriot movement, but not the Batavian revolution of 1795. He died in 1801, the year in which Chateaubriand published *Atala*. Dedel also held religious offices. Already at age twenty, he was listed as a member of the board of Amsterdam's Old Church, and he was a canon in the chapter of St. Marie's in Utrecht (taken over by the Reformed Church during the Revolt) from 1757 until 1775. Partaking of the revival of commerce among Amsterdam's patriciate after midcentury, he was also active as a merchant.[22]

Dedel, it seemed, needed no meticulous strategy, like the one adopted by his predecessor in the case against Donker and Dora. Van Gogh had been arrested in the victim's home, with several witnesses present and the blood-stained knife lying on the floor. And yet, according to the principle of the inquisitorial procedure, even this defendant had to confess that he had actually stabbed Annie. To make him do so, cunning turned out to be necessary. A unique aspect of this criminal trial in early modern Amsterdam is that we have the defendant's later comment on the way the court conducted it. According to Van Gogh, HO Dedel led the interrogations in an authoritarian fashion, which resulted in a biased protocol.

Van Gogh also explained why he cared little about the proceedings at the time. During this first trial he felt as if he were robbed of his senses, barely aware of what went on around him. He wept and groaned incessantly. Having lost his honor, freedom, and beloved—he said in that order—his only wish was to die. Several times he requested the court to finish him off quickly. In that state of mind, his exact words hardly seemed to matter. Looking back, Van Gogh surely exaggerated, since he did care what was recorded in the protocol. Yet the recollection of an intense feeling of despair appears authentic.[23]

A monologue by the defendant took up most of the first trial session. Upon a straightforward question—what had been the occasion for his arrest—Van Gogh gave an account of his relationship with Annie, culminating in a detailed report of the events of the previous day. But he declined to admit he had killed her. For the moment, Dedel pressed the defendant only a little. Why did he turn the knife towards Annie when she grabbed his left hand? Van Gogh had no recollection that he did, but it was probable, he said. He never had the intention to stab her; to the contrary, he had always assured her he would never harass her after an unhoped-for rejection. The protocol resulting from this session was necessarily selective. According to Van Gogh—and we can easily believe him—his account of the affair and the events of the previous night was much more elaborate than the court clerk's written version.

Subsequently, Dedel attempted to get a clearer idea of the circumstances, concentrating on the events of June 24–27. He collected statements from Annie's neighbors and summoned them all in court, five days after the first session. As the HO was only interested in the defendant's reaction to their testimonies, repeated verbally on the spot, he ignored two episodes that Van Gogh added on his own initiative.

Again six days later, the court intended serious business. For the first time, all judges were present, seated next to the prosecutor.[24] The magistrates wanted to know for sure whether Van Gogh had stabbed Annie to death and how. The defendant took a firm stand: He had drawn his knife with the intention to kill himself, and he did not remember what had happened directly after drawing it. Even though he agreed that he deserved to die, he said he would refrain from confessing anything beyond his own recollection. Porter Teunis, his sister, and the charwoman testified that they had seen Van Gogh rushing toward Annie, as if bent on assaulting her. The charwoman first thought he wanted to embrace her, but when she heard a *naar geluid* (nasty sound), she realized something was wrong. The defendant doubted that the three had been in a position to see his exact moves; they were standing in line after each other, and only one lamp burned faintly. If we trust Van Gogh's later statement, the widow confirmed that the lamp badly needed oil, but Teunis suddenly clapped his hands saying it was burning brightly enough. The charwoman supported this statement, and with two witnesses against one, the court accepted it.

Thus, the case remained inconclusive. The witnesses had not actually seen the stabbing, and the defendant claimed amnesia of his actions at the crucial moment. He only admitted to conclusions after the fact, saying this or that was probable. At the fourth session on July 13, however, HO Dedel had recourse to a trick.[25] He presented the murder weapon and asked whether it was "the same knife with which the defendant had injured Anna Smitshuizen?" It actually belonged to his landlord, Van Gogh replied, concluding "that he could tell no better than that it was the same knife as the one with which he had injured Annie." Did he realize he was trapped by a leading question? Satisfied, the HO had the answer recorded in the protocol. He told his clerk to underline it and to add that Van Gogh cried bitter tears when he saw the knife. Whereas the defendant was constantly sobbing during the series of interrogations, this was the only time it entered the protocol.

Van Gogh's mood of intense sorrow makes his various evasive replies all the more intriguing. In fact, he adopted the stance of a modern judge in a fact-finding trial, drawing conclusions about probability from circumstantial evidence. The HO tuned in to this with his first question during the fifth session (July 19): Perhaps the prisoner himself was convinced that he had inflicted the wound from which Anna Smitshuizen had died? The prisoner replied that this was not only probable but even certain, but that he lacked a recollection from that moment. In a modern court of law, the first part of this reply would be highly incriminating. In Amsterdam in 1775 Van Gogh knew exactly that it left room for doubt. Instead of intellectual conclusions, the inquisitorial procedure required first of all the defendant's confession, which he withheld. After the abolition of torture in 1798, the law allowed the country's magistrates to sentence a person because they were convinced of his guilt, even without a confession. Twenty-three years earlier, Van Gogh acted as a post-1798 judge would do, perhaps failing to realize that it might induce his real judges to consent to torture.

This was not yet on the agenda. During the remainder of the interrogation, Dedel went to great lengths to catch Van Gogh in contradictory statements, but he refused to be trapped anew. Nevertheless, he repeatedly requested the court to make him die soon. Each time Dedel retorted, "We are not that far yet."

Dedel now granted his prisoner a reprieve of three weeks. The HO had grown weary of the defendant, it seems; of his intellectual replies, his insistence on the right formulation, alternating with moaning and crying. Dedel wanted to sober him up, not least to make him fit for questioning under torture. According to the jail keeper's bills for the period August–October, he supplied coffee to Van Gogh for the amount of no less than seventeen guilders and seventeen stivers.[26] If we allow for a little speculation, the jail keeper served most of it at the very beginning of this period. On August 9, Van Gogh had his sixth examination.

The official protocol was customarily brief, so let us consider this session from the defendant's point of view. It began with a recital of his confession, that is, the protocols of the previous five sessions. As the secretary was reading, Van Gogh interrupted him more than twenty times to insist upon a correction or an addition. Each time Dedel said in a friendly tone, "OK man, we will have everything changed, but let Mr. Secretary finish his reading first." When he had finished, however, Dedel refused to make the desired changes. They were irrelevant to the case, he said. It only mattered whether or not the defendant agreed with the present text. Did he "persist in negating"? Repeatedly, Van Gogh heard this question hammered at him, while he only persisted in wanting the protocol altered. Tired of his efforts, he finally confirmed his "negation," whereupon the HO immediately concluded that the case required torture.

The judges knew that the HO was likely to demand an examination under torture, so they were all present. One of them, Jan Bernd Bicker, recorded their deliberations in his diary. At first, two of his colleagues consented to the HO's demand. Six, on the other hand, found the case "unsuitable for torture." Bicker himself also rejected the demand, but he did so because "there was a sufficient confession." In other words, Bicker was the only magistrate to take Van Gogh's conclusions about probability for a confession of guilt, sufficient to pronounce sentence. Confronted with a majority of seven, the two others withdrew their consent, now stating that "the defendant was heavily broken." Presumably, they referred to Van Gogh's mental state, echoing contemporary criticism of judicial torture. To abolitionists, it was an act of cruelty to subject any suspect to this method of questioning, while the outcome was always untrustworthy. The two Amsterdam judges conceded that the state of mind of this defendant precluded a lawful use of the method.[27]

The corollary of the judges' refusal of torture was a new trial. The Amsterdam magistrates occasionally granted this to manslaughter suspects and also to persons of humble condition, if the circumstances of the act appeared a little fuzzy. The procedure was called *"ordinary,"* but it actually happened in a minority of cases. The court now changed its method from pressure on the suspect to a consideration of pleas and counterpleas. Van Gogh continued to be jailed; but he obtained three advantages: He was allowed legal assistance; he could summon witnesses for the defense; and because the judges could pronounce a sentence without the defendant's confession this time, appeal to a higher court was possible. On August 29, the magistrates granted Van Gogh a *pro deo* trial, making the services of two defense lawyers and a notary available to him.[28]

∾

At that point, at the end of August or in early September, Van Gogh's mental state completely reversed. From a sobbing wretch he turned into a self-conscious man. He stopped crying and concentrated fully on his physical survival. Being spared torture and having the prospect of a new trial suggested that he might escape the death penalty. With it, he shook off the conviction that he deserved and wished to die. He convinced himself that Annie's tragic demise had been an accident, with no guilt whatsoever on his part. The "ordinary" procedure allowed contact with the outside world, at least with his lawyers. No doubt, they informed him about the great fascination with his and Annie's person. Van Gogh heard that half the country was interested in his case, that many people thought he had been duped by a whore, and that "thieves of honor" like Hoefnagel really were to blame for all this. His friends and supporters awaited the day of his release, when he would crush Hoefnagel with his pen or sue him for slander. Undoubtedly, Van Gogh's newly won confidence owed much to this perceived support. He saw the legal battle about to enroll as a surrogate for his battle with Hoefnagel. From that idea, he drew renewed strength.

Among Van Gogh's supporters were his landlord, Barend Moreu, and his wife, who had acted as surrogate parents. Moreu, however, could no longer do the defendant a favor; he was buried at the cemetery near the Leiden Gate on September 19.[29] Neither was his widow's testimony of much help to their former boarder. She merely confirmed that her husband had allowed him to borrow one of his knives.

The defense witnesses made oral testimonies in court at the beginning of October. Van Gogh's lawyers had summoned three other women, including Johanna Barendina van Gogh—his sister, presumably—and a friend of hers. They had visited porter Teunis on the day after Annie's death, urging him not to incriminate Van Gogh. According to these two women, the porter had replied, "I am unable to do so, because I was not present; we both stood in the corridor." The fourth witness was Johanna Leeman, the woman who had met that mysterious gentleman dressed in black on the morning of June 29. Possibly, the testimony about this event served to make clear that strange visitors appeared in the attic at the Herengracht. Johanna confirmed that Teunis had threatened to kick Van Gogh down the stairs, which the porter had denied at his confrontation with the defendant during the first trial. Additionally, the witness declared: On October 7 or 9 the widow (who lived with Teunis and his sister) came to her house, saying she had just been in court. The widow had not dared to tell the gentlemen that Teunis was Van Gogh's sworn enemy, fearing her neighbor's retaliation. She was glad, therefore, that this witness had testified earlier about Teunis's impertinence.[30] Obviously, the accused's lawyers wished to suggest that the porter had made a false testimony out of hatred for Van Gogh.

The witnesses for the defense failed to impress the HO. In his conclusion, he only referred to Teunis's alleged statement that he and his sister had stood in the corridor at the fatal moment. Not only were the two women biased witnesses, the HO posited, they merely recounted an "extrajudicial chat." Teunis surely had meant to say he had been unable to see the actual stabbing. Had it been a judicial conversation, apparently, the HO would have suggested to the witness the correct interpretation of his own testimony. Dedel concluded that Teunis, his sister, and the charwoman had clearly seen the defendant assault the victim. He also adopted the charwoman's statement that a nasty sound emanated from Van Gogh's mouth. The accused, he concluded, had inflicted a lethal wound on Annie—on a person to whom he had communicated the most passionate feelings of love before. After his deed, he had expressed satisfaction at her death. All this led the HO to demand that the accused be hanged on the scaffold, with the murder weapon above his head. His dead body was to be hanged at the gallows field, again with the murder weapon. Presumably, the fact that Barend Moreu, who had died in the meantime, no longer needed his knife was no matter for consideration. The defense pleaded for acquittal with the obligation to appear again if there was new evidence.

The judges reached a verdict on January 16, 1776, and publicly pronounced their sentence on the following day. Van Gogh trusted them to set him free. In the morning he told the jail keeper he would have lunch that afternoon with his family or one of his lawyers.[31] Later, his attorney in appeal confirmed that the verdict was quite unexpected. The judges sentenced Van Gogh to decapitation, "granting his corpse the earth." The attorney immediately announced his client's appeal to the Court of Holland. The HO notified his colleagues in The Hague.[32]

The Court of Holland apparently had other business first, leaving the defendant in his Amsterdam cell for almost six months. The total sum that the jail keeper charged the Amsterdam court for keeping Van Gogh for just over a year amounted to 266 guilders and 12 stivers, almost a worker's annual wages. On July 10, 1776, a deputy and two court officials escorted the prisoner to The Hague.[33] This move also brought a change of lawyers. From now on, one attorney assisted Van Gogh: Mr. Leonard Thomeeze, who had been the legal representative of Nathaniel Donker's guardian in the late 1750s.

As few new facts or points of view had been put forward during the second trial in Amsterdam and the HO had largely based his conclusion on the written protocol of the first, Thomeeze focused his attention on that text. He procured a copy of the published confession and told his client to indicate which passages he disagreed with. Van Gogh's comments, written in October 1776, were detailed indeed. He exhausted his supply of paper with it, enclosing a request to his attorney to send him some more.[34]

Most of the suspects tried in Amsterdam were humble people, who would never discuss the exact meaning of the words attributed to them by the court clerk. Van Gogh did. According to the protocol of the third session, the defendant had said he believed he had stabbed in the direction of the victim, in *woede* (anger). Van Gogh claimed never to have used the word *woede*, but *wanhoop* (despair). He had recurrently insisted on an emendation of the protocol, which Dedel had conceded each time but failed to do. To his attorney Van Gogh explained: "Anger is always accompanied by maliciousness and malevolent intent, but despair can be without both and wholly quiet and perplexed."[35] By this time, Van Gogh had completely shaken off the mood of desperation and the death wish that plagued him in the summer of the previous year. Bent solely on survival, he invented incredible excuses for his most incriminating statements. He claimed, for example, that his notorious exclamation, "it is good that you are dead," had been meant as a satire on the neighbors' misleading cries. He had never meant those words in earnest. With so many corrections and additions refused, he concluded, his "so-called confession" was a worthless document.

One more point of detail gives pause for thought. Van Gogh emphatically disclaimed the witnesses' interpretation, adopted by the HO, that he had rushed toward Annie. In particular, he was indignant at the suggestion that he had done so with "a nasty sound." This was "an absolute lie." Remember that Van Gogh imagined himself an actor in the play of his life. He had insisted that the neighbors formed the audience. The thought that the audience accused him of an error unworthy of actors was unbearable. In his biography of Jan Punt, Simon Styl explained that actors learned to speak with a delicate, quasi-singing voice, with different nuances for comedies and tragedies. If they were unable to learn to speak in this way, Styl sneered, they had better become funeral announcers or news reporters.[36] Evidently, a nasty sound was the exact opposite of such a delicate voice. Van Gogh denied any faltering in his acting tone at the moment his own play turned into a tragedy.

With only the formal pleas extant, it is unclear to what degree Van Gogh's commentary was useful to his attorney. In the appeal procedure, the HO counted as the defendant. Thomeeze had summoned Dedel, requesting the justices of the Court of Holland to annul the sentence pronounced in Amsterdam. Given the stakes, the written pleas of both parties were rather disappointing. Thomeeze summarized the procedures in Amsterdam so far, emphasizing that the prosecutor had used "irrelevant and abusive methods." The HO's attorney repeated the conclusions his client had reached at the end of the second trial: Not only had Van Gogh assaulted Annie, but the autopsy report proved he had inflicted a lethal wound. Both lawyers probably went into greater detail during the oral session that followed, where no record was taken. From the Court of Holland's final judgment, we must conclude that it condoned Dedel's methods of questioning and recording. The justices pronounced their verdict on December 19, 1776: The Amsterdam sentence was no injustice to the accused. Thomeeze announced his client's appeal to the High Council.[37]

The *Hoge Raad van Holland en Zeeland* (High Council) was a remnant of the abortive centralization of the sixteenth century. The Habsburgs had installed a Grand Council at Malines, as a supreme court for all of the Netherlands, North and South. In the 1580s, when the North had definitively broken with its sovereign, Holland and Zeeland instituted a *Hoge Raad* of their own, whose jurisdiction never was extended to the other five provinces.[38] Two centuries later, the existence of this institution offered Van Gogh the possibility to appeal to an even higher court and, with it, to prolong his life. Since the High Council, like the Court of Holland, held its sessions in The Hague, he remained in the same jail.

The High Council admitted the case on January 11, 1777. It looked indeed as if a brief prolongation of his client's life, rather than saving it, was Thomeeze's primary goal. His written pleas contained no new arguments;

they were identical copies of those presented to the Court of Holland. Again, we do not know the content of the oral pleas. Convinced of winning in this court too, Dedel likewise had his conclusions of the previous trial copied. On July 8, 1777, the High Council reached the same verdict as the Court of Holland seven months earlier: the accused had no reason to complain about the Amsterdam sentence.[39]

It was not over yet. Thomeeze knew another, obscure route of escape. The possibility existed to subject a verdict by the High Council to the judgment of a committee of revision, whose task it was to establish whether any error had slipped into the earlier trials. This procedure applied first of all to civil suits, but Van Gogh's lawyer used it in a criminal case. Such last-review procedures were a rare occurrence, and legal historians have only recently begun to investigate them. One thing they discovered is that revision of a sentence meant no suspension of its execution, unless this caused irreparable damage for the party concerned.[40] That clause obviously applied to our protagonist. To obtain a revision of his sentence, the accused had to petition the Estates of Holland. They decided favorably, allowing Van Gogh to plead his case *pro deo* again. The committee once more examining it consisted of all members of the High Council, two justices of the Court of Holland, and the *pensionarissen* (chief secretaries) of the towns of Delft, Amsterdam, Rotterdam, Brielle, and Enkhuizen. The latter five all had a law degree as well.[41] Van Gogh was to stand trial for the fifth and last time.

Finally, both Thomeeze and Dedel had to do their home work. The first produced a plea of 1,495—admittedly brief—articles. The HO outdid him with a reply of no fewer than 2,611 articles. Both texts were printed, the first occupying 83 pages and the second 121. They probably had gone to print because of the number of people who had to read them professionally. There are no indications that copies were sold on the market; no booksellers are listed, for example.[42] These two texts alone could easily form the basis of a book-length study in legal history. We must consider them here for what they reveal about the moral judgment of contemporaries. That judgment takes us back to the eighteenth-century revolution in love.

The first three articles of the defense's plea showed that Thomeeze was finally prepared to assail the HO head-on. He began: "(1) A certain Anna Smitshuizen, then living in Amsterdam, being in her room on June 29, 1775, with the defendant and a few other persons, is unexpectedly found injured and dies, (2) without any of the persons present having seen anything, however minor, of the infliction of the wound. (3) Nevertheless, the defendant has the misfortune that the other persons accuse him of being the perpetrator, whereupon he is taken into custody in Amsterdam aforesaid."[43] His client's life, Thomeeze continued, depended upon convincing the committee members that, in legal terms, the crime had not been satisfactorily proven. If they still thought his client had been negligent in some way, they should at least find the Amsterdam sentence too severe.

In his turn, Dedel assailed Van Gogh without mercy. Who on earth was prepared to trust such a strange fellow? It sufficed to consider that infamous piece of writing he had addressed to the victim, "a *romanesque* and horrible letter," which he pretended to have written with his own blood and "the reading of which is bound to impart a very unfavorable idea about the Defendant's way of thinking to the Judge from the start."[44] In the course of his reply, Dedel returned to the blood letter several times. For want of negative epithets, he tended to be repetitive. It was a godless letter. It contained the most chilling curses and damnations, with the sole aim of inducing Annie to change her mind about leaving him. In short, this letter said it all. The HO had presented the other pieces of writing for the consideration of the Amsterdam judges, merely to prevent any reproach that he had withheld evidence.

To the contrary, according to Van Gogh's attorney, the ensemble of letters formed a sure proof that the defendant cherished an intense love for the victim, no hate whatsoever. He never had the intention to harm Annie; a regrettable accident had occurred. This was no new argument, but Thomeeze tried to bolster it with citations from legal authors. He had consulted an even greater mass of juridical literature in an attempt to demonstrate irregularities in the earlier trials. Most of his claims failed to impress the other party. Thomeeze had a particularly hard time with the passage "that he could tell no better than that it was the same knife as the one with which he had injured Annie." Dedel now capitalized on it: "Here . . . his conscience flew in his face and forced him to confess."[45] It was unfair to take this expression literally, the defense argued. The court had recurrently asked the accused to draw conclusions, and this was one more conclusion. For a true confession, it was necessary that the accused recollected his real intention at the fatal moment, which he did not. Thomeeze's argument implied that Annie's death was an accidental by-product of Van Gogh's true intention, to commit suicide.

The HO argued the contrary. The defense's portrayal of the situation was an invention after the fact, with the sole purpose of finding an escape route from the death penalty. The only thing that this proved, Dedel sneered, was that Van Gogh had recanted from his wish to die publicly for Annie. According to the HO, there was sufficient evidence to conclude that the defendant had intentionally stabbed the victim, out of jealousy and revenge. The HO's elaborate plea, with a detailed discussion of the witnesses' testimonies, is primarily an intellectual statement. What strikes the modern reader most, nevertheless, are the occasional normative judgments and negative epithets. They betray Dedel's deep abhorrence of the person of Van Gogh. *Romanesque* was the key word. In present-day English it refers to an architectural style, which was not meant of course. A derivative of *roman* (novel), the word had entered Dutch from the French only recently. Its most general meaning was "like in a novel," but this implicitly referred to a sentimental novel. In the second half of the eighteenth century, *romanesque* was closely associated with melancholy and sentimentality. The word further connoted adventure, passion, and fantastic chimeras; one could also speak of a romanesque path in a landscape.[46] Clearly, the word had a positive meaning to romantic readers of sentimental novels. To Dedel, it connoted the dangers inherent to acting out these novels in real life.

Next to dangerously sentimental, the Amsterdam HO considered Van Gogh blasphemous. Without explicitly siding with those who thought him a freethinker, Dedel did find the defendant an ungodly person. Whereas Van Gogh had dwelled on his horrendous descent into hell to impress Annie with the sincerity of his love, to Dedel this passage in the blood letter was no more than a piece of infamous cursing and swearing. Forced to listen to such a godless text, the witnesses had every reason to side with Annie, the HO admitted, while denying their partiality. The blood letter haunted Dedel: It testified to the extravagance of the defendant's passion—an ego-centered passion at that. In this and the other writings, Dedel read not love or affection, but an "excessive desire to have Anna Smitshuizen for himself alone."[47]

On this obsession with having her alone, Dedel based his claim that the defendant had killed the victim on purpose. True, Van Gogh had not planned the act for days, but on the fatal night, when he realized Annie rejected him for good, anger took the upper hand. At the homicidal moment, still according to Dedel's plea, Van Gogh's bosom was filled with nothing but hatred, jealousy, and evil intent. Why else had he relished his deed afterward, saying a married pimp would not have her either? For the committee members, Dedel explained that the killer had referred to a journeyman tailor, his rival, whom he detested. The plea omitted an explanation why this tailor had been mysteriously absent throughout the succession of trials. The HO did provide his own model of how to react if the stabbing really had been accidental: A man who injures his beloved by accident, who feels her blood flowing over his hands, sees her collapse and hears others exclaim she is dead, will never say such a vile thing. No, he is quiet and sad and bursts into a sea of tears. Not so Van Gogh. He comforted himself with the thought that neither he nor his rival could enjoy possession of her now. "The defendant did not bemoan that, for this satisfaction, he had sacrificed to his jealousy and anger the former object of his adoration."[48] Triumphantly, the HO showed the committee the knife, still stained with dry blood up to the handle. Van Gogh, he concluded, never acted like a real lover.

Why did the HO make such a great effort to demonstrate that the defendant had committed the act intentionally out of revenge? We might simply say it is always a prosecutor's task to maximize the charges. After all, decapitation was the lightest of all death penalties, which Dedel neatly pointed out. The standard punishment for premeditated murder, imposed on Nathaniel Donker among others, was breaking on the wheel. But the HO could no longer obtain this sentence. The revision committee's only task was to find out whether an error had occurred during the previous trials. The committee had no authority to aggravate the defendant's punishment. In order to have Van Gogh's death sentence maintained, it sufficed to convince the committee that he had attacked Annie with a knife. Since Dedel nevertheless went at length to prove vengeful intent, something more fundamental, it seems, was at stake.

Behind the negative judgment of Van Gogh's lifestyle and way of thinking lay a fear to be contaminated by him. This should be prevented at all cost. Dedel distanced himself from Van Gogh as far as he could, to avoid any temptation of empathy. Already he came close, by revealing he could imagine himself in the shoes of a real lover. As this was a criminal trial, the repudiation of Van Gogh's character was necessarily couched in legal terms— circumstances, motive, intent. A deeper psychological urge, however, underlay all this. It is no coincidence that Dedel vented his disdain of so-called *romanesque* ideas time and again. He wished to redefine Van Gogh's romanticism and the resulting act of despair into something more traditional and familiar: an ungodly and infamous crime of jealousy and hatred. No room for dramatic pleas and ruminations about killing oneself; no recognition of a tragic and uncontrollable love! It had to be that way, precisely because Dutch elite men, of whom Dedel was one, felt vulnerable themselves. Many patricians, male and female, appreciated sentimental novels. Husbands and wives indulged in the fashion of writing intimate letters to their beloved spouse.[49] The Dutch patriciate partook of the cultural changes of their time. Therefore, Dedel and the lawyers who assisted him were able to imagine themselves in Van Gogh's shoes to some extent. They were conscious of living through a revolution in love, but they refused to accept its occasional darker consequences: these ought not to exist. They wished to exorcise the demons.

The very last articles of Dedel's plea formulated the exorcism almost literally. He exhorted the gentlemen of the revision committee "as servants of the Highest Judge, not carrying the sword in vain, to help avenge, as a deterrence to all others, the innocently shed blood, and to lift the curse from the country."[50]

9
Van Gogh's Last Blood

Almost by definition, fatal attraction leads to disaster. Our story, in each of the two tales, has no heroes, only victims and losers. In the spring of 1778, Cecilia, Nathaniel, and Annie had lain in their graves for years and Dora was about to perish in prison. Van Gogh had been a loser for most of his life, but he thought he could win the last appeal procedure. He was wrong. On March 26, 1778, the revision committee reached a verdict: The High Council had arrived at its judgment without error.[1] By implication, the committee endorsed the sentence pronounced in Amsterdam twenty-six months earlier. Van Gogh had to return to his native town to be executed.

If we count prosecutor Dedel among the principal protagonists, the story has at least one winner. Without leaving for posterity a written appreciation of his plea, the revision committee allowed the HO to cast out the demons. The executioner's sword was to spill Van Gogh's last blood, avenge Annie's, and take away the curse from the country.

No reason for delay any longer. Van Gogh arrived back in Amsterdam on Monday, March 30.[2] The magistrates scheduled the execution for the following Saturday, the customary day for public punishment. April 4 was a mere ten weeks since the previous justice day. Consequently, a modest supply of convicts was available. Only three, condemned to a whipping, were to mount the scaffold together with the notorious killer. As usual, a clerk inserted the four names in advance in the register of justice days. He began with Van Gogh, noting that he was "to be beheaded and the body granted the earth, for stabbing Anna Smitshuizen to death." So well known were the victim and the whole case after almost three years. The clerk gave number two to Neeltje Donker, a female thief, unlikely to be a relative of Nathaniel. Benjamin Salomon Levy was condemned for theft and fraud in trading meat and Johannes van Sitteren for breaking into a ship.[3] A woman, a Jew, a man with an ordinary Dutch name, and his inveterate enemy—how would Hoefnagel have depicted this company?

Booksellers and writers of occasional verses, to whom an execution meant an economic opportunity, had to act quickly, too. This one promised big business. Since the market was most favorable on the justice day itself, the material needed to be ready within a week. Despite this short notice, one company managed to adorn the broadside they published with a drawing, admittedly a simple one. It showed Van Gogh's head, blindfolded, about to be severed from his body. The anonymous artist provided him with short hair and beard stubble, which reminds us of Hoefnagel's epithet "calimanco face." The verse, with the convict as the putative speaker, began with "trust no sighs, nor a stream of briny tears, which you see flowing from the eyes of a whore." That set the tone. Although this execution verse repeated the ancient stereotype that the convict had been bad from youth on, his principal offense was weakness. He shared that weakness, moreover, with men of fame such as Samson and Hercules, who had conquered mighty opponents, but against whom whores' tears had proved too formidable a weapon. The verse remained silent about Van Gogh's actual crime. He suffered capital punishment, not because he had stabbed a fellow human being to death, but because he had been unable to resist the temptations of a prostitute. This was a crass example of blaming the victim.[4]

Another would-be poet composed an acrostic, meant to accompany an engraving representing the execution. This verse deviated from traditional patterns by its lack of an unequivocal moral. The verse has the form of a dialogue among several spectators at the scaffold, including the one kneeling on it. It consists of two columns with thirty-eight lines each. The initial letters of each line, capitalized and printed sideways, read "*Johannes Bartholomeus Ferdinandus Van Gogh*" in the first column and "*Anna Smitshuysen, Geweezene Liev Van* [former sweetheart of] *Van Gogh*" in the second. One spectator bemoans the condemned's sad fate, in losing his loved one, although she was an unfaithful whore. Another: "But why did he have to stab her to death? He does look pitiful though." Van Gogh himself intervenes: "Really, I deserve it; let me die for my Annie." After this repeat of the wish he expressed just after the deed, it is the turn of a few moralistic speakers; one of them recollects Jesus' words that even murderers can enter his Father's kingdom. Quickly, another spectator

Van Gogh's Last Blood   193

draws attention to events going on: "Oh, the executioner raises the sword; oh, he leaves the world. May God give to young people, to all lovers, the right object of affection, which will save them."⁵ Taken as a whole, the dialogue perfectly expresses the mood of the day: emotional love, yes; fatal attraction, no.

While the writers they had commissioned were sweating over their manuscripts, the publishers prepared the advertisements for Saturday. Bookseller Dirk Schuurman advertised in the newspapers of Amsterdam and Haarlem. In the first, he announced the drawing of an artistic plate of the execution, which a capable master would set into copper. Those signing up for it could get a discount. The advertisement in the Haarlem newspaper said the plate would be ready for sale within three weeks. In the same paper, another bookseller advertised *Remarkable Life of Anna Smitshuizen.*⁶

Van Gogh's return to Amsterdam and his impending death gave rise to one last myth concerning his person: his conversion and ultimate confession of guilt. The myth has come down to us in a condensed and an embellished version.⁷ The latter has the form of a dialogue between Annie's murderer and one of the prisoners placed in his cell to guard him. The court customarily selected two inmates of the rasphouse, who earned their freedom with it, to accompany a capital convict through his last night and prevent suicide. This prisoner, however, with the unusual name of Koenraad Stroefhart, was a fictional character.⁸

Although impressed with his ward's intelligence and calling him "master" sometimes, Koenraad identifies with him to some degree: They are both no good, having sought godless company and visited brothels from youth on. But why does he have such a melancholic look on his face? Surely, Van Gogh must know yet another trick to prolong his life for a week or so! But the notorious killer just wants some sleep. Forgetting his duty, the other guard dozes off as well, but Koenraad keeps himself awake by chewing tobacco and swallowing it with coffee. He notices that the condemned sleeps very unquietly and offers him a cup of coffee when he wakes up. An awful nightmare, Van Gogh explains, has finally made him realize what an irreligious and blasphemous life he has led: "I saw Annie standing in front of me with burning eyes, bleeding chest, and threatening hands. My sins would be unforgivable, she said, if I were to enter eternity with a godless lie on my lips. She showed me the blood-stained knife and her pierced heart. Convinced that she was right, I wanted to embrace her, but she pushed me away from her into a deep pit. Then I woke up." Koenraad ironically remarks that falling into a pit is the wrong dream, the standard one for those sentenced to hanging, but Van Gogh is utterly serious. He waits for the assistant minister, who arrives in the early morning.

To the minister, he expresses his repentance and conversion to respect for God. Then the HO and the judges arrive. In a theatrical scene, Van Gogh asks them forgiveness for disappointing them and obstructing justice for so long. He confesses that he caused Annie's death on June 29, 1775, on purpose and with premeditation. His so-called suicidal intent was only a pretext. Thus far the embellished version, which like the condensed one ends with Van Gogh's exclamation on the scaffold, "oh Savior, have mercy on my poor soul." This was a satisfying and comforting account for everyone who preferred solid old religion over radical Enlightenment rubbish.

In reality, the condemned spent the eve of his execution in the customary fashion. First, he went through the ritual of death announcement. If the HO made a speech at the occasion, an optional part of the ceremony, the text has not survived. Afterward, the condemned had his gallows meal in the interrogation room, with the assistant minister and a few court officials.[9] At home, the magistrates laid out their black tabards and sashes with Saint Andrew's crosses ready for the next morning. The execution was to proceed according to the town's ancient ceremonial. Meanwhile, the secretary had recorded the official sentence in the court's register of sentences. The crucial passage proclaimed once more that Van Gogh had rushed toward Annie with a nasty scream and that he had rejoiced in her death saying, "then you won't be for another."[10] With all the publication the case had received over the years, highlighted anew by the rumor of his ultimate "conversion," it mattered little in practice what exactly the secretary would read to the assembled public. We do know that Van Gogh himself never confessed to premeditation.[11] He was to die with at least the satisfaction of not complying with Willem Dedel's view of his deed.

On the morning of April 4, 1778, J. B. F. Van Gogh, former actor in the city's theater, appeared on stage for his ultimate performance. Like the previous one, it was a real-life performance. Unlike in the previous case, his opposite player was a man: Jan van Aanhout, who carried out Donker's capital punishment and still held the office of provincial executioner.

Although Van Gogh played a leading role, he was a "silent character," as was Urania in The Jubilating Theater. In the series of three plays, the number of spectators had fluctuated. Several hundred had been present in 1763, but then Van Gogh was merely an extra. The real-life tragedy featuring him and Annie had boasted three or four spectators. At his very last performance, he drew an audience considerably larger than most actors could ever dream of. Thousands of spectators watched the hero of the play kneel down in a heap of sand on the scaffold, blindfolded. Van Aanhout raised his sword. He severed Van Gogh's head from his body in one perfect stroke, making for a quick and unproblematic execution.[12] The bloodtrack had come full circle: from the first blood the desperate lover had taken from his vein to serve as ink, via the warm blood from his beloved's heart streaming over his hands, to his own blood again, now imbuing the heap of sand on the scaffold with a deep red color.

Since the original sentence granted Van Gogh's corpse the earth, the theater was over. Van Aanhout, assisted by indoor executioner Carel Kleijne, laid the torso and the head in a coffin and arranged a quick burial. Van Aanhout charged the court a total of twenty-seven guilders for executing Van Gogh. In addition, Kleijne presented a bill of four guilders and ten stivers for nailing the coffin.[13]

Whereas Dutch newspapers seldom reported executions, the Antwerp *Gazette* of April 10 paid a great deal of attention to this one. World news came first though, including a report about the American War of Independence, praising the magnanimity of George Washington. The entire passage under the heading "Netherlands" concerned Van Gogh's execution. The reporter called him "a certain sea surgeon, well known in Amsterdam." He further mentioned the long appeal procedures and the HO's arguments for premeditation. The last paragraph was devoted to Van Gogh's supposed conversion, concluding with a moral: His example has shown to others the possible consequences of a licentious way of life.[14]

Toward the end of the month, the engraving announced by publisher Schuurman was ready for sale. A copy still survives today. We see the gentlemen watching from the windows of the town hall as usual. Interestingly, a number of ladies seem to accompany them. The audience is considerable indeed. In front, at the left, one spectator has a recognizable face with individual traits.[15] Could it be that Annie's paramour, the journeyman tailor missing since June 27, 1775, is looking at us here?

Van Gogh's execution: detail. At the bottom left "the journeyman tailor" appears. Photo: Gemeentearchief Amsterdam.

At the beginning of the next year, another side character reappeared. On January 6, 1779, HO Dedel decided to empty a brothel near the Long Bridge. This was a routine measure, probably occasioned by complaints from the neighbors. A deputy and a few court officials busted the house at night, arresting the madam and all women present. The magistrates interrogated them the next day. The madam was a forty-six year-old woman, who gave her name as Geertruyd van Kesteren, born in Nijmegen and living in Amsterdam for twelve or thirteen years.

The name failed to ring a bell with her interrogators, whether or not because she omitted the alias of Black Truy. They charged her with keeping a brothel at five subsequent addresses, lastly in the house in which she had been arrested the previous night. The first location was no less than the Oudezijds Achterburgwal canal near the Old Men's Home. The record gives no hint that the magistrates realized what had happened there in the afternoon of January 12, 1775. The suspect confirmed that she had lived at the addresses mentioned, except the second. She merely had charged the girls boarding money, she claimed, allowing them to bring in a man now and then. Thereupon, two deputies and four court officials declared they knew well enough that Geertruyd van Kesteren was a madam and that she had kept prostitutes at the addresses mentioned. Obviously, her activities had been known and condoned for years. On January 12, 1779, exactly four years after she had introduced Van Gogh to Annie, the court sentenced her to exposure on the scaffold, three years in the spinhouse, and three years banishment from the city. Public punishment was scheduled for January 30, without any capital case this time. While six criminals received a corporal chastisement, Geertruyd stood fastened to the scaffold's railing with a sign saying "whores' hostess." It was the first justice day since Van Gogh's decapitation.[16]

What shall we conclude, apart from the fact that Black Truy first arrived in Amsterdam around the time when Nathaniel and Dora murdered Cecilia? The name of Geertruyd van Kesteren had received full publicity before; she was the only person related to Van Gogh's case mentioned by her full name in the printed editions of his confession. Had most of the public forgotten about Annie and Van Gogh? The previous April, when he finally mounted the scaffold, everyone still remembered the case. Did his execution end all this? If so, Dedel had successfully cast out the demons.

The story ends today, with a new mystery. Since it involves the author of this book, I can speak for myself for the first time. Prosecutor Dedel neverl bothered to prove that Van Gogh merely claimed to have written the famous letter with his own blood. The confiscated original got lost, it seemed, after the HO had it copied. When performing research, however, I discovered a tiny piece of paper, which lay hidden in one of the criminal dossiers in the Amsterdam archive. It has fragments of the text in question written on both sides. The handwriting is similar to that of the comment on his confession that Van Gogh wrote for his attorney.[17] Unquestionably, it is a remnant of the original. I wanted to have this piece of paper tested in a lab for blood traces, but in that process it regrettably disappeared. As long as it is lost, we remain unsure whether Van Gogh really wrote that letter with his own blood.

Notes

Abbreviations Used in the Notes

DB   = *Gemeente-Archief* Amsterdam, Interrogations of Dorothea Bosselman
GA   = *Gemeente-Archief*
HvH = Archive of the Court of Holland (*Hof van Holland*)
J002 = *Gemeente-Archief* Amsterdam, Library, nr. J002
ND   = *Gemeente-Archief* Amsterdam, Interrogations of Nathaniel Donker
VG   = *Gemeente-Archief* Amsterdam, Interrogations of J. B. F. van Gogh

Notes to Prelude

1. GA Amsterdam, archive nr. 5020: *keurboek* U, fol. 141; Nieuwe Nederlandsche Jaarboeken, 1775: 28 June. Because the Ouderkerk ordinance was earlier, I assume that rabies had spread to Amsterdam from the countryside.

2. For the technique of bloodletting: van Andel 1933; Jütte 1991: 72–73; Cook 1993. For Van Gogh's right-handedness: VG3.

3. Copies of the letter in: J002; GA Amsterdam, archive nr. 5061, inv. nr. 441 (confession book); inv. nr. 640N (two copies). In two of these four copies the letter is dated June 28, in the others June 29. In one copy the passage about Annie's alleged pregnancy is underlined. Several printed copies of the letter were published.

Notes to Preface

1. See, among others, Wiltenburg 1992; Cohen (Daniel) 1993; Halttunen 1998. Compare also the interest in *crimes passionnels*, mainly in late-nineteenth-century France: Guillais 1986; Harris 1989. The shift, described by Halttunen, from an exclusively religious crime narrative to a more variegated murder literature (including the gothic genre) took place in the Netherlands a little earlier than it did in America.

2. Cohen and Cohen 1993; Srebnick 1995.

3. Ginzburg 1980; Davis 1983.

4. Elias 1969b: chapter 5 and passim. See also Elias 1983.

Notes to Chapter 1

1. Buisman 1992: 158–62; de Leeuwe in Erenstein 1996: 332–39.
2. *Naamlooziana* 1772: 121–52. See also Styl 1781: 70–74.
3. *Naamloziana* 1772: 187.
4. Barnouw 1963: 21.
5. Rasch 1991; Erenstein 1991: 382–83.
6. Buisman 1992: 164; de Leeuwe in Erenstein 1996: 332–39.
7. Buisman 1992: 165–87. On the Christian character of the Dutch Enlightenment also: Schama in Porter/ Teich 1981: 66–71.
8. The main works serving as the basis for the conclusions of this paragraph are: Blom et al. 1995; Bos 1998; Burke 1974; Davids/ Lucassen 1995; Diederiks 1982; Hart 1976; Jonker et al. 1984; Knevel 1994; van Leeuwen/ Oeppen 1993; Levie/ Zantkuyl 1980; Lourens/ Lucassen 1998; Nusteling 1985 & 1997; de Vries/ van der Woude 1995.
9. Popkin in Jacob/ Mijnhardt 1992: 273–75.
10. Mijnhardt in Jacob/ Mijnhardt 1992: 197–223.
11. Jacob 1981: 190–95; Jacob in Jacob/ Mijnhardt 1992: 224–40.
12. Darnton 1982. For a critique of Darnton, from the perspective of a more traditional history of ideas, see Eisenstein 1992.
13. Rogers 1970.
14. Jacob/ Mijnhardt 1992: 285 (Popkin) and 224–40 (Jacob). The writers Weyerman, Kersteman, Hoefnagel and Ockers are absent from the index of this volume.
15. Jacob 1981: 195–96; Bostoen/ Hanou 1997; van de Pol 1999.
16. Kersteman 1994.
17. ARA, HvH: inv. nr. 184 (26 August 1752).
18. ter Horst 1937; Huussen 1985. Kersteman 1792 is his semi-fictional autobiography. Since nothing is heard of him since that year, it is commonly assumed that he died then or shortly afterwards.
19. On imprisoned writers, see de Haas ed. 2002.
20. Jongenelen 1998: introduction. On Swiss publishers, notably the *Société Typographique de Neuchâtel*: Darnton 1982.
21. Sturkenboom 1998: 135–99. For an English version of some of these ideas: Sturkenboom 2000.
22. Sturkenboom 1998: 295–344.
23. GA Amsterdam, archive nr. 5061, inv. nr 434, pp. 47, 95, 115, 161, 176, 215.
24. Noordam 1995; van der Meer 1995. Spierenburg 1996b is a review article based on these two books.
25. Laqueur 1990; Cadden 1993.
26. Spierenburg 1998b: 326, 334–38 (based upon, among other works, van der Heijden 1998).
27. Sturkenboom 1998: 319–21.
28. On church discipline in early modern Amsterdam: Roodenburg 1990. The

recent book by Helmers (2002) on marital failure in late-eighteenth-century Amsterdam says little about long-term change. On marriage and honor: pp. 367–72.

29. In particular, van de Pol 1996. Unless otherwise mentioned, the information on prostitution in Amsterdam is from this book.

30. On domestic servants, see the contributions by van de Pol, Lucassen, Carlson and Dekker in Kloek et al. 1994.

31. Naamlooziana 1772: 235.

32. See my introduction and chapter in Spierenburg 1998a.

33. These figures deviate a little from those given in Spierenburg 1996a: 91, since I found a few more homicide trials since then.

34. For a set of passionate love letters by an inhabitant of sixteenth-century Pistoia, see Weinstein 2000: 123–28.

Notes to Chapter 2

1. Description of Batavia based on Blussé 1986 & 1997 and van der Brug 1994: 31–45.

2. Jan Booy and Immina Sterk, whose relationship to the family remained unrecorded, were witnesses: ARA, Centraal Bureau voor Genealogie: DTB Batavia. The original records, not the copies, are in a bad state.

3. GA Amsterdam, Archive nr. 5073, inv. nr. 1379 (testament of Pieter Donker); ARA, HvH, inv. nr. 188, f01.137vs.

4. As a rule of thumb (for the Western part of the Republic, 1680–1780) one can put the average workingman's daily wages at one guilder. A year counted about 300 workdays. The amount of 300 guilders, therefore, assumes an absence of sickness. On nominal wages in the Netherlands: de Vries/ van der Woude 1995: 703–13.

5. GA Amsterdam, archive nr. 5073, inv. nr. 1379 (testament of May 6, 1745). In this document, Bunga's name is spelled, in the Dutch manner, as Boenga.

6. GA Amsterdam, archive nr. 5073, inv. nr. 11 (dossier 1747). In 1748, Nathaniel's portion of the inheritance was said to be ƒ 23,900 (idem, inv. nr. 75, dossier nr. 14), but given the size of the estate, this sum must refer to only a part.

7. The Amsterdam copy of Donker's testament mentions that the original was copied at Batavia's Orphan Chamber on July 11, 1747.

8. GA Amsterdam, archive nr. 5073, inv. nr. 76 (dossiers 48–50).

9. GA Amsterdam, archive nr. 5073, inv. nr. 11 (dossier 1747); ARA, HvH, inv. nr. 185: May 24, 1753. Swaandregt is also called Swanendregt, both versions in various spellings.

10. Conclusions from minor financial claims on the Donker family. See: ARA, HvH, inv. nr. 189 (Nov. 12, 1755: Gerrit still alive) & inv. nr. 195, f01.156 (Jan. 22, 1761: Gerrit dead).

11. ND1.

12. Andreae/ Meijer 1968: nrs. 12510 and 12686.

13. ARA, HvH, inv. nr. 3134: June 4, 1753 (art. 3).

14. Jacob Klos was from Gorcum, while his wife was said to be born in Hellevoetsluis in one document and in Den Briel in another.

15. GA Rotterdam, DTB, Gereformeerde Dopen: Sept. 13, 1725; Oct. 10, 1727; March 30, 1732; Feb. 3, 1737; Oct. 25, 1740; Gereformeerd Trouwen: Feb. 4, 1725; Feb. 24, 1732; Gereformeerd Begraven: Oct. 4, 1727; Feb. 6, 1728.

16. ND14 (autopsy report of Dec. 12, 1766).

17. GA Den Haag, Index Ondertrouwen: March 12, 1747; GA Rotterdam, DTB, Gereformeerd Trouwen: March 19, 1747. All Dutch records list Woodrouffe's first name as Jacobus, but originally it must have been James.

18. The exact date is unknown, since his name, in various possible spellings, is absent from The Hague's burial records.

19. Year mentioned by his brother (ARA, HvH, nr. 3134: June 4, 1753) and (in 1759) by Nathaniel himself, confirming that he fell in love with Cecilia (ARA, HvH, nr. 194, f01.70).

20. ARA, HvH, nr. 3134: June 4, 1753 (art. 4–13).

21. GA Leiden, DTB: Kerkelijk Ondertrouwboek QQ (F7 no. 592, la 10), f01.1–19; Trouwboek Pieterskerk, no. 34 (F8 no. 426, la 11), f01.152–71. I am grateful to Aries van Meeteren for checking this for me.

22. I was unable to trace this act, mentioned in several later documents, in the archive of the High Court Martial.

23. GA Den Haag, archive nr. 351 (oud-rechterlijk archief): inv. nr. 3, f01.70; inv. nr. 33, dossier 1751.

24. Meijer 1972: 105. Date confirmed in Huijbrecht et al.: 113.

25. Information from Willem Frijhoff. See also his contribution to Jensma et al. 1985.

26. Information from Corrie Ridderikhoff. See also her contribution to Jensma et al. 1985.

27. Huijbrecht et al.: 113. "Birthday" refers to the day of his baptism.

28. The second petition used the word *geprostitueerd* which may refer either to prostitution or to moral corruption in general. On this word: van der Heijden 1998: 94–95.

29. ARA, HvH, nr. 3134: June 4, 1753 (art. 23–30).

30. ARA, HvH, inv. nr. 185: May 24, 1753.

31. There were several possibilities, such as a legal marriage, which led to majority before a man was 25, but none of them appears to have applied.

32. GA Amsterdam, archive nr. 5073, inv. nr. 1379 (dossier Donker); this document mentions two villages where Pieter Gerbrand went in 1753: Meersel (unidentifiable; perhaps Meerssen or Meerseloo) and Broekhoven (of which there are three, one south of Eindhoven, then in the Southern Netherlands). The May 1754 arrest in Nijmegen is also mentioned in: ARA, HvH, inv. nr. 188, f01.136.

33. GA Delft, Stadsarchief, inv. nr. 2031A.

34. On private confinement: Spierenburg 1991 (chapters 9 and 10) and 1995.

35. GA Amsterdam, archive nr. 5073, inv. nr. 1379 (dossier Donker). The precise amount of the declarations was ƒ 5,405 plus 18 stivers and 8 shillings.

36. GA Amsterdam, archive nr. 5073, inv. nr. 1: f01.100vs.

37. GA Amsterdam, archive nr. 5073, inv. nr. 1379 (dossier Donker); ARA, HvH, inv. nr. 188, f01.136.

38. ARA, Archive nr. 1.01.45 (Hoge Krijgsraad), inv. nr. 272: April 30, 1755 (in the column 'requests': Mr. Pieter Gerbrand Donker, *voogd* of his minor brother Nathaniel, asks for a *curator* for the latter; the column 'dispositions' left blank). The prolongation of the act of confinement in: GA Delft, Stadsarchief, nr. 2031A: April 21, 1755.
39. Frank-van Westrienen 1983.
40. ARA, HvH, inv. nr. 188, fols. 137vs (Pieter Gerbrand's request) & 143vs (Bitter's request) & inv. nr. 193, f01.65vs (revealing that Pieter Gerbrand went to Germany and Italy). Date of the Court's act of confinement confirmed in GA Delft, Stadsarchief, nr. 2031A.
41. *Mandement* procedures were numerous and the pronouncements are not indexed, but from later documents we know that the justices declared the Leiden marriage invalid.
42. ARA, HvH, inv. nr. 310: Feb. 26, 1756.
43. Demographic data in: Keyser 1956: 247. The description of Cleves is based mainly on Kleefsche Waterlust 1752 and the collection of travel accounts in the Stadtarchiv Kleve. See also Langendyk 1747 and Gorissen 1977.
44. Each year, when the churches reported on the number of baptisms, weddings and funerals, the Catholics and Mennonites did so in Dutch: Stadtarchiv Kleve, inv. nr. A VIII 23.
45. Stadtarchiv Kleve, inv. nr. A XXI 2 (Oct. 27, 1741).
46. Stadtarchiv Kleve, Reformed baptisms: Feb. 24, 1757.
47. ARA, HvH, inv. nr. 191, f01.35 (March 8, 1757). The actual amount of the debts was f 21,034 and 18 stivers.
48. Stadtarchiv Kleve, Reformed marriages: Aug. 21, 1757.
49. ARA, HvH, inv. nr. 193, fol. 65vs (a tailor as creditor), f01.254vs; inv. nr. 194, f01.85 (the victuals); inv. nr. 195, f01.118 (the boarding school).
50. Showalter 1996.
51. ARA, HvH, inv. nr. 193, f01.65vs. This source mentions the certificate of good conduct but has no copy of it. I was unable to trace a copy in the Stadtarchiv Kleve. The precise amount of the debts was f 11,573, 7 stivers and 7 shillings.
52. ARA, HvH, inv. nr. 193, f01.272; inv. nr. 313 (1759: Feb. 16, March 5, March 9, April 23, May 23, July 25).
53. ARA, HvH, inv. nr. 194, fol. 71vs (quote).
54. ARA, HvH, inv. nr. 194, fol. 70; inv. nr. 313: Nov. 1 and 15, 1759.
55. GA Den Haag, Index Ondertrouwen: Dec. 2, 1759; ARA, HvH, inv. nr. 313: Dec. 10, 1759.
56. ARA, HvH, inv. nr. 194, f01.85; inv. nr. 313: Nov. 2, 1759.
57. ARA, HvH, inv. nr. 195, f01.118. The precise amount of the debt was f 3,328, 3 stivers and 6 shillings.
58. ARA, HvH, inv. nr. 196 (May 1761); inv. nr. 315 (1761: April 21, 29, May 1, 4).
59. ARA, HvH, inv. nr. 316: May 3, 1762; inv. nr. 197, f01.123vs (May 4, 1762). On May 3 the Court already agreed to end the guardianship, so the session of May 4 must be considered a confirmation.
60. Name and age (five) mentioned in ARA, HvH, inv. nr. 203, f01.127 (Aug. 11, 1767). Name also mentioned in GA Nijmegen, Oud-Rechterlijk Archief, inv.

nr. 2650, f01.123vs-125. This son is absent from the baptismal registers of The Hague, Stompwijk (the village under which Visvliet resorted, which had only a Catholic church), Wilsveen and Leidsendam (two Reformed parishes serving Stompwijk).
61. GA Amsterdam, archive nr. 5073, inv. nr. 1379 (dossier Donker), March 14, 1763.
62. ARA, HvH, inv. nr. 317: June 28 and July 1, 1763.

Notes to Chapter 3

1. ARA, HvH, inv. nr. 200, f01.34. Cecilia's words are paraphrased, not literally quoted.
2. GA Amsterdam, archive nr. 5061, inv. nr. 426, after p. 530 (letter by Maria Steffens, Jan. 8, 1767).
3. DB7 (statement by Johanna Le Boeuf); GA Amsterdam, Notarieel Archief (H. D. van Hoorn), inv. nr. 14263: Dec. 24, 1766 (statement by Hendrik Hoendervoogd and Geertruy Steltman).
4. ND2.
5. DB1.
6. On Jan. 5, 1767 she said she was 25 and that she had been in The Netherlands for about seven years.
7. GA Amsterdam, archive nr. 5061, inv. nr. 19, p. 135.
8. GA Amsterdam, archive nr. 5061, inv. nr. 426, after p. 530 (letter by Maria Steffens, Jan. 8, 1767).
9. GA Nijmegen, Oud-Rechterlijk Archief, inv. nr. 2650, fols. 107-vs, 109vs-110, 112-13, 123vs-125. There is no accessible register of decisions by burgomasters (which might contain the final judgment).
10. All records since 1765 call Mrs. Steffens a widow, but her second husband is absent from Rotterdam's and The Hague's burial registers. The names of their two sons are too common to identify them with certainty. One Maria Steffens, buried in The Hague at age ten on Nov. 17, 1747 (GA Den Haag, Index Begraven), is probably their daughter.
11. ND14 (statements by Caatje van Bemmelen and Margaretha van Hantzin). Originals, with marks, in: GA Amsterdam, Notarieel Archief (H. D. van Hoorn), inv. nr. 14263: Dec. 19, 1766.
12. ND10.
13. The whereabouts of Nathaniel and Dora in 1765 and 1766 reconstructed from his own statement (ND2) and his mother-in-law's (GA Amsterdam, archive nr. 5061, inv. nr. 426, after p. 530, letter of Jan. 8, 1767). The latter dated the escape from the Leiden inn in the summer of 1766, but, in view of the sequence of events following, the spring is more likely.
14. See, for example, Gowing 1994.
15. ND19.
16. GA Amsterdam, Notarieel Archief (H. D. van Hoorn), inv. nr. 14263: Dec. 24, 1766; ND2; ND16; DB1.
17. DB1; DB4.

18. GA Amsterdam, Notarieel Archief (H. D. van Hoorn), inv. nr. 14263: Dec. 19, 1766. The type of ring is made explicit in the list of belongings (see next note).
19. GA Amsterdam, archive nr. 5061, inv. nr. 426, after p. 530: list drawn up by Cecilia's mother, who confirmed she had accompanied Cecilia to the barge. The list included the clothes Cecilia wore, mentioned in the previous paragraph. Details about some of the items supplemented from DB5 (where it is said that her mother packed the basket) and DB15. The mother's list mentions only one snuffbox; DB5 mentions two.
20. DB5.
21. GA Amsterdam, archive nr. 5061, inv. nr. 426, after p. 530: nailed to the statement of Dec. 19, 1766.
22. Boat schedule (end of seventeenth century): de Vries 1978: table 3.1. According to personal information from Jan de Vries, this schedule would have changed only in minor details by 1766. Since the sources mention that Cecilia left at 10 A.M., whereas in De Vries' schedule the boat leaves The Hague at 10.30 A.M., I also put the other arrivals and departures at thirty minutes earlier. This is congruent with the time Cecilia and Nathaniel checked into the Amsterdam inn.
23. DB2.
24. ND5 (the innkeeper's statement).
25. ND1.
26. ND6.
27. ND19 (p. 244 of the transcript).
28. ND5 (statements paraphrased, not literally quoted); ND19.
29. ND19. The phrase "you have pursued us long enough" is a literal quote (p. 248 of the transcript).
30. ND5; ND21.
31. de Vries 1978: 54–55.
32. ND19.

Notes to Chapter 4

1. DB5; DB13.
2. ND19; DB13.
3. DB13.
4. ND15; DB4.
5. ND19; ND20.
6. ND3; ND20. The spoken words are paraphrased.
7. Today, sunset is not yet completed in Amsterdam at 5 P.M. in early December, but the present Central European Time is ca. 45 minutes ahead of sun time.
8. ND3; ND16; ND19. Stalli was able to write his signature, see GA Amsterdam, Notarieel Archief (H. D. van Hoorn), inv. nr. 14263: Dec. 24, 1766.
9. On porter being a free trade: Wagenaar (folio ed.), vol. II, p. 475.
10. Determined by the author, who rewalked the same route, at a pace likely to have been the porter's with his loaded wheelbarrow, on May 4, 2000.
11. "zoo Juffrouw, ga je zoo uijt de stad; je zult mij Goddomme zoo niet verneuken": ND16 (pp. 199 & 206 of the transcript).

12. ND3; ND16; DB3; GA Amsterdam, Notarieel Archief (H. D. van Hoorn), inv. nr. 14263: Dec. 24, 1766 (statements by Michiel Stalli, Hendrik Hoendervoogt, Geertruy Steltman and Cornelia Voeteloos). The porter testified that Dora ran back to Nathaniel. She said that Nathaniel gave her the key to the house then (and that Verhoef had the only other key), but this is impossible, since she was the last to leave the house. Therefore, I assume the exchange concerned the key of the basket.

13. ND4; ND16; GA Amsterdam, Notarieel Archief (H. D. van Hoorn), inv. nr. 14263: Dec. 24, 1766 (statement by Michiel Stalli). On the *Steenenbeer*: note by J. W. E. in: *Maandblad Amstelodamum* 9 (1922): 44–45.

14. ND19.

15. ND18; ND19; DB4.

16. ND5; ND19; DB3. The quote ("wat heb ik op mijn hals gehaald") on p. 262 of the transcript. The grain carrier said he found the basket between 7 and 7.30; Donker said he returned home around 8. I compressed the interval a little, to make their statements conform.

17. University Library Amsterdam (depot): kr. 11, 1766, nr. 150 (Tuesday, Dec. 16, 1766).

18. ND14; GA Amsterdam, Notarieel Archief (H. D. van Hoorn), inv. nr. 14263: Dec. 30, 1766 (also in: archive nr. 5061, inv. nr. 426, after p. 530).

19. GA Amsterdam, Library, nr. B 54 (film nr. 3663): Dec. 9, 1766.

20. GA Amsterdam, archive nr. 5061, inv. nr. 426, after p. 530 (original). Copies in archive nr. 5061, inv. nr. 640g and in ND14.

21. ND14; GA Amsterdam, Notarieel Archief (H. D. van Hoorn), inv. nr. 14263: Dec. 30, 1766: statements 3–6. Copies of these statements and original of the second inspection report in: archive nr. 5061, inv. nr. 426, after p. 530. Copy of the second inspection report in inv. nr. 640g.

22. ND20.

23. GA Amsterdam, Library, nr. B 54 (film nr. 3663): Dec. 9, 1766.

24. DB6. Quote on p. 358 of the confession book.

25. ND8.

26. ND15; ND19.

27. GA Amsterdam, Notarieel Archief (H. D. van Hoorn), inv. nr. 14263: Dec. 24, 1766 (statement by Hendrik Hoendervoogd). According to this statement, Donker himself took the initiative to correct his signature, but it is more logical to assume The Owl wanted it. The correction took place the next morning.

28. GA Amsterdam, Library, nr. B 54 (film nr. 3663): Dec. 12, 1766.

29. ND6; DB1; DB2. The court never questioned Verhoef.

30. ND7 (pp. 91–93 of the transcript).

31. ND11 (p. 125 of the transcript).

32. First quote: ND12 (p. 135 of the transcript); second quote: ND19 (p. 265 of the transcript), which is Nathaniel's confession. That means he confirmed that Gaubert did not believe he was helping a murderer.

33. Donker related the events of Monday, Dec. 15, evasively, telling different versions, in ND6, ND11, ND12, ND13 and ND19. The version offered here is a reconstruction.

34. GA Amsterdam, archive nr. 5061, inv. nr. 633, Dec. 15, 1766.

35. ND7; ND10; ND14. The neighbor stated in court that Mrs. Steffens went

to Amsterdam immediately after receiving Donker's letter, but she must have been mistaken, because this is incongruent with the remark she wrote on the cover. During the trial, the court had this letter and the remark written on it is mentioned in the protocols twice.

36. DB4; DB7.
37. DB2.
38. ARA, HvH, inv. nr. 192, f 0.179 (April 25, 1758).
39. According to Johanna's testimony, given half a year later, Dora said "three weeks ago." I assume Johanna was mistaken. On the 17th, the dumping of the body was exactly two weeks before.
40. Garrioch 1986: 32–33.
41. For the events of Dec. 17–19: DB7; DB8; DB9; DB10. I did not find a reference to the murder in contemporary newspapers. According to Dora, the episode with the song was in the evening of the 18th; according to Johanna it was on the morning of the 19th. Johanna said she had heard about the murder of Cecilia on the 18th and asked Dora about her complicity in the evening of that day. The events are arranged here in the most logical order. Notably, Johanna's reading of the song about "a murder" must precede her hearing in The White Horse that the victim was Cecilia.
42. GA Amsterdam, archive nr. 5061, inv. nr. 19, pp. 131–35.
43. DB2; DB7. "Fattie" is my translation of *Spekje*, an alias connoting that the man was as fat as lard in the soup.
44. GA Amsterdam, Notarieel Archief (Thierry Daniel de Marolles), inv. nr. 11459: Dec. 24, 1766 (nr. 106).
45. ND18.
46. ARA, archive nr. 3.03.08.221 (Rijnland), inv. nr. 99: Jan. 1 & Jan. 4, 1767; GA Amsterdam, archive nr. 5061, inv. nr. 19, pp. 142–45; DB5.
47. GA Amsterdam, Library, nr. B 54 (film nr. 3663): Jan. 1, 1767 (p. 323).

Notes to Chapter 5

1. DB15 (quotes on p. 331 of the confession book).
2. On these procedures: Faber 1983.
3. Elias (Johan E.) 1963: nr. 383.
4. ND1 (quote on p. 10 of the transcript).
5. DB1.
6. DB2; DB3. Since the head remained in the hospital and was shown again in March, I assume it was kept in strong water.
7. GA Amsterdam, archive nr. 5061, inv. nr. 426, after p. 530 (statement by Maria Steffens).
8. ND6.
9. ND7; ND8; ND9 (quote on p. 109 of the transcript); ND10.
10. DB4.
11. DB5; DB6; GA Amsterdam, Notarieel Archief, inv. nr. 14264 (H. D. van Hoorn): March 5, 1767; GA Amsterdam, archive nr. 5061, inv. nr. 127 (year 1767).
12. GA Amsterdam, archive nr. 5061, inv. nr. 633: Feb.–April 1767. There

were unspecified extra expenses for Nathaniel to the amount of eight guilders and fourteen stivers.
13. ND11; ND12; ND13; ND14.
14. ND15; ND16; ND17.
15. DB7; DB8; DB9; DB10.
16. ND18; DB11.
17. ND19 (pp. 242–43 of the transcript).
18. ND19. In the archive, I found no trace of court action against Gaubert.
19. ND20.
20. GA Amsterdam, Library, nr. B 54 (film nr. 3663): July 11, 1767 (p. 329).
21. DB12.
22. ND21; DB13; GA Amsterdam, archive nr. 5061, inv. nr. 633: May–July 1767; ND22 (Donker's original signature in the confession book: GA Amsterdam, archive nr. 5061, inv. nr. 427, p. 284).
23. Spierenburg 1978: 152–61.
24. GA Amsterdam, archive nr. 5061, inv. nr. 81.
25. DB14.
26. GA Amsterdam, Library, nr. B 54 (film nr. 3663): July 18, 1767 (p. 330).
27. ARA, HvH, inv. nr. 203, f01.127 (August 11, 1767).
28. GA Amsterdam, archive nr. 5061, inv. nr. 633: Aug.–Oct. 1767.
29. GA Amsterdam, archive nr. 5061, inv. nr. 427, p. 330. Only the judges' sentence is recorded, with the two clauses deleted, which I assume were part of the prosecutor's demand.
30. Compare Evans 1996.
31. *Confessie van Nathanaël Donker*, 1767: 14–15.
32. GA Amsterdam, archive nr. 5061, inv. nr. 633: Aug.–Oct. 1767.
33. GA Amsterdam, Library, nr. B 54 (film nr. 3663): Aug. 22, 1767.
34. On executions in early modern Amsterdam: Spierenburg 1984.
35. GA Amsterdam, archive nr. 5061, inv. nr. 638: Aug. 22, 1767; inv. nr. 81 (year: 1767).
36. GA Amsterdam, Library, nr. B 54 (film nr. 3663): Aug. 22, 1767. (This witness informed Bicker Raye.)
37. GA Amsterdam, archive nr. 5061, inv. nr. 616: nr. 7.
38. GA Amsterdam, Library, nr. B 54 (film nr. 3663): Aug. 22, 1767. Compare Spierenburg 1984: 39.
39. GA Amsterdam, archive nr. 5061, inv. nr. 127 (year 1767).
40. The Amsterdam newspaper (University Library Amsterdam, depot: kr. 11, 1767, nr. 101, Saturday, Dec. 22, 1767) advertized for, among other books, a "sermon held by the reverend Schepp at the occasion of the punishment of six criminals." This work possibly referred to Donker (although minister Ten Brink assisted him) and the five persons whipped. It is absent (in various spellings) from the Dutch central book catalogue.
41. Confessie van Nathanaël Donker, 1767. Under "F Donker N" the library of the GA Amsterdam also has a handwritten copy of Donker's confession (without the speech), which probably formed the basis for the booklet. Both copies wrongly date his confession on July 16. Unlike the confession, the sentence mentioned neither Pieter Gerbrand nor Gaubert.

42. GA Amsterdam, Library, nr. B 54 (film nr. 3663): pp. 333–34.
43. Kersteman 1784: 150–53. Kersteman's authorship and date of this edition mentioned in the catalogue of the Amsterdam University Library.
44. The only candidate for being Cecilia's mother in The Hague's burial registers is a Maria van der Linden buried on May 3, 1768 at age 66. There is a slight chance that she is the Maria Stevens buried on April 25, 1789 at age 89. She may of course have left The Hague.
45. GA Amsterdam, Archive nr. 5073, inv. nr. 1379 (dossier Donker), Nov. 29, 1774.
46. GA Amsterdam, archive nr. 5061, inv. nr. 427, p. 479.
47. GA Amsterdam, Library, nr. B 54 (film nr. 3663): Oct. 14, 1767.
48. GA Amsterdam, archive nr. 5061, inv. nr. 633: Aug.–Oct. 1767.
49. Spierenburg 1991: passim; van de Pol 1996: 187–96.
50. GA Amsterdam, archive nr. 195 (Bicker family), inv. nr. 152, p. 33. This is an old reference, which I originally owe to Sjoerd Faber.
51. GA Amsterdam, archive nr. 5061, inv. nr. 437, pp. 386–98.
52. GA Amsterdam, archive nr. 195 (Bicker family), inv. nr. 152: notes at the beginning, paginated 32–35. The notes are by Jan Bernd Bicker, one of the judges in January 1774. He mistakenly dated Dora's escape attempt in the same year.
53. Gijsen s.a.: 330. Compare van de Pol 1996: 30.

Notes to Chapter 6

1. VG1; Hoefnagel, Brief aan Ockers, 1772: 21. According to Merkwaerdige Samenspraak (1778: 20), Van Gogh was born in Vianen, but the baptismal records of that town fail to corroborate this claim. The period knew no uniform spelling, so his name was also spelled as "Van Gog" and "Van Goch."
2. "welke waarschynlyk is ymant van des Impetrants familie": J002, *deductie* by Dedel, p. 56, art. 1193.
3. Hoefnagel, Antwoord aan de Jonker, 1775: 1 (one of the epithets is *'t Stikziende Vroedvrouwszoontje*).
4. Haarlem, RA Noord-Holland, archive nr. 184, inv. nr. 2591: March 26, 1782. I was unable to trace this widow in Ouderkerk's burial registers; the burial registers of one of the two Catholic parishes are missing for this period. Although the auction register did not say the widow was deceased (sometimes widows sold goods after their husband's death, to provide their children with an inheritance portion), most of the auctions listed in it concerned the goods of someone who had died. In Haastrecht, a comparable village, auctions with returns up to ƒ 120 constituted the lowest quarter of the total of auctions, but these included the sale of furniture (information from Johan Kamermans).
5. She signed her statement with "Johanna B. Van Gog": GA Amsterdam, Notarial Archive, inv. nr. 16135, nr. 169.
6. No Van Gogh appears in Vreeland's baptism, marriage, or burial registers.
7. Waarachtig Bericht: 41–45 (written by his friend); *Hollandsche Toneelbeschouwer*, nr.11 (18 Jan. 1763): 184–85.
8. "O Batavieren, die, in Amstels ruime wallen/ Eene ongestoorde rust, een vry verblyf geniet/ En daaglyks aantoont dat de Kunsten u gevallen/ Wanneer ge in

deezen Burg haar juichend hulde bied. . . . Dat de oorlog, als voorheen, met Janus tempeldeuren/ Te ontgrendlen, nimmer weêr dit vrolyk Zangchoor sluit/ Maar 't lief genot der Vrede u altoos doe bespeuren/ Dat tevens met den palm, waarmeê zy Neêrlands bruid/ De schoone Vryheid strooit, uw welvaart aan blyv' groeijen/ Dan zal, tot aller heil, de Kunst door Yver bloeijen" (Pater 1763: 18–19).

9. *Hollandsche Toneel-beschouwer*, nr. 11 (18 Jan. 1763): 183–84. The Amsterdam University Library's copy of this journal is one bound volume, with reviews of plays performed from August 30, 1762 until May 24, 1763. Another journal, *Schouwburg Nieuws of Merkwaardige Berichten*, published in two volumes in 1764–65, has reviews from September 1762 on. However, according to Hanou (in Erenstein 1996: 326–31), the first issue of *Schouwburg Nieuws* was published in July 1762, which makes it the first Dutch-language journal devoted to theater. It mostly deals with the contents of plays and does not even mention *The Jubilating Theater*.

10. *Hollandsche Toneel-beschouwer*, nr.11 (18 Jan. 1763): 185–87.
11. *Hollandsche Toneel-beschouwer*: 201, 208, 211, 219.
12. *Waarachtig Bericht*: 41–44. According to the author, this letter was dated Saturday, February 18, 1763. However, Feb. 18 was a Friday. The theater's archive was destroyed in the 1772 fire.
13. *Hollandsche Toneel-beschouwer*: 509.
14. *Gedicht Geschreven in de Treurkamer*, 1778.
15. Pratasik 1997
16. See the bibliography in Groot (Hans de) 1980.
17. Cf. Erenstein 1991. Other information on the theater and acting from Wybrands 1873; Brandt/ Hogendoorn 1993; Erenstein ed. 1996.
18. *Antwoord aan de Rotterdamsche Klik-Spaan*, 1773: 6.
19. *Nodige Aanmerking*, 1773: 6.
20. *Dubbele Overweeging*, 1772: 11.
21. *Hollandsche Toneel-beschouwer*, 1763: 517.
22. Styl 1781: 2, 8, 17, 31, 61.
23. Corver 1786: 81. Punt actually was sixty-one.
24. GA Amsterdam, archive nr. 366, inv. nrs. 255 (16 Nov. 1760) & 252 (15 Nov. 1762).
25. VG1.
26. Jacob 1981; Jacob in Jacob/ Mijnhardt 1992: 224–40.
27. Hoefnagel, Brief aan Ockers, 1772: 29; Amsteldamsche Democriet: 7.
28. *Naamlooziana*: 5. According to Hoefnagel (Brief aan Ockers, 1772: 56) Ockers had written the first fourteen issues of this journal, whereupon Hoefnagel himself wrote the next fifteen. Issues 12–16 deal with the Amsterdam theater fire. They treat it rather factually, without moralism, but issue 16 suddenly concludes with a passage attacking atheist writers. This is consistent with the claim of a change of authors.
29. On La Mettrie: Thijssen 1982; Wellman 1992. Wellman refers to La Mettrie's notion of the fundamental similarity of animals and humans several times, but mostly in relation to Descartes' philosophy. She does not list Thijssen's book in her bibliography. On Descartes' ideas serving as a legitimation for humans' callous treatment of animals: Thomas 1983: 33–35. However, Thomas

repeats the mistaken notion that La Mettrie simply extended Descartes' animal-machine theory to humans.

30. Ockers 1766. The date 1766, written with a pencil on the copy of the Amsterdam University Library, also appears in the catalogue of the library of the GA Amsterdam. The catalogue of the Amsterdam University Library dates it 1768. Hoefnagel (Brief aan Ockers, 1772: 56) also attributed this work to Ockers.

31. van Merken 1768 (printed with a privilege from the Estates of Holland).

32. Ockers 1769.

33. Quoted in Knuttel 1914: 53 (nr. 171); he dates the book 1769. Compare Hoefnagel, Brief aan Ockers, 1772.

34. Hanou 1972-73: 65-68.

35. *Alle de Magistraatsgezinde*, 1782: 18.

36. Jongenelen 1998: nr. 110.

37. "Zoo krygt gy Pasquiljant, dan eindelyk uw loon/ Die niet bekeerdt zyt door den doodval van uw zoon." The poem is one of a dozen publications pro and contra Hoefnagel, bound into one volume with the Amsterdam University Library's copy of Neerlandsch Echo (hereafter in the notes as "after Neerlandsch Echo").

38. Brief van een voornaam heer (after Neerlandsch Echo). This pamphlet and the verses against Hoefnagel are cited in Roef-discours (65-72), a work which Hoefnagel also ascribed to Ockers.

39. Hoefnagel, Echte en waare verantwoording (after Neerlandsch Echo; also in Ghent University Library).

40. *Brief aan Hoefnagel . . . Kortegaart* (the author signed with "N.N. in Monnikendam"); Hoefnagel, Antwoort op Johannes Naweeger (after Neerlandsch Echo).

41. Hoefnagel, Brief aan Ockers, 1772: 21-24. Hoefnagel called the German Pieter Wever; his name is re-germanized here. Quotations are a little paraphrased.

42. *Alle de Magistraatsgezinde*, 1782: 22.

43. Hoefnagel, Brief aan Ockers, 1772: 29-30, 51.

44. Hoefnagel, Brief aan Ockers, 1772: 23-24, 30, 53-55.

45. *Alle de Magistraatsgezinde*, 1782: 22. Waarachtig Bericht (10-14) alleges that Van Gogh had secretly treated Hoefnagel for venereal disease. This story lacks credibility, because it is hard to tell why Van Gogh kept the secret when Hoefnagel turned against him later.

46. *Naakte Waarheid*, 1782: 28.

47. *Dubbele Overweeging*, 1772: 15; *Waarachtig Bericht*: 14-19; Corver 1786: 129; Rössing 1874: 20, 77; Coffeng 1965. Waarachtig Bericht dates the funeral to Nov. 12 and says the collection was done on 11 and 12 Nov. According to Coffeng, Zuiderhout was buried on Nov. 11. He was baptized on Dec. 11, 1746. Tithoff's name was also spelled Tethoff or Tiethoff. According to Rössing, the amount of f 34, contributed by the youngest regent, was for the cost of the funeral.

48. *Waarachtig Bericht*: 16-19.

49. *Waarachtig Bericht* says Van Gogh found out that she had behaved badly in the past. According to Hoefnagel (Antwoord aan de Jonker, 1775), all three of Van Gogh's lovers had jilted him. Both authors agree that Van Gogh had had three affairs in all.

50. It is only two independent sources if Hoefnagel wrote Annie's biography: see the discussion in the next chapter.

51. *Waarachtig Bericht*: 68–71.
52. GA Amsterdam, archive nr. 5061, inv. nrs. 419, pp. 71, 101 & 420, pp. 329, 342. However, her sentence was six months, whereas Waarachtig Bericht says Eva served in the spinhouse for three years.
53. Hoefnagel, Antwoord aan de Jonker, 1775: 9. Compare *Merkwaardige Levensgevallen*: 232, 248. This source agrees with Waarachtig Bericht that the widow lived in the Vijzelstraat.
54. The 1774 libel is referred to in Waarachtig Bericht: 10, 20 and Brief aan Hoefnagel . . . Magog: 5 (which says "five stones" instead of seven).
55. Cf. Ryswykze Vrouwendaagze Courand, 1774. Of Hoefnagel's parody, called Ryswyksche Vrouwendaagsche Na-Courant, no copies are extant. Cf. Hanou 1973.
56. *Rotterdamse Klik-Spaan*, 1773; A*ntwoord aan de Rotterdamsche Klik-Spaan*, 1773; *Missive Leijden*, 1774; Styl 1781: 83; Corver 1786: 137; Rössing 1874: 77. Tithoff's new husband, H. Hencke, was no actor.
57. *Naauwkeurige Hollandsche Almanach*, 1775: 136–40; Rössing 1874: 61–69; Wolterson 1947: 160. Having married a widower in the meantime, Van Merken was known now as Lucretia van Winter.
58. Mijnhardt in Hunt 1993: 283–300.
59. Darnton 1982: 117 (on hatred of the system: 34, 121).
60. Hoefnagel, *De Nederlandsche Faam*. Anonymous and undated. The catalogue of the Dutch Royal Library ascribes it to Hoefnagel and dates it ca. 1775.

Notes to Chapter 7

1. However, another daughter was named Antje and three sons were named Jan, with only one child buried in the meantime. Possibly, not every child burial was registered. On the index card of the first Anna, a later writer incorrectly wrote "murdered by Van Gogh."
2. Regionaal Archief Alkmaar, DTB, nrs. 14–16 (Gereformeerde Doopboeken), 31 and 33 (Gereformeerde Huwelijken), 52 (Begraven op het Kerkhof); GA Amsterdam, DTB, nr. 586, p. 132.
3. *Merkwaardige Levensgevallen*: 18–24. That Annie's first master was an apothecary is from Waarachtig Bericht: 62.
4. *Merkwaardige Levensgevallen*: Voorreden.
5. *Waarachtig Bericht*: 1, 16, 37–40. Probably based on this work, the catalogue of the library of the Alkmaar archive, which has a copy of Merkwaardige Levensgevallen, ascribes it to Hoefnagel. The woman was actually termed "Mrs. E . . . h" with her husband sometimes calling her Betje. This can only refer to the name Elisabeth.
6. *Alle de Magistraatsgezinde*, 1782: 22.
7. Buijnsters 1980: 41. Repeated in Zevenbergen 1985: 72.
8. The author of *Waarachtig Bericht* had not (yet) noticed this; he apparently reacted to an earlier version of *Merkwaardige Levensgevallen* (no longer extant), consisting of the first two chapters only.
9. Hanou in *Spektator* 3 (1973–74): 574–76. Hanou cites the judicial records,

which are more trustworthy than Kersteman's embellished autobiography, in which he claims he was allowed a desk and pen in the Rotterdam prison from the beginning (Kersteman: 1792: 33).

10. *Zeldzaame Droom*, 1773; *Hekke-Sluiter*, 1792.

11. This causes another problem, since the index of Amsterdam's burial records has no Smitshuizen or Kluiten in 1775.

12. *Merkwaardige Levensgevallen:* 24–59. The information about Annie's whore's name is from Waarachtig Bericht (44), whose author chides the author of Merkwaardige Levensgevallen for not knowing this. Annie's stay in The English Haystack and the threesome with the tailor and his wife are confirmed in Waarachtig Bericht (65–66).

13. J002: Van Gogh's comment on his confession, p. 3; *Waarachtig Bericht*: 22–27, 37–40, 63–65. The latter source also reports that Annie had lived in concubinage with a sailor, named Dirk or Jan Smit, in 1770–71, but this is unconfirmed by other sources.

14. That Moreu had three children is mentioned in GA Amsterdam, Begraafboek nr. 1243, f01.56 (because the children are not mentioned in the records of Van Gogh's case, I assume they had left home). His wife's illiteracy is revealed in: GA Amsterdam, Notarieel Archief, inv. nr. 16135: nr. 169.

15. VG1; *Waarachtig Bericht*: 65–66.

16. Sturkenboom 1998: 322–23.

17. VG1; *Waarachtig Bericht*: 66–71.

18. *Waarachtig Bericht*: 62–64.

19. Suggested in *Waarachtig Bericht*: 48.

20. *Merkwaardige Levensgevallen*: 231–42.

21. *Waarachtig Bericht*: 53–56; Hoefnagel, Antwoord aan de Jonker, 1775: 13–14. Both agree that Hoefnagel met Van Gogh in the pub in the Nes.

22. *Brief aan Hoefnagel . . . Magog*, 1775: 2.

23. VG2.

24. VG2. Van Gogh used the verb *beproeven*, which means to test as well as to put to an ordeal.

25. Although unconfirmed in Amsterdam's burial records, Waarachtig Bericht (48–50) is very precise about the date; on May 26, 1775, the same day that the agreement for the room at the Herengracht was made and a day after Annie and Van Gogh went to his mother.

26. VG2.

27. *Waarachtig Bericht*: 50–53.

28. J002: transscriptions of letters by Van Gogh and Annie.

29. The date of May 10 for the first pamphlet is mentioned in the second (*Brief aan Hoefnagel . . . Magog*, 1775: 3), which itself is dated May 19; the third pamphlet (Hoefnagel, Antwoord aan de Jonker, 1775) has no date on it, but Waarachtig Bericht (56) dates it on the 26th.

30. Information from Irene Groeneweg.

31. I assume this, because May 24 is the earliest date recorded on which Annie was concerned about Van Gogh's public notoriety.

32. Hoefnagel, Antwoord aan de Jonker, 1775: 5. The words translated as "dresses" and "mender" are *palieze* and *verkielder*. The first does not appear in the

Woordenboek der Nederlandse Taal; the second only with another meaning, but here it must be related to *kiel* (a lower-class piece of clothing).

33. The original statements taken from the neighbors by a notary, with signatures and marks, in: GA Amsterdam, Notarieel Archief, inv. nr. 14269: nr. 38. Copies in VG2. The statements are our source for events up to June 27.

34. GAA, J002: witnesses for the defense; VG4.

35. VG3.

36. VG2; J002: Van Gogh's comment on his confession, p. 3.

37. J002: Van Gogh's comment on his confession, pp. 2–3. Truy and her daughter declared they had never seen another man but Van Gogh in Annie's room (VG2), which Van Gogh called a lie. Van Gogh was probably wrong in thinking the last time he fought with the tailor was on the 26th: the widow insisted that it was on the 27th and she described another incident than Van Gogh did for the 26th, which he said was omitted from his confession.

38. VG2.

39. *Waarachtig Bericht*: 22–29.

40. Kloek 1985, vol. II: 10.

41. Sturkenboom 1998: 344–52.

42. This holds true for the average Dutch, German, and English sentimental novel. In France, *Manon Lescaut* by Prévost (1731), in which the heroine is a sort of semi-prostitute, forms a partial exception. In Dutch erotic novels of the seventeenth century and the first half of the eighteenth, men often fall in love unknowingly with a prostitute who pretends to be a lady. Information from Inger Leemans.

43. VG2.

44. Francken 1733: 63–66 and information from Frank Huisman.

45. *Waarachtig Bericht*: 19.

46. VG5.

47. J002: witnesses for the defense. The incident with the wedge is confirmed in VG3. Teunis denied having used threatening language to Van Gogh, but the latter and Johanna said he did.

48. VG1. The rendering of the following events, until the murder scene, is based, unless indicated otherwise, on VG1 and VG3.

49. Both notes in J002: transsscriptions of letters by Van Gogh and Annie; also in GA Amsterdam, archive nr. 5061, inv. nr. 640N.

50. J002: transsscriptions of letters by Van Gogh and Annie.

51. The description of the murder scene and Van Gogh's behavior immediately afterwards, is an interpretation based on VG1, VG3, VG4, VG5, and J002: Van Gogh's comment on his confession, p. 7. This scene was the one most contested in court: see chapter 9.

52. Wording based on several, slightly different versions in VG3 and VG5. The word translated as pimp was *pol*, an eighteenth-century word with an imprecise meaning; it stood for a man in (any) negatively valued relationship to a woman, among others a brothel keeper.

Notes to Chapter 8

1. "Hier bijd een martelaar der teederste aller liefde/ Anna Smitshuijsen wast, die hem het Hert dus griefde/ Zij had hem't hart geroofd, gaf hem in schijn haar min/ Maar spande saamen met een snoode hoerwaardin/ Misleijde hem dus zeer vals, dies zij't ligt ontrukte/ Wijl hij Niet kon weerstaan die rampe die hem drukte/ Gij wandelaar neemd een voorbeeld aan 't geen hem wedervoer/ Vertrouwd u nimmer op de listen van een hoer": J002: transscriptions of letters by Van Gogh and Annie.
2. VG5. Nevertheless, the clerk who copied the poem, wrote *"grafschrift"* (epitaph) on the back.
3. *Confessie van Johannis B., F., van Gog*, 1775 (the Amsterdam University Library has two identical copies). There were a few other minor mistakes.
4. *Ondervragingen en antwoorden van Johannes Barth. Ferdinandus van Gog*, 1775 (quoted footnote on p. 12). The Amsterdam University Library has one copy; another is inserted in J002. Possibly, there were separate editions also of the letters and notes, which have not survived.
5. de Vries 1978: 79, 116, 210. For chatting in barges, see the quotations in the *Woordenboek der Nederlandse Taal*, under *roef*.
6. *Merkwaardige Levensgevallen*: 80.
7. *Merkwaardige Levensgevallen*: 116–17.
8. *Merkwaardige Levensgevallen*: 125–30.
9. *Merkwaardige Levensgevallen*: 200.
10. *Waarachtig Bericht*: 50–60.
11. *Merkwaardige Levensgevallen*: 11–16; *Waarachtig Bericht*: 1–9, 35, 45–47. The two pamphlets probably appeared in 1776. According to *Waarachtig Bericht*, Van Gogh wrote a refutation of both on Dec. 12 of that year.
12. *Waarachtig Bericht*: 31–37.
13. On the spiritualization of honor, see my introduction to Spierenburg 1998a.
14. *Merkwaardige Levensgevallen*: 195–215 (quote on p. 212).
15. See Walker 1981.
16. Compare van de Pol 1996: 320–21.
17. *Merkwaardige Levensgevallen*: 17, 71, 191–95.
18. VG4.
19. *Merkwaardige Levensgevallen*: 250–52.
20. Delaney 1977. Daniel A. Cohen (1997) argues that the motif of the beautiful female murder victim appeared in England and America around 1800, while prefigurations of it date back another two hundred years.
21. GA Amsterdam, archive nr. 5061, inv. nr. 640g: June 30, 1775. Copy in VG4.
22. Elias (Johan E.) 1963: nr. 393.
23. Account of the first trial based on the interrogation protocol (VG 1–6) & J002: Van Gogh's comment on his confession.
24. According to the confession book all judges were present; the copy in J002 has only Deutz and Munter present.

25. The dating, in the confession book, of the fourth and fifth sessions on July 13 and 19 is in accordance with the cases immediately preceding and following; the copy in J002 incorrectly dates them on July 23 and 29.

26. GA Amsterdam, archive nr. 5061, inv. nr. 633: Aug.–Oct. 1775.

27. GA Amsterdam, archive nr. 195 (Bicker family), inv. nr. 152: Aug. 9, 1775.

28. Request inserted in J002.

29. GA Amsterdam, DTB, Begraafboek nr. 1243, f01.56.

30. GA Amsterdam, Notarial Archive, inv. nr. 16135, nr. 169 (Oct. 30, 1775). Copies in J002. (Notary Mastenbroek officially registered the statements on the 30th.)

31. *Waarachtig Bericht*: 74–77.

32. GA Amsterdam, archive nr. 5061, inv. nr. 1906, f01.63vs. (registration of ordinarius trial); J002 (pleas in ordinarius trial).

33. GA Amsterdam, archive nr. 5061, inv. nrs. 128 (deputy's bill of 10–11 July, 1776, in dossier for 1778) and 633, 634 (jailkeeper's bills).

34. Confession, with markers added by Thomeeze, and Van Gogh's handwritten comments in J002.

35. J002: Van Gogh's comment on his confession, p. 5.

36. Styl 1781: 50–51.

37. ARA, HvH, inv. nr. 1004 (civiele sententiën 1776), nr. 29. Copy in J002.

38. Verhas 1997: 25–33. Holland instituted the *Hoge Raad* in 1582 and Zeeland joined its jurisdiction in 1587.

39. ARA, archive nr. 3.02.02 (Hoge Raad), inv. nr. 861 (geëxtendeerde sententiën, 1775–77): f01.172–82vs. Copy of verdict in J002.

40. Verhas 1997: 144–47.

41. Composition of committee, with their names, in J002. I was unable to trace the granting of the revision procedure in the archive of the Estates of Holland.

42. In all probability, J002 (containing a complete set of trial papers, the printed confession with handwritten annotation and Van Gogh's handwritten comment for his attorney) was Thomeeze's personal copy of the dossier of the revision procedure. The Amsterdam Archive bought this dossier at an auction at the end of the nineteenth century. A bound volume in print, containing the plea by Thomeeze and Dedel's reply (with identical article and page numbers) plus the sentences of the various courts, survives in the library of the Alkmaar Archive.

43. J002, Deductie: art. 1–3. Also in this procedure, Van Gogh technically was the party who took the initiative, demanding a revision of his sentence. The record denotes him as the *impetrant*. Since, after all, he was accused of a crime, I have translated *impetrant* as defendant.

44. J002, Dedel's reply: art. 51–53. Italics in the original.

45. J002, Dedel's reply: art. 1126.

46. See the quotations in *Woordenboek der Nederlandse Taal* (under 'romanesk').

47. J002, Dedel's reply: art. 2079.

48. J002, Dedel's reply: art. 2306.

49. Hokke 1987. The "spectatorial" writers' ideal of the restrained man of feeling was primarily a middle-class man. Both the elite and the lower classes, they claimed, had more passionate feelings: Sturkenboom 1998: 355.

50. "om als dienaars van den oppersten Regter, en het zwaard niet te vergeefs

dragende, het onschuldig vergoten bloed, alzoo ten affschrik van alle anderen, te helpen wreken, en den vloek uit den lande weg te doen." J002, Dedel's reply: art. 2609–11.

Notes to Chapter 9

1. J002 (following on the printed pleas).
2. J002 (*Antwerpse Gazette*). Although the jailkeeper (GA Amsterdam, archive nr. 5061, inv. nr. 634: Feb.–April, 1778) wrote that Van Gogh arrived on the 26th, he charged the court for six days, which is consistent with an arrival on the 30th.
3. GA Amsteram, archive nr. 5061, inv. nr. 639: April 4, 1778.
4. *Gedicht Geschreven in de Treurkamer*, 1778. Published by Johannes van Seggeren and Son (copy in University Library Amsterdam; also inserted in J002).
5. *Overdenkende Beschouwing*, 1778 (copy in University Library Amsterdam; also inserted in J002).
6. *Amsterdamse Courant*, 1778, nr. 41 (Saturday, April 4); *Oprechte Haerlemse Courant*, 1778, nr. 14 (Saturday, April 4).
7. Report in the *Antwerpse Gazette* (inserted in J002) and *Merkwaerdige Samenspraak*, 1778 (the essence identical in both).
8. No name resembling that of Koenraad Stroefhart can be found in the confession books or jailkeeper's bills. Nor is he on a list of inmates of the rasphouse dated February 1, 1777 (GA Amsterdam, archive nr. 345, inv. nr. 3).
9. GA Amsterdam, archive nr. 5061, inv. nr. 634: Feb.–April 1778.
10. GA Amsterdam, archive nr. 5061, inv. nr. 617: nr. 64.
11. His name is absent from the confession book for 1778 (GA Amsterdam, archive nr. 5061, inv. nr. 445). If a convict made an additional confession shortly before death, the magistrates always had it recorded.
12. *Antwerpse Gazette* (inserted in J002).
13. GA Amsterdam, archive nr. 5061, inv. nr. 128 (year: 1778). Since there were four convicts altogether, I counted Van Gogh's share in the day money, rope money, cost of travel and assistance as one-fourth.
14. *Antwerpse Gazette* (inserted in J002).
15. Inserted in J002.
16. GA Amsterdam, archive nr. 5061, inv. nr. 446, pp. 146, 147; inv. nr. 639: Jan. 30, 1779.
17. Confirmed by two experts at the GA Amsterdam.

Bibliography

Primary Sources

Archival Sources

Interrogations of the defendants

The interrogations of Nathaniel Donker are in *Gemeente-Archief Amsterdam*, archive nr. 5061, inv. nrs. 426 (pp. 170, 183, 193, 207, 248, 270, 351, 449, 514) and 427 (pp. 1, 59, 171, 225, 284, 330). These are so-called confession books. There were 22 interrogations altogether (the 16th beginning at the end of inv. nr. 426 and ending in inv. nr. 427). In the notes these interrogations are listed by their rank number (because some interrogations followed immediately on the previous one in the book, there are fewer page numbers than interrogations).

Inv. nr. 640 M-2 (dossiers, 1762–71) has a copy of Donker's interrogations, with page numbers of its own. Literal quotes from Donker's interrogations are from this copy. Both versions are identical, save for a few differences in spelling.

The interrogations of Dorothea Bosselman are only in the confession books: inv. nr. 426 (pp. 227, 282, 319, 335, 354) and 427 (pp. 17, 64, 231, 258, 282, 331, 479). There were 15 interrogations altogether, listed by their rank number in the notes.

The six original interrogations of J. B. F. van Gogh (spelled as Van Goch), listed in the notes by their rank number, are in the confession book: inv. nr. 441 (pp. 180, 192, 214, 234, 253, 276). All quotes from these interrogations are from the copy in the appeal trial dossier: Library of the Amsterdam Archive, nr. J002 (in the notes: J002). Both versions are identical, save for the spelling and a few minor words.

A third copy of the interrogations is in archive nr 5061, inv. nr. 640N. This dossier included the fragment of the original of the blood letter and it has copies of the sentences in all further procedures (with a note saying that oral pleas were delivered).

Further Archival Sources

Gemeente-Archief Amsterdam
Archive nr. 195: *Familie-Archief Bicker*, inv. nr. 152
Archive nr. 366: *Gilden*

Archive nr. 5020: *Keurboeken*
Archive nr. 5061: *Oud-Rechterlijk Archief*
Archive nr. 5073: *Weeskamer van Amsterdam*
Oud-Notarieel Archief
DTB = Doop-, Trouw en Begraafbocken (Baptism, Marriage, and Burial Registers)
Library: nrs. B 54; F Donker N; J 002
Algemeen Rijksarchief, The Hague (now: *Nationaal Archief*)
Archive nr. 1.01.45: *Hoge Krijgsraad*
Archive nr. 3.02.02: *Hoge Raad van Holland en Zeeland*
Archive nr. 3.03.01.01: *Hof van Holland*
Archive nr. 3.03.08.221: *Rechterlijk Archief Rijnland*
Centraal Bureau voor Genealogie, DTB Batavia
Rijksarchief in de Provincie Noord-Holland, Haarlem
Archive nr. 184 (*Oud-Rechterlijke en Weeskamer Archieven*), inv. nr. 2591
Regionaal Archief Alkmaar, DTB
Gemeente-Archief Den Haag
DTB
Archive nr. 351: *Oud-Rechterlijk Archief*
Gemeente-Archief Leiden, DTB
Gemeente-Archief Nijmegen, Oud-Rechterlijk Archief
Gemeente-Archief Rotterdam, DTB
Stadtarchiv Kleve (Germany)
Baptisms, marriages and various

Eighteenth-Century Works

Alle de Magistraatsgezinde, benevens alle de Hertogs aanhangende publique schryvers, met naam en toenaam, een iegelijk in zijn carakter en bestaan zeer natuurlijk beschreeven. Waar in onder alle uitmunten de schryvers van de Diemer-of Watergraaf-Meersche Courant, de Politique Hollandais en de zo zeer berugte en bekende Nicolaas Hoefnagel. Door een Liefhebber van 't Vaderland. (*All persons of the Patriot Party . . . Described . . . and the very notorious and well-known Nicolaas Hoefnagel. By a lover of the Fatherland.*) Den Haag s.a. [1782]

Antwoord aan de Rotterdamsche Klik-Spaan . . . onder de zinspreuk "deze verandering baard voor Amsterdam verbetering." (*Reply to the Rotterdam tattle-tale . . . with the motto "This change is an improvement for Amsterdam."*) Te Amsterdam. 1773.

Confessie van Johannis B., F., van Gog, van Amsterdam, na gissing oud 38 of 39 jaar. Met desselfs ondervraaging en antwoorden. En copia brief aan Annaatje Smitshuyzen, en wederom-brief aan Van Gog, en grafschrift van J.B.F. (*Confession of Johannis B. F. van Gogh, from Amsterdam, thought to be 38 or 39 years old. With his interrogation and answers. And copy of the letter to Annie Smitshuyzen, and letter back to Van Gogh, and epitaph of J. B. F. van Gogh.*) van Gog. [1775].

Confessie van Nathanaël Donker, oud 36 à 37 jaaren, geboortig van Batavia, gevangen binnen de stad Amsterdam seedert den 15 December 1766, en geëxecuteert den 22 Aug. 1767. Dus agt maanden en seeven daagen. Alsmede de aanspraak door den heer Hoofd-Officier gedaan aan Nathanaël Donker. (*Confession of Nathaniel Donker, 36 or 37 years old, born in Batavia, jailed within the city of Amsterdam since 15*

Bibliography 221

December 1766, and executed on 22 August 1767 . . . and the speech by the honorable Hoofd-Officier to Nathaniel Donker.) [1767].
Corver, M[arten]. *Toneel-Aantekeningen vervat in een omstandigen brief aan den schrijver van het leven van Jan Punt.* . . . (*Theater noitces in the form of an elaborate letter to the author of* The Life of Jan Punt.) Leiden, 1786.
Dubbele Overweeging op den brief van een heer te Dordrecht aan zyn vriend te Amsteldam . . . (*Double consideration about the letter of a Dordrecht gentleman to his friend in Amsterdam.*) 1772.
Francken, Johan Herman. *Nieuwe oeffenings verhandelingen der vier hoofdhandgrepen over* . . . *het snyden van alle darm-, water-, bloed-, vlees-en vet-breuken zonder de teeldeelen te extirpeeren.* . . . (*New treatise of practice of the four principal operations in cutting ruptures of intestines, water, blood, muscles, and tissue without removing the testicles.*) Amsterdam, 1733.
Gedicht geschreven in de treurkamer door J. B. F. van Goch. (*Poem writtten in the room of sorrow, by J. B. F. van Goch.*) 1778.
Hekke-Sluiter of vrolyke missive van Meester Franciscus aan zyne landgenooten, ontwikkelende alle de geheimen van het tegenwoordig wonderjaar 1792 . . . gebouwd op de voorzeggingen van den beroemde astrologist Joh. Christoph Ludeman. (*Fence-closer or merry message from Master Franciscus to his countryman, disclosing all secrets of this year 1792* . . . *based on predictions by the famous astrologist Joh. Christoph Ludeman.*) 1792.
Hoefnagel, Nicolaas. *Neerlandsch Echo.* 1770–1771 (followed by several short publications for and against Hoefnagel).
———. *De Nederlandsche faam vliegende over de Amsteldamsche Nieuwe Jaar-dag.* (*The Dutch fame flying over Amsterdam's New Year's Day.*) [1775].
Hollandsche Toneel-beschouwer. (*Theater Observer of Holland.*) 1762–1763.
Kersteman, Franciscus Lievens. *Gedenkwaardige levensbeschrijving van den wereldberoemden Johan Christophorus Ludeman.* . . . (*Noteworthy biography of the world-renowned Johan Christophorus Ludeman.*) s.l., s.a. [1784].
———. *Het leven van F. L. Kersteman, professor honorair en doctor der beide rechten . . . door hem zelven beschreven.* (*The life of F. L. Kersteman, honorary professor and doctor of two branches of law . . . written by himself.*) 2 vols. Amsterdam, 1792.
Kleefsche Waterlust ofte beschrijving van de lieflyke vermakelykheden aen de wateren te Kleef. . . . (*Cleves water-pleasure, or description of the pretty attractions at the waters in Cleves.*) Amsterdam 1752.
Langendyk, Pieter. *De stad Kleef . . . in kunstprenten verbeeld, berymd.* . . . (*The town of Cleves . . . depicted in artistic prints and in rhymes.*) Haarlem, 1747.
Merken, Lucretia Wilhelmina van. *David. In twaalf boeken. Tweede druk.* (*David. In twelve books. 2d ed.*) Amsterdam: Pieter Meijer, 1768.
Merkwaardige en zonderlinge Levensgevallen van Anna Smitshuizen, gewezene minnares van den thans gevangen zittende J. B. F. van Gog. Vervat in samenspraaken. (*Remarkable and unique life of Anna Smitshuizen, former mistress of J. B. F. van Gogh, now imprisoned. In the form of conversations.*) [c. 1776].
Merkwaardige Samenspraak tussen J. B. F. van Goch, dezer dagen te Amsterd. geëxecuteerd, en een' van zyne wakeren, als ook met den ziekentrooster, neevens eenige byzonderheden van zyn losbandig leven, en bedenkingen over de smerte en ysselykheid van een te laat uitgesteld berouw, en den angst eener verwaarloosde bekeering: zynde dit

geschikt, om behoorlyk gebruikt wordende, elk van de zonde af, en ter deugd op, te leiden. (Remarkable dialogue between J. B. F. van Gogh, executed in Amsterdam one of these days, and one of his guards . . .) [1778].

Missive van een heer in Leijden aan zijn vriend in 's Gravenhage vervattende eenige nieuwigheeden betreffende de Amsteldamsche en Rotterdamsche schouwburgen. (Message of a gentleman in Leiden to his friend in The Hague, comprising some news about the Amsterdam and Rotterdam theaters.) 1774.

Naakte Waarheid; of de onverwagte ontdekking. T'samenspraak tusschen een welmeenend Amsterdammer en een opregte Hagenaar, zynde een weerklank op den O.N.P. ontmaskerd. . . . In 's Hage by Hans Vouwbeen, in den Hoefnagel. *(Naked truth, or unexpected discovery. Dialogue between a well-meaning Amsterdamer and a sincere The Haguer, being a reaction to "the demasking of the O.N.P.")* February 1782.

Naamlooziana, of vertoog zonder naam over vraagen zonder vinding, zynde iets over alles [. . .] door het genootschap van de zevenstar, gezegd het naamlooze twee-stuivers collegie. (Namelessness, or treatise without a name about questions without evidence, being something about everything . . . by the society of the seven stars, called the nameless college of two stivers.) Amsterdam: C. Philips J. Z., 1772.

Naauwkeurige Hollandsche Almanach. (Precise almanac of Holland.) 1775.

Nieuwe Nederlandsche Jaarboeken. (New Dutch yearbooks.) 1775.

Nodige Aanmerking op de engagementen der acteurs en actrices van eenen nieuwen op te rechten Nederduitschen schouwburg. (Necessary remark about the contracts of the actors and actresses of a new Dutch theater that will be constructed.) Amsterdam, 1773.

Ockers, Willem. *Amsterdams Honden-Mirakel, of de geest van Schout Bondt op het honden-congres. (Amsterdam dog miracle, or the spirit of officer Bondt at the dog conference.)* [1766].

———. *De Waare Held. Lierdicht aan jufvrouw Lukretia Wi[l]helmina van Merken, dichteresse van de David. (The true hero. Lyre poem for Mrs. Lukretia Wilhelmina van Merken, author of "David.")* [1769].

———. *Geestige mengel-stukjes. (Humorous miscellanea.)* Amsterdam 1784.

Ondervragingen en Antwoorden van Johannes Barth. Ferdinandus van Gog van Amsterdam, oud na gissing 38 of 39 Jaaren. [1775]

Overdenkende Beschouwing van de gedaane executie aan J. B. F. van Gogh, op Zaturdag den 4 April, Anno 1778. (Thoughtful consideration of the execution performed on J. B. F. van Gogh, on Saturday, 4 April, A.D. 1778.)

Pater, Lucas. *De juichende schouwburg. Zinnebeeldig divertissement.* Te Amsteldam, bij Izaak Duim. *(The jubilating theater. An allegorical play.)* 1763.

Roef-discours tusschen een man van den tabbaard en een man van den degen . . . over den zogenaamden zwindelhandel . . . alsmede over . . . Neerlandsch Echo en Overweger en over de pourtrettering van de schryver dier prullen. (Upper-deck discourse between a man of the robe and a man of the sword, about the so-called swindler's trade as as about "Netherlands Echo" and "Consider" and a portrait of the author of that trash.) [c. 1772]

Rotterdamse Klik-Spaan, gevende een waar en waarachtig bericht. . . . (Rotterdam telltale, presenting a true and sincere message.) 1773.

Ryswykze Vrouwendaagze Courant. (Ryswyk women's day newspaper.) 1774.

Schouwburg Nieuws of merkwaardige berichten. . . . (Theater news, or remarkable messages.) 2 vols. 1764–1765.

Styl, Simon. *Het leven van Jan Punt.* (*The life of Jan Punt.*) Amsterdam 1781.
Waarachtig Bericht, meerendeels getrokken uit echte brieven en geschriften van den thans op de Gevangen-Poort geconfineerde J. B. F. van Goch. Aan zyn famielje en goede vrienden geschreven, zynde een zaakelyk verhaal van al 't rampzalige dat op 29 juni 1775 en vervolgens tot heden is voorgevallen; benevens een waarachtige beschrijving van de persoon, het carakter en leven van Anna Smitshuizen van haar weglopen uit Alkmaar tot aan haar overleyden ten toon gestelt, werdende in dit verhaal klaar aangetoond dat al die schandige logenachtige en lasterlyke paskwillen, die voor en na valschelyk op naam van Van Goch verspryt zyn, niet anders behelzen als een saamenstel vol loogenen, pasquilleuse en eerloose lasteringen ten nadele van J. B. F. van Goch. Verspryt en van tyt tot tyt aan 't publiek medegedeelt. Veritas temporis filia. (*Truthful messsage, mostly compiled from actual letters and writings of J. B. F. van Gogh, presently incarcerated in The Hague's jail . . .*) [c. 1777].
Wagenaar, Jan. *Amsterdam in zyne opkomst, aanwas, geschiedenissen, voorregten, koophandel, gebouwen, kerkenstaat, schoolen, schutterye, gilden en regeeringe.* (*Amsterdam: Its origins, growth, history, privileges, commerce, buildings, types of churches, schools, civil militia, guilds, and government.*) Quarto edition. 13 vols. Amsterdam 1760–1768.
Zeldzaame Droom door Meester Franciscus gedroomd. Zynde de nageblevene corespondent van den beroemden astrologist Johannes Christophorus Ludeman . . . afgehandeld in een koddige zaamenspraak over het engageeren van de meeste acteurs en actrices der gewezene schouwburg te Amsteldam voor den tyd van zes jaaren te Rotterdam en staande eerstdaagsch op haar vertrek na gemelde stad. (*Rare dream dreamt by Master Franciscus, being the surviving correspondent of the famous astrologist Johannes Christophorus Ludeman . . .*) [1773].

Secondary Sources

Andel, M. A. van. "De aderlating in theorie en practijk. III: hygiëne en techniek. *Nederlandsch Tijdschrift voor Geneeskunde* 77, no. 1 (1933): 1015–21.
Andreae, S. J. Fockema, and Th. J. Meijer, eds. *Album Studiosorum Academiae Franekerensis, 1585–1811, 1816–1844.* Franeker, 1968.
Barnouw, Pieter Jacobus. *Philippus van Limborch.* Den Haag, 1963.
Berg, Willem van den, et al. "Residentiële segregatie in Hollandse steden. Theorie, methodologie en empirische bevindingen voor Alkmaar en Amsterdam, 16e–19e eeuw." *Tijdschrift voor Sociale Geschiedenis* 24 (1998): 402–36.
Blom, J. C. H., et al., eds. *Geschiedenis van de joden in Nederland.* Amsterdam, 1995.
Blussé, Johan Leonard. "Strange Company. Chinese Settlers, Mestizo Women and the Dutch in VOC Batavia." Dissertation, University of Leiden, 1986.
———. *Bitters bruid. Een koloniaal huwelijksdrama in de gouden eeuw.* s.l. 1997.
Bos, Sandra Beatrice. *"Uyt liefde tot malcander." Onderlinge hulpverlening binnen de Noord-Nederlandse gilden in internationaal perspectief, 1570–1820.* Amsterdam, 1998.
Bostoen, Karel, and André Hanou, eds. *Geconfineert voor altoos. Stukken behorend bij het proces Jacob Campo Weyerman, 1739, vermeerderd met een autobiografie.* Leiden, 1997.

Brandt, George W., and Wiebe Hogendoorn, eds. *German and Dutch Theatre, 1600–1848.* Cambridge: Cambridge University Press, 1993.
Brug, Peter Harmen van der. "Malaria en malaise. De VOC en Batavia in de 18e eeuw." Dissertation, University of Leiden, 1994.
Buisman, Jan Willem. *Tussen vroomheid en Verlichting. Een cultuurhistorisch en sociologisch onderzoek naar enkele aspecten van de Verlichting in Nederland, 1755–1810.* Zwolle, 1992.
Buijnsters, P. J. *Levens van beruchte personen. Over de criminele biografie in Nederland gedurende de 18e eeuw.* Utrecht, 1980.
Burke, Peter. *Venice and Amsterdam. A Study of 17th-Century Elites.* London, 1974.
Cadden, Joan. *Meanings of Sex Difference in the Middle Ages: Medicine, Science and Culture.* Cambridge: Cambridge University Press, 1993.
Coffeng, Johan M. *Lexicon van Nederlandse tonelisten.* Amsterdam, 1965.
Cohen, Daniel A. *Pillars of Salt, Monuments of Grace: New England Crime Literature and the Origins of American Popular Culture, 1674–1860.* New York: Oxford University Press, 1993.
———. "The Beautiful Female Murder Victim: Literary Genres and Courtship Practices in the Origins of a Cultural Motif, 1590–1850." *Journal of Social History* 31, no. 2 (1997): 277–306.
Cohen, Thomas V., and Elizabeth S. Cohen. *Words and Deeds in Renaissance Rome: Trials before the Papal Magistrates.* Toronto: University of Toronto Press, 1993.
Cook, Harold J. "Physical Methods." in W. F. Bynum and Roy Porter, eds. *Companion Encyclopedia of the History of Medicine.* Vol. 2. London, New York, 1993: 939–60.
Darnton, Robert. *The Literary Underground of the Old Regime.* Cambridge, MA: Harvard University Press, 1982.
Davids, Karel, and Jan Lucassen, eds. *A Miracle Mirrored: The Dutch Republic in European Perspective.* Cambridge: Cambridge University Press, 1995.
Davis, Natalie Zemon. *The Return of Martin Guerre.* Cambridge, MA: Harvard University Press, 1983.
Delaney, Susan J. " 'Atala' in the Arts." In Jacques Beauroy et al., eds. *The Wolf and the Lamb: Popular Culture in France from the Old Regime to the 20th Century.* Saratoga, CA, 1977, 209–31.
Diederiks, Herman. *Een stad in verval. Amsterdam omstreeks 1800, demografisch, economisch, ruimtelijk.* Meppel, 1982.
Eisenstein, Elizabeth L. *Grub Street Abroad: Aspects of the French Cosmopolitan Press from the Age of Louis XIV to the French Revolution.* Oxford: Oxford University Press, 1992.
Elias, Johan E. *De vroedschap van Amsterdam, 1578–1795.* 2 vols. 2d ed. Amsterdam, 1963.
Elias, Norbert. *Über den Prozess der Zivilisation. Soziogenetische und psychogenetische Untersuchungen.* 2 vols. 2d ed. Bern, München, 1969 (1969a).
———. *Die höfische Gesellschaft. Untersuchungen zur Soziologie des Königtums und der höfischen Aristokratie.* Neuwied, Berlin, 1969 (1969b).
———. *Die Gesellschaft der Individuen. Eine Studie von Norbert Elias herausgegeben von Nils Runeby.* Stockholm: Idéhistoriska Uppsatser 5, 1983.

Erenstein, R. L. "De emancipatie van de acteur in de 19e eeuw." In *Tijdschrift voor Geschiedenis* 104 (1991): 381–95.

———, ed. *Een theatergeschiedenis der Nederlanden. Tien eeuwen drama en theater in Nederland en Vlaanderen.* Amsterdam, 1996.

Evans, Richard J. *Rituals of Retribution: Capital Punishment in Germany, 1600–1987.* Oxford: Oxford University Press, 1996.

Faber, Sjoerd. *Strafrechtspleging en criminaliteit te Amsterdam, 1680–1811. De nieuwe menslievendheid.* Arnhem, 1983.

Frank-van Westrienen, Anna. *De Groote Tour. Tekening van de educatiereis der Nederlanders in de 17e eeuw.* Amsterdam, 1983.

Garrioch, David. *Neighbourhood and Community in Paris, 1740–1790.* Cambridge: Cambridge University Press, 1986.

Ginzburg, Carlo. *The Cheese and the Worms: The Cosmos of a 16th-Century Miller.* Baltimore: Johns Hopkins University Press, 1980.

Gorissen, Friedrich. *Geschichte der Stadt Kleve. Von der Residenz zur Bürgerstadt, von der Aufklärung bis zur Inflation.* Kleve, 1977.

Gowing, Laura. "Language, Power and the Law: Women's Slander Litigation in Early Modern London." In Jenny Kermode and Walker Garthine, eds. *Women, Crime and the Courts in Early Modern England.* London, 1994, 26–47.

Groot, Hans de. "Bibliografie van in Nederland verschenen 18e en 19e eeuwse toneeltijdschriften, 1762–1850, en toneelalmanakken, 1770–1843." *Scenarium* 4 (1980): 118–46.

Guillais, Joëlle. *La chair de l'autre. Le crime passionnel au 19e siècle.* Paris: Olivier Orban, 1986.

Gijsen, Aafje. *Het dagverhaal van Aafje Gijsen, 1773–1775. Toegelicht en van aantekeningen voorzien door J. W. van Sante.* Wormerveer s.a.

Haas, Anna de, ed. *Achter slot en grendel. Schrijvers in Nederlandse gevangenschap, 1700–1800.* Zutphen: Walburg Pers, 2002.

Halttunen, Karen. *Murder Most Foul: The Killer in the American Gothic Imagination.* Cambridge, MA: Harvard University Press, 1998.

Hanou, A. J. A. M. "Een 18e eeuws broodschrijver: Nicolaas François Hoefnagel, 1735–84." *Spektator* 2 (1972–1973): 62–81.

———. "Bibliografie van Nicolaas Hoefnagel, 1735–84." *Documentatieblad Werkgroep 18e Eeuw* 18 (January 1973): 21–43, and 21 (September 1973): 15–38.

Harris, Ruth. *Murders and Madness: Medicine, Law and Society in the Fin de Siècle.* Oxford: Clarendon Press, 1989.

Hart, Simon. *Geschrift en Getal. Een keuze uit de demografisch-, economisch-en sociaalhistorische studiën op grond van Amsterdamse en Zaanse archivalia, 1600–1800.* Dordrecht, 1976.

Helmers, Dini. *"Gescheurde bedden." Oplossingen voor gestrande huwelijken, Amsterdam 1753–1810.* Hilversum: Verloren, 2002.

Heijden, Manon van der. *Huwelijk in Holland. Stedelijke rechtspraak en kerkelijke tucht, 1550–1700.* Amsterdam, 1998.

Hokke, Judith. " 'Mijn alderliefste Jantielief.' Vrouw en gezin in de Republiek: regentenvrouwen en hun relaties." *Jaarboek voor Vrouwengeschiedenis* 8 (1987): 45–73.

Horst, D. J. H. ter. *Franciscus Lievens Kersteman. Het leven van een 18e-eeuwschen avonturier.* Amsterdam, 1937.
Hunt, Lynn, ed. *The Invention of Pornography: Obscenity and the Origins of Modernity, 1500–1800.* New York, 1993.
Huussen, A. H., Jr. " 'Het leven van F. L. Kersteman' (1792). Een autobiografie?" In Peter Altena et al., eds., *Feit en fictie in de misdaadliteratuur, 1650–1850.* Amsterdam: Vrije Universiteit, Juridische Faculteit, 1985, 57–68.
Huijbrecht, R[ob], et al., eds. *Album advocatorum. De advocaten van het Hof van Holland, 1560–1811.* Den Haag: Algemeen Rijksarchief, s.a.
Jacob, Margaret C. *The Radical Enlightenment: Pantheists, Freemasons and Republicans.* London, 1981.
―――, and Wijnand W. Mijnhardt, eds. *The Dutch Republic in the 18th Century: Decline, Enlightenment and Revolution.* Ithaca, NY: Cornell University Press, 1992.
Jensma, G. Th., et al., eds. *Universiteit te Franeker, 1585–1811. Bijdragen tot de geschiedenis van de Friese hogeschool.* Leeuwarden, 1985.
Jongenelen, Ton. *Van smaad tot erger. Amsterdamse boekverboden, 1747–1794.* Amsterdam: Stichting Jacob Campo Weyerman, 1998.
Jonker, Michiel, et al., eds. *Van stadskern tot stadsgewest. Stedebouwkundige geschiedenis van Amsterdam.* Amsterdam, 1984.
Jütte, Robert. *Ärzte, Heiler und Patienten. Medizinischer Alltag in der frühen Neuzeit.* Munich, Zürich, 1991.
―――. *Zeldzaame levens-gevallen van J. C. Weyerman. Heruitgave op basis van de 2e druk (1763). Bezorgd door M. van Vliet.* Leiden, 1994.
Keyser, Erich. ed. *Rheinisches Städtebuch.* Stuttgart, 1956.
Kloek, Els, et al., eds. *Women of the Golden Age: An International Debate on Women in 17th-Century Holland, England and Italy.* Hilversum, 1994.
Kloek, J. J. *Over Werther geschreven. Nederlandse reacties op Goethes Werther, 1775–1800. Proeve van een historisch receptie-onderzoek.* 2 vols. Utrecht, 1985.
Knevel, Paul. *Burgers in het geweer. De schutterijen in Holland, 1550–1700.* Hilversum 1994.
Knuttel, W. P. C. *Verboden boeken in de Republiek der Verenigde Nederlanden. Beredeneerde catalogus.* Den Haag, 1914.
Laqueur, Thomas. *Making Sex: Body and Gender from the Greeks to Freud.* Cambridge, MA: Harvard University Press, 1990.
Leeuwen, Marco H. D. van, and James E. Oeppen. "Reconstructing the Demographic Regime of Amsterdam, 1681–1920." *Economic and Social History in the Netherlands* 5 (1993): 61–102.
Levie, Tirtsah, and Henk Zantkuyl. *Wonen in Amsterdam in de 17e en 18e eeuw.* Purmerend, 1980.
Lourens, Piet, and Jan Lucassen. "Ambachtsgilden binnen een handelskapitalistische stad. Aanzetten voor een analyse van Amsterdam rond 1700." *NEHA-Jaarboek voor Economische, Bedrijfs-en Techniekgeschiedenis* 61 (1998): 121–62.
Meer, Theo van der. *Sodoms zaad in Nederland. Het ontstaan van homoseksualiteit in de vroegmoderne tijd.* Nijmegen, 1995.
Meijer, Th. J., ed. *Album Promotorum Academiae Franekerensis, 1591–1811.* Franeker, 1972.

Mönch, Walter. *Das Sonett. Gestalt und Geschichte.* Heidelberg: F. H. Kerle, 1955.
Noordam, Dirk Jaap. *Riskante relaties. Vijf eeuwen homoseksualiteit in Nederland, 1233-1733.* Hilversum, 1995.
Nusteling, Hubert. *Welvaart en werkgelegenheid in Amsterdam, 1540-1860.* Amsterdam: Dieren, 1985.
―――. "The Population of Amsterdam and the Golden Age." In Peter van Kessel and Elisja Schulte, eds., *Rome, Amsterdam. Two Growing Cities in 17th-Century Europe.* Amsterdam, 1997, 71-84.
Pol, Lotte van de. *Het Amsterdams hoerdom. Prostitutie in de 17e en 18e eeuw.* Amsterdam, 1996.
Porter, Roy, and Milulas Teich, eds. *The Enlightenment in National Context.* Cambridge: Cambridge University Press, 1981.
Pratasik, Bennie. "De moeizame weg van het theaterleven in de provincie in de 18e eeuw." *Holland* 29 (1997): 226-39.
Rasch, Rudolf. "Om den armen dienst te doen. De Amsterdamse schouwburg en de godshuizen gedurende het laatste kwart van de 17e eeuw." *Holland* 23 (1991): 243-67.
Rössing, J[ohannes] H[erman]. *Geschiedenis der stichting en feestelijke opening van den schouwburg op het Leidseplein te Amsterdam.* Utrecht, 1874.
Rogers, Pat. *Grub Street. Studies in a Subculture.* London, 1972.
Roodenburg, Herman. *Onder censuur. De kerkelijke tucht in de Gereformeerde gemeente van Amsterdam, 1578-1700.* Hilversum, 1990.
Showalter, Dennis E. *The Wars of Frederick the Great.* London, New York, 1996.
Spierenburg, Pieter. "Judicial Violence in the Dutch Republic: Corporal Punishment, Executions and Torture in Amsterdam, 1650-1750." Dissertation, University of Amsterdam, 1978.
―――. *Elites and Etiquette: Mentality and Social Structure in the Early Modern Northern Netherlands.* Rotterdam: Centrum voor Maatschappij-Geschiedenis. Vol. 9, 1981.
―――. *The Spectacle of Suffering. Executions and the Evolution of Repression: From a Preindustrial Metropolis to the European Experience.* Cambridge: Cambridge University Press, 1984.
―――. *The Prison Experience: Disciplinary Institutions and Their Inmates in Early Modern Europe.* New Brunswick, NJ, London, 1991.
―――. *Zwarte schapen. Losbollen, dronkaards en levensgenieters in achttiende eeuwse beterhuizen.* Hilversum, 1995.
―――. "Long-Term Trends in Homicide: Theoretical Reflections and Dutch Evidence, Fifteenth to Twentieth Centuries." In Eric A. Johnson and Eric H. Monkkonen, eds., *The Civilization of Crime. Violence in Town and Country since the Middle Ages.* Urbana, Chicago, 1996, 63-105 (1996a).
―――. "Homoseksualiteit in preïndustrieel Nederland. Twintig jaar onderzoek." *Tijdschrift voor Geschiedenis* 109, no. 4 (1996): 485-93 (1996b).
―――, ed. *Men and Violence: Gender, Honor and Rituals in Modern Europe and America.* Columbus,: The Ohio State University Press, 1998 (1998a).
―――. *De Verbroken Betovering. Mentaliteit en Cultuur in Preïndustrieel Europa.* 3d ed. Hilversum, 1998 (1998b).
Srebnick, Amy Gilman. *The Mysterious Death of Mary Rogers. Sex and Culture in 19th-Century New York.* New York: Oxford University Press, 1995.

Sturkenboom, Dorothée. *Spectators van hartstocht. Sekse en emotionele cultuur in de 18e eeuw.* Hilversum, 1998.

———. "Historicizing the Gender of Emotions: Changing Perceptions in Dutch Enlightenment Thought." *Journal of Social History* 34, no.1 (2000): 55–75.

Thomas, Keith. *Man and the Natural World: A History of the Modern Sensibility.* New York, 1983.

Thijssen, Willem Theodorus Maria. "De mens-machine theorie. Een studie over de ontwikkeling van het mechanicistische mensbeeld bij La Mettrie." Nijmegen. Meppel,1982.

Verhas, Christel Madeleine Odile. "De beginjaren van de Hoge Raad van Holland, Zeeland en West-Friesland." Leiden: Den Haag 1997.

Vries, Jan de. "Barges and Capitalism. Passenger Transportation in the Dutch Economy, 1632–1839." *AAG-Bijdragen* 21 (1978): 33–398.

Vries, Jan de, and Ad van der Woude. *Nederland, 1500–1850. De eerste ronde van moderne economische groei.* Amsterdam, 1995.

Waardt, Hans de. "Breaking the Boundaries: Irregular Healers in 18th-Century Holland." In Marijke Gijswijt-Hofstra et al., eds., *Illness and Healing. Alternatives in Western Europe.* London, New York, 1997, 141–60.

Walker, D[aniel] P[ickering]. *Unclean Spirits. Possession and Exorcism in France and England in the Late 16th and Early 17th Centuries.* London, 1981.

Weinstein, Donald. *The Captain's Concubine: Love, Honor and Violence in Renaissance Tuscany.* Baltimore: Johns Hopkins University Press, 2000.

Wellman, Kathleen. *La Mettrie. Medicine, Philosophy and Enlightenment.* Durham, NC: Duke University Press, 1992.

Wiltenburg, Joy. *Disorderly Women and Female Power in the Street Literature of Early Modern England and Germany.* Charlottesville, London, 1992.

Wolterson, Bertha. "Amsterdamsch tooneel in de achttiende eeuw." In E. A. d'Ailly, ed., *Zeven eeuwen Amsterdam.* Vol. 4. Amsterdam [1947]: 139–72.

Wybrands, C[hristiaan] N[icolaas]. *Het Amsterdamsche toneel van 1617–1772. Bewerkt naar merendeels onuitgegeven authentieke bescheiden.* Utrecht, 1873.

Zevenbergen, Yvonne. "*Het geval Van Goch. Misdaadliteratuur in de 18e eeuw.*" In Altena (Peter) et al. (eds.), *Feit en fictie in de misdaadliteratuur, 1650–1850.* Amsterdam: Vrije Universiteit, Juridische Faculteit,1985, 69–85.

Index

acting, 121–24, 168
Amsterdam
    criminal procedures in, 95–96
    hack writers in, 135–37
    theater fire in, 1–4
    theater, opening of new, 134–35

Batavia, 21–22, 25
Bicker Raye, Jacob, 48, 82–83, 94
Bosselman, Dorothea
    arrest of, 93–94
    background of, 48
    escape attempt, 113–15
    flight to The Hague, 88–92
    impersonation of Cecilia by, 64–66
    imprisonment of, 112–16
    lawsuit against Cecilia Klos, 49–50
    looks of, 48–49
    sentence of, 112
    trial of, 97–105. *See also* Donker, Nathaniel

Cleves, 32, 39–42, 91
Corver, Marten, 119, 123
crime, historiography, xvi–xviii

Darnton, Robert, 6, 135
Davis, Natalie Zemon, xviii
Dedel, Willem Gerrit, 115, 135, 178–90, 191
Donker, Nathaniel
    adolescence of, 25–26
    affair with Dora, beginning, 51–55
    annulment of first marriage, 31–32
    discharge from Prussian army, 36–37
    escape from private prison, 38–39
    execution of, 107–10

    family background of, 22–25
    fleeing Amsterdam, plans, 83–87
    marriage with Cecilia: first, 28–29; second, 40; third, 42–43
    meets Cecilia, 27–28
    murder of Cecilia: carrying it out, 63–64; the day after, 67–69; events preceding, 59–63; preparations for, 55–57
    sentence of, 106–107
    settles on estate, 44–46
    sons of, 40, 45, 105–6
    trial of, 96–103. *See also* Bosselman, Dorothea; Klos, Cecilia
Donker, Pieter Gerbrand, 23, 25–26, 29–33, 37–38, 43, 54, 84–86, 91–92, 111

Effen, Justus van, 5
Elias, Norbert, xviii
Enlightenment
    breakthrough in the Netherlands, 4–6
    emotional standards of, 8–9

Gaubert, Jan, 32, 85–87, 100
Ginzburg, Carlo, xviii
Gogh, Johannes Bartholomeus Ferdinandus van
    affair with Lizette, 133
    arrest of, 167–68
    background of, 117–18
    blood letter: disappearance of, 197; reciting of, 165; text of, xi–xiii; writing of, ix–x
    conflicts with Annie, 158–60
    and emotional standards, 8–9, 147
    estrangement from Hoefnagel, 132
    execution of, 194–95
    freethinker, considered as, 174–75

killing of Annie: carrying it out, 167; events during the day, 162–64; events immediately preceding, 165–66
literary production about, 170–71, 192–94, 195
medical condition of, 162
meets Annie, 146–47
meets Hoefnagel, 129–31
pamphlets against, 153–55
proposes to Annie, 147–48
sentence of, 194
spies on Annie, 150, 152
surgeon's career, 124
theater performance by, 117, 118–21
trial of: first, 178–81; second, 181–84; third, 184–85; fourth, 185–86; fifth, 186–90. *See also* Smitshuizen, Anna

Hoefnagel, Nicolaas François, 7, 117, 127–34, 137, 140–41, 150, 153–55, 176, 182, 192
homicide, 9–11, 18–19
honor, 14, 16–18, 30, 97–98, 136, 169–70, 171–74

imprisonment, private, 33–36

Jacob, Margaret, 6, 125
Jaunis, Johanna (Madam Sjoenis), 88–91, 101

Kersteman, Franciscus Lievens, 7, 141
Klos, Cecilia
  clothes of, 57–59
  corpse of: discovered, 77–79; displayed, 78–79, 80; dumped 75–77; transported 72–75
  dismemberment of, 69–70
  family background of, 26–27
  lawsuit against Dorothea Bosselman, 49–50
  petitions Court of Holland, 47–48. *See also* Donker, Nathaniel
knife fighting, 18

La Mettrie, Julien Offray de, 7, 125–26

Linden, Maria van der, *see* Steffens, Maria
love, revolution in, 13–14, 19–20, 54–55, 134, 151–52, 176–77, 189–90
Ludeman, Johan Cristoph, 7, 110–11, 141

marriage, 12-13
microhistory, xviii–xix

Nijmegen, 32–33, 36, 49–50, 91

observing magazines, 6, 34, 151–52, 161
Ockers, Willem, 7, 124–27, 128–32, 152, 176
Ouderkerk, ix, 118, 151

Paris, hack writers in, 135–37
Pol, Lotte van de, 14
Popkin, Jeremy, 6
prostitution, 14–16, 196–97
Punt, Jan, 119–20, 123

sentimental novels, 9, 160–62, 188
Smitshuizen, Anna
  adolescence of, 139–40
  and atheism, 175–76
  biography of, 140–42
  corpse of: displayed, 177–78; inspected, 178
  family background of, 138–39
  first years in Amsterdam, 142–46
  moves to Herengracht, 155–58
  resumes prostitution career, 148–49. *See also* Gogh, Johannes Bartholomeus Ferdinandus van
sodomy, 11
Stalli, Michiel (porter), 70–75, 81–82, 100-101
Steffens, Maria (mother of Cecilia Klos), 26–27, 53, 80–81, 83–84, 87, 98, 105–6
Sweers, Isaac, 96–107

Thomeeze, Leonard, 38, 184–87

Verhoef, Pieter, 56, 60, 70

Weyerman, Jacob Campo, 6

THE HISTORY OF CRIME AND CRIMINAL JUSTICE SERIES
David R. Johnson and Jeffrey S. Adler, Series Editors

The series explores the history of crime and criminality, violence, criminal justice, and legal systems without restrictions as to chronological scope, geographical focus, or methodological approach.

Controlling Vice: Regulating Brothel Prostitution in St. Paul, 1865–1883
Joel Best

The Rule of Justice: The People of Chicago vs. Zephyr Davis
Elizabeth Dale

Prostitution and the State in Italy, 1860–1915, Second Edition
Mary Gibson

Murder in America: A History
Roger Lane

Violent Death in the City: Suicide, Accident, and Murder in Nineteenth-Century Philadelphia, Second Edition
Roger Lane

Cops and Bobbies: Police Authority in New York and London, 1830–1870, Second Edition
Wilbur R. Miller

Crime, Justice, History
Eric Monkkonen

Race, Labor, and Punishment in the New South
Martha A. Myers

Homicide, North and South: Being a Comparative View of Crime against the Person in Several Parts of the United States
H. V. Redfield

Men and Violence: Gender, Honor, and Rituals in Modern Europe and America
Edited by Pieter Spierenburg

Rethinking Southern Violence: Homicides in Post–Civil War Louisiana, 1866–1884
Gilles Vandal

Five Centuries of Violence in Finland and the Baltic Area
Heikki Ylikangas, Petri Karonen, and Martti Lehti

www.ingramcontent.com/pod-product-compliance
Lightning Source LLC
Chambersburg PA
CBHW020945230426
43666CB00005B/175